Also by Sue Hubbell:

A Book of Bees
A Country Year
On This Hilltop

BROADSIDES
FROM THE
OTHER ORDERS

BROADSIDES
FROM THE
OTHER ORDERS
A BOOK OF BUGS

SUE HUBBELL

Illustrated by Dimitry Schidlovsky

RANDOM HOUSE

NEW YORK

Grateful acknowledgment is made to the following for permission to
reprint previously published material:
The Canadian Entomologist: Excerpt from an article by Richard
Merritt from the January/February 1991 issue of *The Canadian
Entomologist* 123 (1): p. 184 (1991). Reprinted by permission.
Ecology: Excerpt from "Studies on Territorialism and Sexual
Selection in Dragonflies" by Merle Jacobs from the October 1955
issue of *Ecology*. Reprinted by permission.
Davison G. Grove: Excerpts from doctoral thesis by Davison
Greenawalt Grove. Reprinted by permission.
W. W. Norton & Co., Inc. and Weidenfeld Publishers: Excerpt from *The
Natural History of Flies* by Harold Oldroyd. Copyright © 1964, 1992
by Harold Oldroyd. Rights throughout Canada are controlled by
Weidenfeld Publishers. Reprinted by permission.
Portions of Chapter 3 appeared in slightly different form in *The New
Yorker*; portions of Chapter 6 appeared in slightly different form in
Smithsonian magazine.

Library of Congress Cataloging-in-Publication Data
Hubbell, Sue.
   Broadsides from the other orders: a book of bugs / by Sue
Hubbell.—1st ed.
      p.   cm.
   Includes bibliographical references.
   ISBN 0-679-40062-1
   1. Insects.   I. Title.
QL463.H89   1993
595.7—dc20   92-27165

Book design by Michael Mendelsohn

Manufactured in the United States of America

9   8   7   6   5   4   3   2

First Edition

Hey, Tazbo

The Praying Mantis
Visits a Penthouse

The praying Mantis with its length of straw
Out of the nowhere's forehead born full armed
Engages the century at my terrace door.
Focused at inches the dinosaur insect sends
Broadsides of epic stillness at my eye,
Above the deafening projects of the age.
My love, who fears the thunder of its poise,
Has seen it and cries out. The clouds like curls
Fall in my faith as I seize a stick to stop
This Martian raid distilled to a straw with legs,
To wisps of prowess. Bristling with motionlessness
The Mantis prays to the Stick twice armed with Man.
I strike, the stick whistles, shearing off two legs
Which run off by themselves beneath some boards.
The Mantis spreads out tints of batlike wing,
The many colored pennants of its blood,
And hugs my weapon; the frantic greens come out,
The reds and yellows blurt out from the straw,
All sinews doubtless screaming insect death.
Against the railing's edge I knock the stick
Sending that gay mad body into the gulf.
Such noisy trappings in defeat wake doubts.
I search my mind for possible wounds and feel
The victim's body heavy on the victor's heart.

—OSCAR WILLIAMS

Acknowledgments

This book has come from the entomologists, who were kindly and generous with their time. My grateful thanks to them all; you will meet them in the pages that follow, and will, I hope, remember that although mistakes are mine, theirs was the knowledge and love of subject that made the book possible. Others, not named in the text, also contributed. Important research help was cheerfully given by Mary Jane Dunlap, Mary Beth Markey, Kati Hanna, Barbara Wilson, and Charles Corliss. Charlie Cooper provided sensitive and telling Russian translations. Cecilie Sieverts, Ursula McManus, and Suzanne Frischling helped undo the mysteries of entomological German. Nancy Stacel, the families Martin and Vaughan, and most especially Martha Echols proved to be stout camel-cricket hunters for the cause of Science. My thanks go to the USDA staffers, particularly to Janna Evans, for making my trip to Guatemala not only informative but pleasurable. And my special thanks also to Carla Flug, who tenderly baby-sat camel crickets.

Fortune favors me with a remarkable family. The help and support of Asher Treat, Liddy Hubbell, Brian Hubbell, and Arne Sieverts were vital to every stage of my work.

Contents

Introduction

A few years ago Arne, my husband, and I were taking our dog, Tazzie, for her morning walk near our home in Washington, D.C. We were cutting through an elegantly landscaped residential area on our way to Rock Creek Park, where Tazzie likes to run before her breakfast. It was springtime, the hour was early, the sun not yet high. Its rays slanted low through the foliage of shrubberies, and there about two or three feet off the ground, backlighted in the sunshine, was a congregation of tiny, dancing insects. We stood watching them shimmering, glinting and silvery. Arne knows all about American foreign policy, but he directs his bug questions to me.

"What are they?" he asked. "And what are they up to?"

"Well, I guess they're midges," I said. "And what they're doing probably has something to do with mating."

It was a lame reply, rather like that of the amateur archaeologist who calls every mysterious shard "an object with a ritual purpose." The truth was I had only the haziest idea about what they were up to, and I wasn't even sure they were midges. "Maybe they're gnats," I suggested. "I don't really know the difference, if there is any. Maybe 'gnat' and 'midge' are common names for the same animal. I know they belong to the order Diptera, though. You know—flies, mosquitoes, that sort of bug."

It wasn't an answer. I was just hiding behind words, and Arne's questions nagged me as did those of my son, Brian, when I visited him and his wife, Liddy, in Maine. Black-fly season, Maine's early summer, was just ending and both of them were still scratching the red bites left by the black flies. I'd sent them bee suits—white coveralls complete with zippered bee veils and gloves—hoping these would protect them enough so that they would be able to work out-of-doors when the flies were biting. But the black flies were small enough to get through the veils' screening, and eager enough for blood to bite through the cotton fabric. Brian and Liddy's cats, wise to the northern wilds, refused to come outdoors at all; the flies bit the tender inner surfaces of their ears and burrowed into their thick coats to get at their flesh. There were, Brian told me, more car accidents with moose during the season because the big animals, perhaps crazed by bites, ran out on the highways to escape the woods, where the flies tormented them. He asked me what I knew about them. "Nothing, really," I told him. "Like all other flies they belong to the order Diptera, which means they have two wings, and I've been reading up on other small Diptera recently. Gnats, midges. Some of them, like the midges you see dancing in swarms in the air, never bite at all. They have mouths, but don't use them. I'm finding out what their lives are like and how they live."

"If you ever find out about black flies, I'd like to know," Brian said, as he watched Liddy scratching her ankles. "Are they some part of a food chain? Do they do anyone any good? What are they up to, anyway?"

What *are* they up to? It was the same question Arne had asked me about the midges. Little wonder, I suppose, that those close to me echoed the question I've spent years asking others. It isn't a very dignified question, not one an adult should ask in these times when most questions are quantity questions, ones that can be tabulated and processed by a computer. To me, the astounding thing is that for the past twenty years, the years I've had a writing life, I've been able to talk editors into letting me go around asking that question—What are they (he, you, she) up to?—and make a living out of it. It seems presumptuous, and it has been so much fun that I am afraid one day a grown-up will come along and put an end to it.

I read in *The New York Times* not long ago that for every pound of us there are 300 pounds of bugs. Now that is a perfect love of a statistic. It would be easy enough to generate the number on a computer, and it is the kind of fact people seem to want to know these days; once we can assign a number value we are satisfied we know something.

My first husband is an electrical engineer, and it was he who made me suspect that I was not going to be comfortable in these times, although he certainly had no intention of making me think so that day back in 1957, when he was explaining to me the difference between analog (the comparative, the sweep of a clock's hand, figure and ground, this but maybe partly that, too) and digital (yes or no; one, two; off, on; this, not that). After he had done so he said, "And the future is digital," and I realized with one of those flashes of understanding that come now and again that I was going to be analog in a digital world.

A few years ago, when my commercial beekeeping operation was still big enough to require hired help for the honey harvest, I had a teenager working for me. I knew the boy was a star pupil in the local high school and was headed for a career in computer science. He was a pleasant young man, and we worked together companionably for several weeks. He had a lively mind, and was full of questions. How long does a bee live? How much does a gallon of honey weigh? How many bees are there in this hive? How big? When? How heavy? My answers disappointed him: It depends on what they are doing. More than water. A whole bunch, more than we have time to count. Bigger than a bread box. I don't know. More than I can carry. He was left dissatisfied, hungry for exactitude. I wish I'd known then that there were 300 pounds of bugs for each pound of us. He'd have found that more nourishing.

One afternoon, while we were working in the beeyards, I wondered aloud whether we'd be able to work another yard or whether we'd better go back home and call it a day. He looked at his digital watch and crisply told me the time to the second. His answer made me smile. The falsity of precision: Just having a number doesn't mean we *know* something. My question had more to do with the difficulty of driving over the bad road to the next beeyard, the amount of daylight remaining, the touchiness of the bees late in the afternoon, and the tiredness of our muscles rather than with the minutes and seconds past 4:00 P.M. All unbidden, a picture unfolded inside my head: I could see my first husband and me, then only a few years older than my young helper, standing in the aisle of a drugstore in El Paso, Texas, where the words "digital" and "analog" had first floated into my brain. "And the future," he was saying, "is digital." He was right: My helper was the future. Most people ask and answer quantity questions now, in part because we have the tools to answer them and the tools' capabilities often drive research.

I'm glad that there are people asking those quantity questions, because my own questions sometimes grow out of their answers. But my own questions are those of process: What does he like to eat? Who is he, anyway? Does she behave differently from those over there, the ones who look like her? What limits the population? What does he do when he gets into a pickle? How does she get along with her own kind? Are they having any fun? How does he grow up? Where are they when they aren't here? What is he up to? My mother tells me that when I was able to string words together my first question was "Who made God?"

The need to make a living out of writing has made me ask questions about a lot of things besides bugs, of course, but bug questions are my favorite ones because I like bugs and because the people who can answer my questions, entomologists, are such extraordinarily nice people. My favorites are field biologists, men and women who go outdoors, mess around, look, watch, take notes, and see what there is to be seen. I suspect they were the kids who got their jeans dirty and wet because they sat down in the weeds to watch the ant find a bit of dead moth and then followed her on their hands and knees to see what she was going to do with it. As they've gotten older they've kept on doing pretty much the same thing, and they always seem to be mildly astonished that they are paid enough money to live on while they are doing it.

My favorite entomologist is my cousin, Asher Treat. He is a modest man, startled to be the world authority on moth ear mites. It is a specialty he created, willy-nilly, when he discovered the animals tucked away in a moth's ear. He went on to study the connection between bat predation upon moths and ear mites, who courteously infest and thereby deafen their moth host in only one ear, ensuring that both they and the moth survive. Asher is retired from an academic career, but goes on with his work in a home laboratory, corresponding with and helping younger men and women all over the world who are broadening our understanding of mites. He is a French-horn player, learned to play the viola when he was past eighty, and makes music with friends who gather in his house. He had not intended to be an entomologist, although he had collected bugs even as a youngster. With a smile, he once told me that his ambition had always been to be a horn player in a circus.

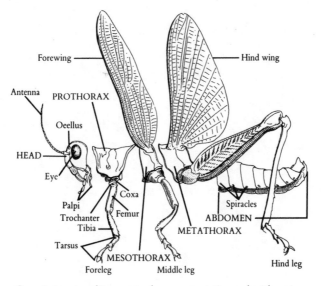

Generic insect, split apart to show segmentation and with major body parts labeled

But all my entomologist friends are similar. Their delight in their subject has the furtive modesty of someone who expects that any time now an adult is going to tell them to stand up, put on dry clothes, and, for heaven's sake, grow up. They have been generous to me with their time, patient with my questions, and shared their delight. What follows is what I have learned from them.

BROADSIDES
FROM THE
OTHER ORDERS

CHAPTER I

ORDER LEPIDOPTERA: BUTTERFLIES

"Hot damn!" said Ernest Williams. "It's *ursadentis!*"

"*Ursa . . . dentis,*" I said, translating. "Bear . . . tooth."

"Yep," said Ernest, sounding enormously pleased. "*Ursadentis,* the Beartooth butterfly. *Boloria eunomia ursadentis.* It's a subspecies, actually."

Ernest Williams, a rangy, bearded biology professor from Hamilton College, in Clinton, N.Y., and I were standing ankle-deep in wildflowers and butterflies, high in the Beartooth Mountains of northern Wyoming. We were participants in the 1987 Xerces Society's annual Fourth of July Butterfly Count, and we had just counted the first of the mountain range's own subspecies of butterfly, named for the locale in which it is found.

Ursadentis is one of the butterflies called fritillaries, a group of medium-sized orange butterflies with stylish black spots on the forewings and, underneath the hind wings, pale, silvery, iridescent spots that look like dewdrops. In the late morning sun, we watched *ursadentis* flutter close to the ground and the flowers. As the animal lit on smartweed to sip nectar (lepidopterists give the noun a gerund's push toward the verb, and say that butterflies are nectaring), Ernest bent close to it and pointed to its wings. "See those circles with the dark borders? This one, a male, is a little ratty, really. His wing edges are torn, so he's been around for a while." In butterfly terms, "a while" is anywhere from eight to ten days—the life span of a typical butterfly.

"There's another!" Ernest called. "*Ursadentis* lives and breeds near these alpine willows. Well, that's great! It's good to have them on the count. We're seeing some nice species. If we get a *gillettii* we'll have had our share—but we'll take whatever we can get."

Gillettii is a butterfly banded with orange stripes, one of a group called checkerspots. It is Ernest's research specialty. Its full name is *Euphydryas gilletti. Euphydryas,* the genus or grouping name, means "comely wood nymphs"; *gilletti* is the species, or specific, name, which it received in 1897 from the lepidopterist William Barnes, who described the butterfly for the scientific community and named it after Clarence P. Gillette, a collector who had sent him the specimen. (Entomologists call the bug they are talking about by its species name and assume the genus is understood.)

The whole system of lepidopteran names has been undergoing a lot of changes in recent years. Genus names have been subject to the most scrutiny, and people who have not been involved in the changes are now finding it hard to look up butterflies in their field guides as a result, because listings in them are alphabetical by genus name. There is much public tut-tutting in the entomological journals over the changes, and various factions—liberals and conservatives, empiricists and theoreticians—have lined up against one set of names or another.

The tally Ernest and I were making for the Fourth of July Butterfly Count was one of more than a hundred that were taking place across the United States. The counts are not necessarily held precisely on the Fourth—we did ours on July 20—but are scheduled in a given area on a fine sunny day when butterflies are abundant at that latitude. In some ways, the Xerces Society's Fourth of July Butterfly Count is analogous to the Audubon Society's Christmas Bird Count; indeed, many of the butterfly counters are also bird counters. But the Butterfly Count is a less celebrated affair, and the Xerces Society is a younger organization than the Audubon Society. It was born in England on December 9, 1971,

4

when Robert Pyle, then a young Fulbright scholar, was studying at Monkswood, a national nature reserve dedicated to insect conservation. Pyle had spent the evening at a Linnaean Society meeting in London, listening to a lecture by a British Museum entomologist about the large blue, a butterfly that had become extinct in Great Britain. If the large blues should disappear (and they did), let us make them a symbol, the speaker had said.

On the train back to Monkswood, Pyle remembered that another blue—*Glaucopsyche xerces*—was the first butterfly species to have become extinct in North America owing to human interference: In the early 1940s, a practice field for army tank units had been built on its last breeding grounds, the dunes outside San Francisco. After Pyle had returned to the U.S. and was working on a doctorate in insect ecology at Yale, he formally established the Xerces Society with the help of Jo Brewer, a popular writer on butterflies. The World Wildlife Fund provided money for a secretary and Pyle became the only graduate student at Yale with a paid assistant.

Today Xerces has more than a thousand members and a professionally staffed headquarters in Portland, Oregon. Eminent zoologists have lent their names to the organization—E.O. Wilson, Spencer Beebe, Roger Tory Peterson, and S. Dillon Ripley among them. Grant money has funded a variety of projects, including the preservation of habitat in California and Mexico for the monarch butterfly; copublication with the Smithsonian of a book on butterfly gardening; the establishment of a butterfly educational center on Staten Island; and the acquisition of land in Puerto Rico, where the butterfly habitat is threatened.

The first butterfly count, taken at only a couple of dozen places, was in 1975. Fewer than twenty years' worth of count data is not yet much but, incomplete as it is, a significant census report is being created and is beginning to give a picture of butterfly abundance across the country. Changes in numbers in repeated counts indicate habitat lost or altered. Relationships such as that between butterflies and plants on which they nectar and that between caterpillars and host plants are still not well understood. Sometimes an area that, to human eyes, looks perfectly fine for butterflies is scorned by them. Some researchers, Bob Pyle among them, believe that the most important research problem in lepidoptery is to figure out "the subtle and elusive character we call 'habitat fit.' " What is it that causes butterflies to be happy in some areas and not in others? "The ability to manage habitats in ways that preserve biological diversity depends upon a clear understanding of the limiting factors, and we generally lack that knowledge," Bob told me. The Butterfly Count is helping to fill that lack.

I found myself in the Beartooth Mountains, at 10,000 feet, a little dizzy from altitude, in the sunshine and wildflowers, through a concatenation of events. The previous autumn I had been in upstate New York, near Hamilton College, working on a magazine story about loons. The woman I was interviewing there invited me to the local bird-club meeting. Before the meeting began a gangly, bearded, bespectacled young man with a warm smile stood up, introduced himself as Ernest Williams, and announced that during the coming summer he would be again conducting a butterfly count near Utica. If any of the birders wanted to sign up, they should get in touch with him. I asked my loon lady about the butterfly count. She didn't know much about it, she said, but she had heard it was going on nationwide. If I was interested, why didn't I give Williams a call? He was a professor she knew. She scribbled his telephone number on a scrap of paper and I tucked it into my billfold.

I had a busy winter and forgot all about the butterfly count until one morning in May when I was sitting in the spring sunshine at my farm in the Ozarks drinking a cup of coffee. A zebra swallowtail joined me, flying down from the overhanging branch of a hickory tree. He perched on my shoulder, walked up and down my arm, flew away briefly and returned for another saunter, walking daintily and calmly. He glistened in the sunshine. I could see every detail of the big triangular wings, the hind wings ending in long tails with bright scarlet spots that set off the bands of chalky greenish-white and black which gave him his common name. He was so shiny and fresh that he must have just emerged from his chrysalis. Perhaps he was still drying his wings, because he waved them gently back and forth in the light morning breeze.

After I had finished my coffee and he had flown away for good, I went into the house and rummaged through my books. I read that the zebra swallowtail caterpillar, which is green with broad, yellow-edged black stripes, feeds on pawpaw leaves, and that the female lays her eggs on them. There are lots of pawpaws down by the river, so that handsome new adult was not far from where he originally hatched. I read that the males are often found in groups, sipping moisture from the sand, alongside streams. True enough, I had many times seen them there. I read that the adults have shorter proboscises (those coiled tube-tongues that butterflies use for taking up nectar) than other swallowtails, and therefore usually feed on shallow flowers like blueberry, redbud, lilac. Well, they could find all those on my farm. I also read that they are common in the countryside but tend not to adapt to suburban development.

I wanted to know a lot more, and then I remembered that I still had the telephone number of the tall, soft-spoken professor who was going to count butterflies that summer. When I telephoned Ernest Williams he said he would be happy to have me come along on the Utica count, but that he did another one in the Beartooth Mountains. Would I like to come along on it, too? I did.

I had known before linking up with Ernest that butterflies belong to the order Lepidoptera, which means "scaly-winged." The order also includes moths. There are something like 135,000 species of Lepidoptera, and of those only about 24,000 are butterflies. Human beings are a single species, or so we say. Much of moth and butterfly classification is based on small external differences in genitalia, and if the moths and butterflies were doing the classifying, the numbers might be different. I had also thought I knew the difference between a moth and a butterfly. Butterflies, I assumed, were those bright, colorful, slim-bodied day fliers who alight with folded wings. They had antennae in the shape of little clubs. Moths were dull, drab, furry, large-bodied night fliers who came to rest with open wings and have plumed, feathery-looking antennae. A moth spun a cocoon to make the change from caterpillar to adult,

Moth

Skipper

Butterfly

but a butterfly completed its metamorphosis inside a chrysalis, the tough hard covering that is the product of the caterpillar's final molt. As a child I had often plucked chrysalises off twigs and taken them home to watch the butterflies emerge.

Well, yes . . . but there are, it seems, exceptions to all those neat descriptions. There are day-flying moths, as I soon discovered when I began counting butterflies with Ernest and mistook them for butterflies. Some butterflies—the western parnassians—emerge from thin cocoons on the ground. There are colorful moths—the pale green lunas and the big, showy cecropias, the latter as brightly patterned as any butterfly. There are dull-colored, large-bodied, furry butterflies that appear mothlike to the untutored eye. They are skippers, which have antennae that are clubbed, with a little hooked point extending from them. Skippers are not what lepidopterists call "true" butterflies like swallowtails or monarchs; nevertheless taxonomists include them among the butterflies. Lepidopterists talk about such things as wing venation to make the distinction between moths and butterflies, which begins to sound like rather small potatoes to most of us.

I took my confusion to the man who might be described as the federal lepidopterist. He is Robert Robbins, one of the butterfly and moth experts at the Smithsonian. Robbins is what is called in biological circles a taxonomist or systematist—a person who studies the similarities and differences in related organisms. (Ernest Williams likes to characterize such entomologists as "dead-bug people" because they work from killed specimens; he and his fellow field entomologists he calls "live-bug people.")

It is generally agreed today that butterflies are descended from mothlike ancestors, and that the separation occurred somewhere between fifty and a hundred million years ago. It helps, Robbins told me, not to worry too much about the distinction between moths and butterflies. "After all, butterflies are just moths—special moths," he said. "However, I think it is interesting to pose a question: If birds are animals with feathers and mammals are animals with mammary glands, what are butterflies? I don't know the answer. I wish I did."

I joined Ernest Williams for the Utica butterfly count on the last weekend in June. With us were two local high school science teachers, a cooperative extension agent, and Ernest's summer research assistant at Hamilton College. The area in which we were working, a circle that included Utica and its southern environs, is also used by the Audubon Society for its Christmas bird count. For the most part, it is what biologists call a "disturbed habitat"— a place where humans have moved in and rearranged the land to their liking: farmed, made roads, franchised McDonald's restaurants. It was therefore not surprising to Ernest that out of 564 butterflies counted that day we ended up seeing a preponderance of two introduced species that are considered to be the English sparrows of the butterfly world: 419 examples of the European skipper and 82 European cabbage butterflies. The latter is the familiar yellowish-white, black-dotted butterfly that gardeners don't like to find among their vegetables. Like other introduced species —kudzu, gypsy moths, English sparrows—cabbage butterflies are tough and opportunistic. They were introduced accidentally into Quebec in 1860 and have spread rapidly since then through most of North America. The females can produce several broods a year and will do so as long as weather permits. Birds avoid the adults (and maybe the caterpillars) because the caterpillars feed on plants with high mustard-oil content—garden plants such as cabbage and broccoli, and also wild plants such as mustard and peppergrass—which make both caterpillar and butterfly taste awful from a bird's standpoint.

The European skipper, our other exotic—as biologists term introduced species—is not as well known to most of us as the cabbage butterfly, in part because it is less distinguished in appearance. It is small, brownish-orange, and has a fat, furry body, characteristic of skippers. It, too, was introduced in Canada (London, Ontario, in 1910), and is now found throughout the Northeast. It has also turned up in isolated populations, having possibly come in on loads of shipped hay, in British Columbia and Colorado. It is spreading so fast that one expert, James Scott, the author of *Butterflies of North America,* expects the European skipper to be found throughout the northern Rockies and Alaska within fifty years. European skipper caterpillars eat grasses and are considered a pest on timothy. Timothy itself is an exotic—another European native—but it has been in this country at least since 1747, and the years give everything status and acceptance. An exotic is an exotic only while we still remember that it came from somewhere else. Migration is often the mechanism of species spread. The foreigners' success may be hard on native species, which have generally developed a life suited to the way things are and were. Exactly. Thank you. But change is necessary to the living process. We don't have to like this, of course; conservatism is characteristic of the already born.

Ernest had expected the European cabbage butterflies and the European skippers to be the most numerous in our survey area because the plants there—introduced cultivated garden flowers and farm crops—were not the ones native to the area. The native butterfly species had lost their habitat; we found only a few. Out in the Utica marsh, a nature preserve and the least disturbed place in which we counted, we found America's best-known butterfly, the gaudy orange and black monarch, but it was the only representative of its species we saw all day.

We also saw four question marks, *Polygonia interrogationis,* which are anglewings, as the genus name suggests. Nearly all *Polygonia* species are northern forest butterflies with ragged outlines and mottled brown color; they are good dead-leaf mimics. *Interrogationis* is so named because of a pale question-mark shape on the gray underside of its splotchy forewings. We saw a streak of black and orange at the margin of the road. "Yes, it's a red admiral," Ernest said. "*Vanessa atalanta*. They are very fast, very hard to net." Red admirals cannot stand extreme winter cold; the ones in the north have migrated in the springtime from warmer climates, where as many as three generations a year may grow from egg to caterpillar, pupate in a chrysalis, and emerge as adults to mate, oviposit, and start the cycle anew.

We watched this one disappear into the shadows, and later, back at the van, Ernest showed us its picture. The tops of the forewings are gently curved, and when folded back they look scalloped. The orange appears in bold bars across the forewings and in bands at the bottom edge of the hind wings. The forewings are also dotted with white spots, brilliant against a background of glorious rich black. Butterfly wings are covered with scales, and the colors in the red admiral and the yellows and browns of other butterflies come from the pigment in the scales; other colors—iridescent blues, greens, purples, and silvers—are created by refracted light. In varying lights those scales shimmer and change before our eyes.

Only a few of the showier butterflies were in our count and, except for the light yellow-white cabbage butterfly, most of those we saw were dull brown skippers—seven species in addition to the European one. They were hard to identify, even for Ernest, without netting. He would sweep them up with a deft pass of his white mesh net and allow them to fly into the end of it, where we could look at them and identify them by their markings. There were a few that he could not be sure of in the field; these he killed quickly with a pinch to the thorax and put in paper envelopes that he marked for location and dropped into a tackle box strapped to his waist. Back in his office, he would spread, dry, and identify them.

I had talked to Bob Pyle on the telephone, and when he heard that Ernest and I would be in Wyoming the third week in July he invited us to meet him and Karölis Bagdönas, a zoology professor and another past president of Xerces, at the Audubon camp at East Fork, in the Wind River Range. Bob is a prolific author who travels, lectures, teaches, talks. He defies categories. With his full and flowing beard he looks rather like Santa Claus. The day we were with him he wore a straw hat, a butterfly-emblazoned T-shirt, white tennis shorts, and Birkenstocks, in which he climbed over rocky terrain and, at one point, waded a river to fetch me a fringed gentian. He carries a butterfly net named Marsha. Marsha has a branch for a handle, worn smooth and silky from use.

Karölis Bagdönas is another lepidopterist with style. Of Lithu-anian descent and intense political consciousness, he slicks back his white-blond hair straight above his high forehead. He is a large man with large enthusiasm and engaging openness. He has headed a team of researchers that became known internationally as the Bagdönas Flying Circus. He would gather a devoted band of fledgling field biologists and travel through the western mountains on what he calls fifteen-pass circuits. "Let's do some biology," he would exhort, and in eight days the group would hurtle eight hundred miles, across fifteen mountain passes, counting butterflies and noting other wildlife matters. He was studying the effect of acid rain on animals and plant life in the Wind River Mountains. Butterflies reveal a lot about an ecosystem, its health or failure, for they are what biologists call indicator species. When butterfly hab-itat is altered, effects may be felt down the line by other living things.

Ernest, Bob, Karölis, and I put one of the Flying Circuses on the road and then began a walk in the Wind River Mountains. Ern-est and Bob both had butterfly nets. "No net today," Karölis said. "I'm just going to be shucking and jiving and doing biology."

Bob swung Marsha at a butterfly and missed. Laughing, he said that in the trade this is called "an almosty but not quitey." To the admiration of the rest of us, Karölis identified a Queen Alexandra butterfly on the wing. *Colias alexandra* is a sulphur butterfly, hard to differentiate from others like it; Karölis had made the identification by noting the precise shade of yellow in its wings. We were at 8,000 feet of elevation, and the wind was soughing through lodgepole pines. Shifting patterns of sunlight and shade raced across ridges and canyons and the wildflowers underfoot. We spotted a yellow-bellied marmot, the rockchuck of the West, scurrying for cover. Bob captured a *Boloria titania,* a fritillary with wings that were duskier near its body, a shading typical of high-altitude butterflies. When the basal third of the wing is dark enough, it can absorb precious heat in these altitudes and help warm the insect's body. Bob put his captured black-spangled orange *titania* on my nose. It sat there quietly, savoring the saltiness of my skin, and Bob photographed the two of us for his butterfly-on-the-nose slide collection. The evening before, at the East Fork Lodge, he had entertained us with a slide show of butterfly intimacies: pictures of butterflies on people—on their noses, mostly. All the people are laughing. In my picture I am laughing, too. It may be impossible *not* to laugh when a butterfly is on your nose.

Ernest netted an *Erebia theano,* an orange and chocolate-brown butterfly, to show me, and Bob displayed it carefully in order not to hurt it. He grinned at Ernest. "Don't mean to co-opt your butterfly, Ernest," he said, "but this is *such* a lovely little alpine, one of the prettiest among seventy or so species. This species is unusual because of its bright spots. See the purple and green reflections on the wings? The *Erebias* are very charming butterflies. There is something about them that excites passions in people— whole coteries become unhealthily obsessed. Our foremost *Erebia* freak is Paul Erhlich, the population biologist. He did his doctoral dissertation on the biology of some of the *Erebia* and he became the great North American *Erebia* man. I'm writing a novel, and in it I have a character who is a total *Erebia* freak. His specialty is *Erebia magdalena,* a species that is completely black."

13

Bob let the *theano* fly away and deftly netted another butterfly with black-bordered white wings which he identified as a female *Parnassius phoebus*. "Do you know about *Parnassius* sex?" he asked me.

"No," I replied.

"Well! This is one of the most fascinating things in all invertebrate biology," he said, with a perfectly straight face.

"In *all* biology," Karölis added, not to be outdone. "Vertebrate as well as invertebrate."

"In the entire *universe*," Bob said, snatching back the initiative, "this is one of the most interesting things."

I peered at the butterfly he was holding. The white wings were set off not only by the dusky black edges but also by brilliant red spots. The wings were darker near the body, helping to keep the butterfly's ovaries warm. "You very seldom find a virgin female *Parnassius*," Bob explained. "The males mate with them very soon after pupation. Most butterflies have to be dissected to find out if the females are virgins, but parnassian females mate only once, because after the mating the male secretes a fluid that solidifies and forms a structure called the sphragis around the female's reproductive opening." He pointed to a neat little cap that fitted over the end of her abdomen. "This assures that only this particular male's genes will be passed on. Parnassians copulate for three hours or more, during which time the liquid molds exactly to the female's shape and hardens. If the male lets go of her too soon, the sphragis will not be formed and will fall away. On the other hand, if he holds on too long it's *coitus perpetuus!*" Bob lets *phoebus* fly away. "Okay, Karölis," he challenges. "Call *that* butterfly." He pointed to a dazzling blue butterfly that had just flown near us, its whitish hind wings dotted with turquoise and orange studs.

"*Melissa*," Karölis replied at once.

"How do you know it isn't *idas*?" Bob asked, explaining to me that *melissa* and *idas* are two species of *Lycaenidae* that are remarkably similar.

Karölis cast down his eyes in mock humility. "Nine years of college?" he said with a grin. Then he added, "Seems more like *melissa* territory. The elevation is too low." The two species are hard to tell apart at medium elevations, where their ranges overlap, he told me, but *melissa* is seldom found at higher altitudes. At medium altitudes the identification can be made with certainty only by dissection of the genitalia. At one time, Bob added, the authority on these butterflies, known by the common name of blues, was Vladimir Nabokov, who studied the mountain blues so thoroughly that he patterned his descriptions of Lolita after one of them; certain phrases—such as "fine, downy limbs"—come from technical descriptions of this butterfly. It was also Nabokov who once wrote in his autobiography, *Speak, Memory,* "Live organisms are less conscious of specific or subgeneric differences than the taxonomist is."

At 8:30 the following morning, Ernest and I begin our count two hundred miles to the north at Clay Butte in the Beartooth Mountains. The day has dawned sunny, and although frost coats the grass when I awake, by the time we start counting, even in the mountain meadow where patches of last winter's snow remain in protected spots, the tough day-flying moths have been joined by butterflies. The windswept butte is thick with bright orange and red spikes of paintbrush, the yellow of buttercups and mountain dandelions, the pink of sticky geranium, the blue of flax, lupines, asters, gentians. I feel as though I am in an illustration for *Heidi.* Below us a mountain lake shimmers in the morning sun. Lodgepole pines ring the meadows. The mountains that rise above those meadows are gray and steely looking. To the south I can see the black and lowering Absarokas, which are volcanic in origin and, hanging low over their peaks, a heavy cloud of smoke, for it is the summer that Yellowstone is burning. But overhead the sky is blue, deep, double, triple blue. We are at 10,000 feet and the air is thin. I feel a little giddy, perhaps merely from altitude, but also with the tingling richness of intense, sexy diversity, plant and animal, with every organism in a hurry to come to maturity and reproduce in the short alpine summer that is all that the elevation allows. Somewhere in the distance white-crowned sparrows are singing; nearby I can see the flash of red as rufous hummingbirds work up and down the spikes of delphiniums, poking their long beaks into the flowers. And everywhere I look there is the flutter of butterfly wings.

There are so many butterflies that there is no way the two of us can identify and count them. I stand still, gaping at it all, while Ernest, the scientist, methodically goes to work, net at the ready. "There's a *theano*," he says. "And there's another . . . four . . . five." I point to an orange butterfly with greenish hind wings. "That's *meadii*," he says. "*Colias meadii,* one of the sulphurs. Oh, there's a female *phoebus*. Bob was right: you hardly ever see a virgin. See her sphragis?" I point to another pair of wings. "No, that's one of those moths that confuse you. It flew like a butterfly but it landed like a moth. There's a *theano* . . . *theano* . . . another *phoebus* . . . this is a good year for them. A skipper! I'd better net this one. I can't be sure. Oh! Did you see it duck? The technique is to sweep the net through the air, rather than slam it on the ground. We're getting swamped here." He takes out his notepad to start keeping count. Marking tally lines next to the name of each species, he recites quietly to himself, "*Theano, meadii* . . . " I stand still, breathing deeply the scarce air, trying to catch my breath and my wits. For Ernest, the species names are as homey and familiar as the names of his family. For me they are new and harder, but I've put common names behind me because they vary more often than do the scientific ones and are often simply made up at the behest of pocket-guidebook editors, who assume that the public will be flummoxed by Latin. In the respite while Ernest is making notes, I try to place these species in their genus, to remember which one is orange, which white. It is rather like meeting too many people at a party. Meanwhile, butterflies in new shapes, sizes, and colors are flying around in the sunlight. The air is tasty, tangy. Ernest tucks his notebook in his pocket and strikes on ahead, counting, identifying, excited and happy with each new species. "Who are you?" he asks a butterfly. "Oh, you're a *glandon*.

16

Just what I thought, a *glandon*!" and moves on, netting butterflies
he cannot identify, releasing them after showing me the details. I
saw a *theano* closely yesterday with Bob and Karölis, but he nets
one to show me again. "See, it's a little silvery underneath and
orange and chocolate-brown above. Pretty. Very pretty. What a
nice bug!" He looks around in despair at all the butterflies we have
missed while he was showing me this bit of beauty. He laughs.
"It's always exciting up here. One person can't see everything.
The important thing is to be accurate about what we *do* see." Then
he's off again, racing ahead of me. Ernest, I note, has very long
legs and is more than ten years younger than I am.

We drive to a nearby site on the road below the crest of the
butte. There are more of the same butterflies than we can count,
and we find a *melissa* and a *Plebejus icarioides,* both of which, like
the *Agriades glandon* he has recorded on the butte, are members of
the subfamily called blues (even though usually only the males are
actually blue).

Also blue is the grouse that scuttles from cover as we walk
rapidly through the flowers. I'm getting the hang of a few names.
Mormonia is pleasant on the tongue. It belongs to the genus *Speyeria,* and together the two words are delicious. I begin to see *mormonia* everywhere and sing out when I do, counting them . . . two
. . . three . . . five . . . eight . . . for Ernest's notebook. I am
having fun, although I keep being diverted by bird song and flowers: false dandelion, dainty deep-blue lupines, and elk thistle,
which Ernest tells me is edible and tastes like celery when the
tough outer layers are peeled back. In my newly acquired confidence I call out to Ernest. "Isn't that a different fritillary?"

"Yes. It's *atlantis,*" he says, stopping to note it on his pad.
Ernest has told me about Paul Grey, the leading fritillary expert, a
man who revised the entire genus *Speyeria* and spent a lifetime
studying its members. Grey lives in Maine. He is a self-trained
lepidopterist, a carpenter by trade. Ernest once met him up on
Clay Butte on a cold, rainy day. The conditions were too poor for
butterflies to be flying, but Grey, who knows his insects, was

using forceps to pluck butterflies from among the grasses and flower stems, where he knew they were waiting out the bad weather.

We drive to another, higher, spot, where willows are so close to the earth that they look like ground cover. The alpine plants are low-growing and can avoid mountain winds and harsh weather. The willows don't look much like what a lowlander would call willows, except for their long leaves and catkin fluff. Ernest and I are both beginning to feel lightheaded and we each notice the beginnings of a headache from the altitude. I sit down and watch Ernest loping across the rocky outcroppings, netting butterflies and making more entries in his notebook. He returns after a quarter of an hour, and we head back to the car with several new species.

We go down to a meadow with a running brook, where we find *ursadentis,* the Beartooth butterfly, to give our count an eponymic authenticity. Then we descend still lower to a camp at 8,600 feet. Ernest has been coming here summer after summer to study his own specialty, *Euphydryas gilletti.* It is a handsome orange butterfly, easy and serene, in part because as a caterpillar it feeds on twinberry, which makes its flesh distasteful to predators. This is a common defense for butterflies. The cabbage butterflies we found in such numbers near Utica use it; so do the monarchs. Monarch caterpillars—fat, green, stripy—feed on milkweed, storing up the plant's cardiac glycosides, which are an emetic, and as a result the gaudy adults are avoided by birds. They, too, are calm butterflies.

At Ernest's camp we find *gilletti* as well as their eggs on the undersides of the lance-shaped leaves of the twinberry that grows at the boggy edges of forests. In the past few years Ernest has thought that he might be documenting the extinction of this highly localized butterfly, for its numbers, both adults and eggs, have been fewer each season. But the egg masses that we see today and note for the count please Ernest, and he intends to come back tomorrow and search the area thoroughly for more *gilletti* eggs for his own research. He is almost apologetic about his good cheer.

As a scientist, he says, he should be content to note the facts, but as a man who has spent years in thoughtful contact with these beautiful butterflies, he can't help being happy about the abundance of eggs, with their promise of a new generation. Ernest's study area contains a variety of habitats and host plants. On a rocky outcropping, hot and arid, we look for another species in the genus *Euphydryas,* the one called *anicia.* Paul Ehrlich, Ernest tells me, moved his studies from *Erebia* to *Euphydryas*—his researchers, he adds with a smile, insist that the host plant for *anicia* is granite. Lepidoptery joke. We range from the rocks down through meadowland surrounded by trees to a hot swampy spot with a stream cutting across it. Biting horseflies, bumblebees, and mosquitoes like the place too, but we have no time to pay attention to them, so many are the butterflies.

The sun tells us that it is past midday and we still have other places to count. We quickly eat some bread and cheese, then drive on. Throughout the afternoon we stop in meadows, walk around ponds, tramp through bog edges. We see juncos, the gray-and-white birds that suburbanites find at their winter feeders. Here they are nesting in pines, and they chatter at our approach. Red-winged blackbirds are singing wherever there is water. We walk, hip-deep in some places, through blue gentians and wild flax, through wild buckwheat, marsh marigolds, cow parsnip, and everywhere we look there are butterflies. I am trusted now to count *mormonia.* I have learned well enough to be dependable about *glandon,* the blue that is actually rather brown. I am proud to have mastered *Pontia occidentalis,* which is common here, the only big, white, fast-flying butterfly at this altitude.

We speed down the highway at 60 mph, Ernest blitz-counting *Cercyonis oetus,* a small, dark-brown butterfly with an underwing eyespot to trick birds into believing that the hinder end is the head, and which is found only among the sagebrush below 7,500 feet. Its unusual stance and flight pattern make it easy to recognize as it nectars on the juicy rabbit brush at the road's edge. "Twenty-one . . . twenty-two . . ." Ernest intones at the wheel. "Fifty-seven . . . fifty-eight," he is saying as we pull up at a country store, and as we get out of the car, "sixty-nine, seventy . . . *theano* . . . *occidentalis.*" Ernest says he is beginning to feel the sun, and my legs do not want to obey me. We go into the store, drink bottles of cold grapefruit juice, and speed on.

We park at the edge of a swamp and find great bunches of butterflies in a patch of thistle: more *mormonia* than we can count, and with them the similarly patterned *aphrodite.* We slow down our counting to make sure of our identifications. Ducks object to our presence; kingfishers rasp out their calls. The afternoon is drawing to a close. We make a few more stops. Ernest, tireless, strides on ahead, counting, calling out new species to me. I sit down and wait for him in the shade of an aspen grove. My brain has just gone on overload. I've asked it to learn too many new words. But my senses still take in what my brain can no longer process: bird song, the sound of a brook, wildflowers of every color, the flash of butterfly wings everywhere, the scent of pines in clear air, golden patches of sunshine dappled with shade, a light breeze lifting the hair at the back of my neck, my legs aching with pleasant tiredness, Ernest disappearing and reappearing, occasionally netting a butterfly.

At 4:30 we finish. Our day's work, neatly tabulated, will be published by Xerces months later as part of the national count. The numbers are instructive, but they tell nothing of the glory of the thing.

CHAPTER II

ORDER DIPTERA: GNATS AND MIDGES

 The class of insects has been divided up by people who think about this sort of thing into a number of orders that group bugs with common characteristics. The number varies, depending upon the system used by the entomologist who is doing the counting, but it is more than twenty-five. These order names are often words that end with the suffix -ptera, such as Lepidoptera or Diptera (the word I used to give some structure to my ignorance when I was talking to Arne and Brian about midges, gnats, and flies). The -ptera suffix comes from the Greek word for wing, *pteron,* and it is used in naming the orders to describe what kinds of wings the animals in a particular group have.

Thus butterflies and moths, the Lepidoptera, all have wings covered with tiny scales, the Greek word for which is *lepis;* it is these scales, some colored, some reflective, that give butterflies their beauty. Diptera, the flies, are so named because they have only two wings, and *dis* in Greek means "twice." Flies are twice-winged. Most insects have four wings, a forward and hind pair. But during the course of their evolution flies adapted their second pair of wings into balancers, little knobs on their backs called halteres, which help stabilize their flight. Of course, in entomology, nothing is without exception and there are a few flies who have lost all their wings, although their body structure reveals that they once had them. The general rule, however, is that flies have two wings attached to the middle part of their thorax, which is stout and beefy with flight muscles. Commonly we call some other bugs flies, too—fireflies and dragonflies, for instance—but their common name is deceptive, for they have *two* pairs of wings, a total of four, and so are not Diptera at all, but belong to quite different orders. Fireflies are actually beetles and belong to the order Coleoptera. Dragonflies are of the order Odonata.

These names that we use for orders—Lepidoptera, Coleoptera, Diptera, and all the others—do not stand for anything in the real world. This was why I was just playing with words when I told Arne and Brian that midges and blackflies belonged to the order Diptera. The order names are sorting words, or taxa, that we humans use to group a dizzying array of individual bugs that otherwise we would find too many and too confusing to think about. Because of the way we have evolved, we have sorting kinds of brains and feel more comfortable if we put what we see in the world into various piles and categories so that we can get a handle on them. But this says more about us and our brains than it does about the world outside our heads, and we shouldn't mix up these categories—the taxa—with reality.

Because we have backbones, we think that our vertebrae, which organize our inside skeleton and nervous system, are enormously important, and so biologists often sort out animals by dividing them into Vertebrates (animals with backbones) and Invertebrates (animals without them). Some of the characters in this book—the dogs, the tadpoles swimming in

Typical fly body plan. Note the single pair of wings and the halteres, or stabilizers, which are the modification of the second pair of wings that most other insects have.

a mud puddle, and the entomologists—are vertebrates. The bugs are invertebrates. There are more of the latter than the former, but in my experience most people hold vertebrates dearer, perhaps because they are our sort.

The biggest grouping of invertebrates are members of the phylum Arthropoda, which means "joint-legged." This includes the class Insecta, but also other classes, such as spiders (which we commonly lump together with insects and call bugs) and crabs and lobsters. What all these animals have in common are exoskeletons, hard external parts outside their bodies rather than the internal skeletons that we have. All the insects have six legs and three main segmented body parts—head, thorax, and abdomen—which you can see in the illustration on page xix. Animals in other classes within the phylum—spiders, lobsters, ticks, and crabs—have body parts arranged differently. The classes are divided into orders, Diptera, Lepidoptera, and the others. But orders are not the final divisions, for we are still merely inside our own brains, arranging bits of the outside world into our own mental categories or piles.

Orders are made up of families, important groupings that often reflect the common names we use for the insects we see in everyday settings. Within the order Diptera, for instance, mosquitoes are a family. Midges are a family, or at least the nonbiting ones are. Black flies are a family. Entomologists have given each of these families a Latin name ending in -idae—Culcidae, Chironomidae, Simuliidae. The Diptera that Arne and I saw—the creatures that started all this—were not midges (Chironomidae), I found out, but belonged to the family Bibionidae, and, all silvery and dancing in the morning sunlight, were members of another artificial grouping within the Bibionidae, the genus *Bibio,* which go by the common name of March flies.

March flies come in a variety of species. I don't know which species the ones we saw were, because in order to identify them I would have had to capture some and give them to a dipterist who specialized in that family; he could have taken them to his laboratory and then told me which they were. I could not have identified them by sight alone, and I did not have wit enough to capture any.

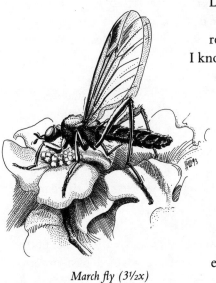

March fly (3½x)

Life is a regretful series of missed opportunities. Now that I have read about March flies, however, I know that they are found throughout North America, typically in parks and suburban gardens, where mated females lay hundreds of eggs in masses in the loose soil before they die. The tiny larvae hatch in the soil, where they feed on decaying plant matter, pupate, and then emerge as winged adults early in the springtime (although not necessarily in March) to swarm in mating dances a few feet from the ground. Their low, clumsy flight, which was what Arne and I saw, was characteristic. These dancing March flies vary in size according to species, and if we had looked at them closely we would have found that they were shiny black or dark brown, with wings clear or whitish with yellow-brown veins.

Species is the basic taxon. Species are defined as those groupings of individuals who readily mate and produce offspring of a like kind. This sounds very precise, and it is sometimes said that species represent the only biological reality in the classification scheme. But the species name is as much a product of our brains as any of the rest of the taxa, and in many ways just as unreal. Taxonomists, the people who study killed specimens, describe them, and assign names, work from animals no longer capable of breeding because they are dead. Their descriptions are of physical difference only; laboratory equipment now allows the establishment of close morphological, chromosomal, and biochemical differentiation. But one is never quite sure whether geographically isolated animals can interbreed. Ernest Williams was interested when I told him about the artificial insemination of queen bees. He wondered whether the techniques and equipment used for the procedure might help in the determination of butterfly species. For instance, could a West Coast butterfly be artificially inseminated and produce fertile offspring using sperm from an East Coast butterfly that was similar but thought to be of a different species? And how would that influence classification? Bob Robbins, the systematicist, said this would not be a helpful approach. "Ernest and I have different ways of looking at the matter," he said. "He's talking about potential and possibility, but I think you've got to stay with reality as it is. We must define species as those animals that interbreed. Whether they are isolated by a mountain range or biological capability is not important."

The various taxa are not fixed. Changed scientific names sometimes bewilder the users of field guides, who think that those binomials, in all their Latin dignity, are immutable and in some way represent reality. Even in my own applied entomological field, beekeeping, names change. Twenty years ago, when I first began keeping bees, the bee from Africa which became known as the killer bee was called *adansonii* (full name: *Apis mellifera adansonii*). Today it is known as *scutellata* (short for *A. m. scutellata*). The first initially capitalized word in a Latin name represents genus, the second lowercase one is the species, and subsequent words are subspecies or races. Anyone who spends much time thinking about bugs must eventually learn different words for the same pieces of scurrying reality that creep and fly about. One reason for the changes is that new fossils and previously undescribed bugs are being discovered all the time, and more is being learned about the biology, chemistry, distribution, and behavior of those already "described," which is the word entomologists use in naming a bug. So taxonomists revise the taxa, regroup the animals within them, and rename them, sometimes creating intermediate categories—subspecies, superfamilies, and the like—which are supposed to clarify relationships. But there are as many fashions in classifying and naming as there are in all human activities.

25

Today these revisions often rely on cladistics to put bugs into piles even without the existence of fossil records, which, for such fragile creatures, are hard to come by. Cladistics (the word is from the Greek *klados,* a branch, twig, or stem) is a branching classification system that attempts to eliminate subjectivity by arranging animals according to their genealogies, inferred from their present states. Its author is Willi Hennig, who in 1950 laid it out in a book entitled *Theorie der phylogenetischen Systematik.* Cladistics assumes that individuals in a single group sharing special characteristics are the descendants of a single ancestor, and that the named groupings should reflect this relationship. The word for this is *monophyletic.* The corollary is that shared primitive characteristics should be ignored in classification because they have been retained from a more remote ancestral form. This sounds precise and neat, but sometimes it is hard to know whether a characteristic is truly special. Animal characteristics have a puckish tendency to turn up here and there independently: Insects, bats, and birds have wings, for instance, but they evolved separately. This is called convergent evolution, and it can sometimes trick classifiers, for there are many subtle cases of it that are not so intuitively obvious as the wings of insects, bats, and birds. Nevertheless, in recent years cladistics has become the hot new way to revise the various taxa to express phylogenetic, evolutionary relationships.

There are other approaches to classification, too. This is hardly surprising, for our relationship with other animals has been chiefly in their naming, and we, being many, have many ways of naming. Those names, and the patterns into which we have put them, have always revealed more about us than the animals they were supposed to describe. Another system is called numerical taxonomy. Made possible by the ability of computers to easily handle large amounts of data, numerical taxonomy is supposed to be a classification system that even those without biological training can use. It was developed by a virtual committee of biological thinkers, C. D. Michener, R. R. Sokal, P. H. A. Sneath, A. J. Cain, and G. A. Harrison, who also wanted to eliminate subjectivity from classification. Numerical taxonomy accords equal importance to

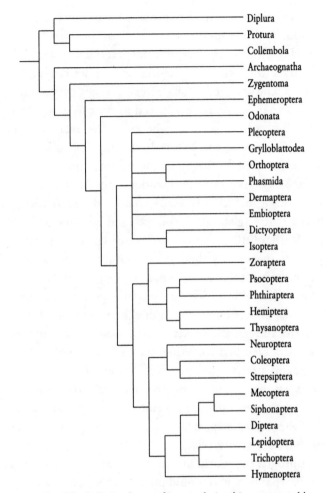

Possible cladistic scheme of insect relationships, as created by
R.G. Davies for his Outlines of Entomology

all the characteristics an animal has, disregards evolutionary relationships, and groups together all animals with shared characteristics. Within this system, the term "species" as a base taxon is
rejected, and is replaced with the inelegant term "operational taxonomic unit," or (what else?) OTU. In point of fact, some characteristics eventually have to be given more weight than others
(what to do about maleness and femaleness and the differences

they require in otherwise similar animals, for instance) and subjectivity is gradually reintroduced.

Another classification method is what is termed traditional classification. Here, the skill, experience, and understanding of the classifier is acknowledged. Characteristics of the animal are weighed and certain ones are considered more important than others. The fossil record is studied wherever it is available, and an effort is made to make use of the branching and divergence of ancestral lines as well as the apparent relationship among living animals. The subjectivity of the classifier is acknowledged.

Naturally, disagreements take place about the particular pile in which this or that bug should be placed, and how the piles should be heaped. With a little effort we can conceive of other categories that do not group bugs by their genetic similarity as expressed in their DNA patterns, their wing venation, their genitalic structure, and the like. Other world views have other species, other specificities. It is rather like looking through a kaleidoscope: We hold it up to the light and see the pretty design made by the patterns of bits of glass arranged just so. When we shift it, the glass falls into another, equally pretty, design. The Algonquin Indians classed some insects by their desire to bite us, lumping together the bugs we would separate and name mosquito, black fly, biting midge. They called them *sawgimay,* which means, roughly, small-person-who-flies-and-bites-so-fiercely.

Artists approach the world in a more visual way than the rest of us. I know one painter who would put together in the same species our new black puppy, Louie the Labrador, and the cat, Black Edith, who is just now doing a little dog fishing. The black cat is sitting on a chair high enough to be out of Louie's reach and is dangling a paw down limply, twitching it slightly. Louie, who has been lying down wondering what on earth to do with all her puppy energy, jumps up to snatch the paw and is given a box on the nose. The two animals are the same color and nearly the same size, and both have long tails. It is easy to see how an artist could group them as a single species for pictorial purposes of shape and color. But an artist might also want to add to the species of color a 1939

Plymouth, black beetles, some telephones, crows, Washington bureaucrats in their dismal suits, and Bob Pyle's *Erebia magdalena.* My painter friend might put into another species, perfectly workable for her, golden retrievers, marmalade, honeybees, butternut squash, Marilyn Monroe in gold lamé, and some nasturtiums.

Our sense of smell, and therefore our appreciation of chemical differences, is limited. Entomologists now have equipment that can detect some of those differences, and use it as an aid to classification. But for dogs it is primary; I suspect they classify the world by odor and, since their sense is so exquisite, subdivide by time: new odors, old odors, in-between odors. One taxon might be *Something that I would like to chase just came by here. Let me at it.* Another might be *Something tasty was here yesterday. Regrets.* I wish I could get inside their brains and know a world so arranged.

There are something like 90,000 known species of flies worldwide, arranged as entomologists arrange them. "There are so many flies that no one can ever truly profess to know them all," lamented Charles Curran in his authoritative *Families and Genera of North American Diptera,* written in 1965 when he was curator emeritus of the American Museum of Natural History. Even the families are large. There are families that entomologists call midges and gnats, which include those that breed near water and those that don't; those that bite humans and those that don't—thus completely mixing up our common understanding of the difference between the two words. I took a brief, unscientific survey and found that most people thought that gnats were the things that bite and live around the water and midges were the things that didn't bite and lived away from the water. Everyone said that they were little-bitty guys.

Midge is a word that comes to us from Old English, *mycg,* and is related to the Greek word for fly, *myia (musca,* in Latin), and lives on in our word *mosquito.* It is identified in Webster II as "any very small gnat." Gnat, on the other hand, is defined in the same dictionary as "any of various small flies, especially such as bite." The definition goes on to list as examples two flies that do bite, the buffalo gnat and the black fly, which are not gnats in the ento-

29

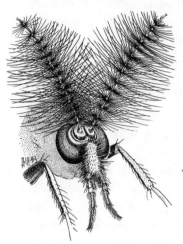

Head of a male midge, showing the antennae with their long, sensitive hairs

mological sense, but members of the family Simuliidae, and gnats that don't bite at all, the fungus gnats.

The word *gnat* comes from the Old English *gnætt,* and is akin to the word *gnaw*. There is a rather unruly and annoying connotation in *gnat*. In the twelfth century, a Parisian canon, Hugo St. Victor, who was a scholar in dispute with Abelard, held that after the Fall some of the animals chafed against serving Man. Indeed, two classes of them escaped his control completely: the Greatest, exemplified by lions and tigers; and the Least, the gnats.

Members of the family Chironomidae, the nonbiting midges that we see and hear dancing in swarms high in the air on a summer evening, look like miniature mosquitoes, to whom they are not related. They are more delicate and much smaller, usually no more than ⅜ of an inch long. The family is a big one, containing several thousand species. The dancing swarms are made up of as many as 50,000,000 individuals. One researcher, D. J. Lewis, dried and weighed samples of one species, *Tanytarsus lewisi,* and concluded that an entire swarm weighed only one ounce. Frail and insubstantial as they seem, however, the collective beating of their wings makes such a murmur that they can be heard before they are seen. Both James Needham (one of this country's most renowned field entomologists, who worked at Cornell during the first part of the century) and Curran mention the poetic and crepuscular experience of one Professor Williston, who, in 1896, standing in a meadow one evening in the Rocky Mountains, watched swarms of Chironomidae rise from the grasses in incredible numbers, producing a sound like that of a distant waterfall.

One hundred years ago the individuals within the swarms of

30

Chironomidae and other midges were thought to be female, but today entomologists tell us that although there are females among them, the aggregations are primarily male. These males with their fine, bushy antennae orient themselves by some marker—a post, a tree, an open patch of ground, or even a human walking along —which explains why they sometimes accompany us on our strolls. Their rapid motion raises their body temperature and may make them more potent. Females, lurking nearby in the grass or bushes, dart into the swarm once the males have become irresistible to them. There they are seized and mated. Both male and female Chironomidae have mouths but will never use them, for the adults live only to breed. They have stored enough food energy in their bodies from their larval days to fuel the furious beating of their wings. One estimate—I wish I knew how it was made —claims that they beat at a rate of 3,000 strokes a minute.

After the females have mated, they lay their eggs, usually in the water, where they and the larvae that develop from them become an important food for the fish and other animals that live there. Some species of chironomid larvae are known as bloodworms (the same that are sold in cans in pet stores for fish food) because they are red in color. This is due to the presence of hemoglobin in their blood. Our blood is red because we have hemoglobin in it too, but most insect blood, called hemolymph, is colorless or a pale greenish-yellow. It circulates freely, not in veins and arteries as ours does, but throughout the insect's body and is the liquid that oozes out squoochily if we smash one. Hemoglobin carries oxygen to body tissue in those of us who have red blood, but most insects don't need it because they get the oxygen their bodies use through a system of finely branching trachea—tubes that spread throughout their bodies

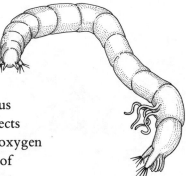

Midge larva (7x)

31

and are connected to the outside by tiny holes (spiracles) that cunningly close in most aquatic insects. But bloodworms, those chironomid larvae, are special among insects because their hemoglobin allows them to transfer oxygen to their body tissue. This seems to be an adaptation that permits them to survive in oxygen-poor conditions, such as the stream beds in which they live. James Needham described raising them in jelly tumblers and reported that they were very shy. "When placed in a jar their chief anxiety is to bury themselves in the mud, and very soon they will gather bits of dead leaves and particles of sand about them, binding them together with viscid threads passed out of the mouth and in a short time will be completely concealed in a rough tube." The larvae pupate at the bottom of a stream, pond, or river, and then emerge as adults, float to the surface, and fly away to mate and begin the process all over again.

The other family of midges, the biting midges, are known to entomologists as the Ceratopogonidae. The best-known species in this family have mouths that they use to bite us. Our blood provides them with the protein needed to produce a new generation. Their popular name is no-see-ums or punkies. They are very small, hence the first name. *Punkie* comes from a Lenape word for ashes, dust, or powder. In 1794, G. H. Loskiel, writing in his *Mission to the Indians of North America,* observed "The most trou-

Punkie (15x)

blesome plague . . . especially in passing thro' the woods was a kind of insects called by the Indians Ponk or Living Ashes." In my circle we always called them no-see-ums (or can't-but-hardly-see-ums or any of a string of variations), and my first introduction to them was years ago, when some friends and I were returning from a camping trip in New England. We stopped overnight in the Adirondacks. Our camping gear was all scattered about, so we planned to sleep in our station wagon, which was fitted with window screens made of mosquito netting. We had barely dropped off when we found our bodies on fire with bites from bugs too small to swat. When we turned on lights we could not find our tormentors but could see their work—we were polka-dotted with bites. Closing the windows merely made us hot, for the invisible plague had already drifted through the netting. Sleep was impossible. We dressed, took out the screens, rolled down all the windows to allow whatever was inside to blow out, and sped through the night for home. A man at a diner where we stopped for coffee laughed at our red polka dots and told us we'd been bitten by no-see-ums. The bites, so ferociously administered, did not itch at all, and the next day they were gone.

Only a few genera of this family contain species that bite us. Most of them feed on flowers or other midges and small mayflies. And of the species that do bite us, only the female has the piercing, stabbing mouthparts that penetrate our skin to give her the blood meal she needs. In the sense that my enemy's enemy is my friend, it is perhaps gratifying for a human to know that one species, *Culicoides anophelis,* chases mosquitoes that have gorged themselves on blood and, by piercing their abdomens, sucks out droplets of it.

There are a number of small flies that, at least in the United States, are called gnats (the Brits do it contrariwise—what we call midges, they call gnats, and vice versa). They are all plant, sap, and nectar feeders: the gall gnats, whose larvae make those bumps and swellings on trees and plants, family Cecidomyiidae; the wood gnats, family Anisopodidae; and the fungus gnats, families Sciaridae and Mycetophilidae. Unless you are a dipterist specializing in

33

these families, the adults of the various species look pretty much alike: They are rather like miniature mosquitoes. But since they do not bite humans, few of us ever take much notice of them while we are out walking in the woods, where we might find them if we were looking. Some of their larvae, however, are highly unusual. Certain species of gall gnats, which usually come together, male and female, in adult winged form to mate and lay eggs in the usual fashion, also have an optional form of reproduction called paedo-genesis, a word used by entomologists to describe reproduction by a juvenile, immature insect. This is not unique to gall gnats; a few other insects—some beetles, for instance—can reproduce the same way, but it is rare and curious.

In the case of the gall gnats, regular, normal larvae, both male and female, have reproductive cells within their bodies. Usually these remain dormant until the gnat becomes a flying, sexually mature adult. But here and there will be a larva that has a few large eggs, up to thirty-five in number, which will mature within the larva's body, hatch into larvae, and devour the parent larva as they free themselves from its body, only to be dealt with in the same way by the larvae which will hatch out within *their* bodies. Several generations of larvae can continue in this way, tumbling together life, birth, and death in an extraordinarily direct fashion without growing to adulthood or resorting to sex. Each hatch, of course, is made up of individuals from the same sex, but since both males and females can reproduce paedogenetically, two populations of both sexes begin to build up under the bark of the tree where the first eggs were laid. Then, suddenly, a generation is produced in which the reproductive cells remain dormant, the larvae mature and, in due time, take wing and mate, male with female.

Any insect that undergoes a complete metamorphosis has sev-eral different life stories, ones that describe how it lives in its immature, larval forms, what goes on in its pupal transformation —if it has one—and how it behaves as a mature sexual adult. Entomologists call the various stages between egg and adult "in-stars." They call the adult an "imago" or "imagine." When we non-entomologists think about bugs, we usually think about them as imagines, for those are the ones we see most often. Of course we may be aware that those tent caterpillars we burn out of our trees turn into moths. When we were children, some of us may even have plucked up a fat yellow-, black-, and white-striped jewel-box caterpillar along with its butterfly-weed leaf and kept it in a jar to watch as it changed, first into a chrysalis and then into a monarch butterfly. But ordinarily, most larval lives proceed without our knowing about them and remain a puzzle to all but the specialists.

Ten years ago I stumbled, quite literally, onto one such larval puzzle and used the incident to conclude a book about natural history I had written. I had seen what I thought, at a distance, was a shed snake skin. But when I came up to it, I found that it was a moving mass of tiny, maggoty-like caterpillars grouped in a snakish configuration, piled more deeply and thickly in the center and tapering at both ends. They were all moving along in the same direction, each synchronous with his fellows so that a wave of motion undulated down the mass. They were following a single leader, and when I picked him up another moved into his place. They were little creatures, half-inchers or a bit more, hairless, creamy white with dark heads. My human brain was groping for a classificatory box to put them into, but I was completely bewildered. I had no idea what they were, what they were up to, where they were going, or why. I couldn't even figure how to look them up. I had called them caterpillars, but they looked like no caterpillars I had ever seen. I didn't capture any, so I had nothing to give an entomologist to identify. They seemed an adequate way to end a book about living the kind of life in which answers have a way of turning themselves into questions, so I passed on my creamy, dark-headed wrigglers to my readers, none of whom evidently knew what they were either, for I never received a letter about them.

I was sitting in the Library of Congress one day, after Arne and Brian had loaded me down with questions about small Diptera, reading through a stack of books about them. I had just discovered Charles H. Curran's satisfying volume *Families and Genera of North*

Sciara ♂ (6x)

American Diptera, and was reading about the family Sciaridae, the dark-winged fungus gnats, when I came on an answer to at least one of my questions. The larvae of these gnats, Curran wrote, "have some very interesting habits —some of them sometimes travelling over the ground in snakelike masses."

I turned to another book, the remarkable and beautifully written *Natural History of Flies,* by the British entomologist Harold Oldroyd, and looked up the family in it. Sciaridae larvae, he wrote, are slender, wormlike creatures with small but distinct dark heads. They are typically vegetable feeders. The larvae of one species, *Sciara militaris,* he went on to explain, are popularly known as army worms, but are not to be confused with the lepidopteran larvae with the same popular name. *S. militaris,* he wrote, "march harmlessly across the leaf mould of a forest floor as a band of worm–like insects an inch or so broad and 10 to 15 feet long. No one knows why they should do so."

Intrigued, I browsed through the bug books to see if anyone else knew more, but could find little in addition. The two standard insect authors, Augustus D. Imms and John Henry Comstock, did tell me that they are called army worms in Europe, but in the United States are usually named snake worms because of their snakelike appearance in the mass. These writers added that they travel at the rate of an inch a minute, that they have been seen marching along in Sweden, Russia, and Germany as well, and that everyone is puzzled by them. Imms reports certain speculations, such as that they may be massed in order to protect one another as they move to a spot where they will pupate, and recommended as the only authoritative study one by O. A. Johannsen, published by the Maine Agricultural Experiment Station as Bulletin No. 172

in 1909. When I was in Maine studying black flies, I found a copy, but Johannsen had simply collected reports of sightings of these long snakelike columns of larvae and had nothing more to add.

At least I now have a name to attach to my questions. But "No one knows why they should do so." It is something, I suppose, to learn that my puzzlement is shared by entomologists.

One last word about a gnat that we humans find pesky and annoying and—well, gnatlike. These gnats don't bite, but they make a summertime walk difficult because of their habit of persistently flying into our eyes. In fact in some places they are called eye gnats. They belong to a large family, the Chloropidae, a common group widely found in grassy places where the larvae live in stems. Most species in this family never come to our attention because we are as irrelevant to their lives as they are to ours, but adults of a few species have a ferocious need for moisture and gather on any source of it they can find—our eyes, or even sores. In the Ozarks we call them pecker gnats, because they congregate around that part of a hound dog's anatomy.

CHAPTER III

ORDER COLEOPTERA: LADYBUGS

When asked what he had learned about the nature of the Creator from his studies, the great British biologist J. B. S. Haldane is said to have replied that "God has an inordinate fondness for beetles." There are more beetles than anything else in the animal kingdom. In numbers of species described, they represent the largest group of animals on the planet, more than 25 percent of them. Some 370,000 species have been named so far, and Terry Erwin, of the Smithsonian, estimates that there are probably ten million kinds of beetles now living.

South American Indian mythmakers may have sensed the truth behind Haldane's witticism; in addition, they neatly put mankind in its proper place in relation to beetles. According to their stories the Creator was a very large beetle, who made men and women from the grains of earth left over after he had constructed the rest of the world. Not only are beetles very many, they are very successful, having adapted to nearly every environment the planet has to offer—water, land, and air. They also have been around for much longer than many other insects—longer, in fact, than most animals now alive. Something rather beetlelike has been scuttling about for more than 225 million years, ever since Permian times, at the end of the Paleozoic era.

Many, but not all, insects have two pairs of wings, forewings

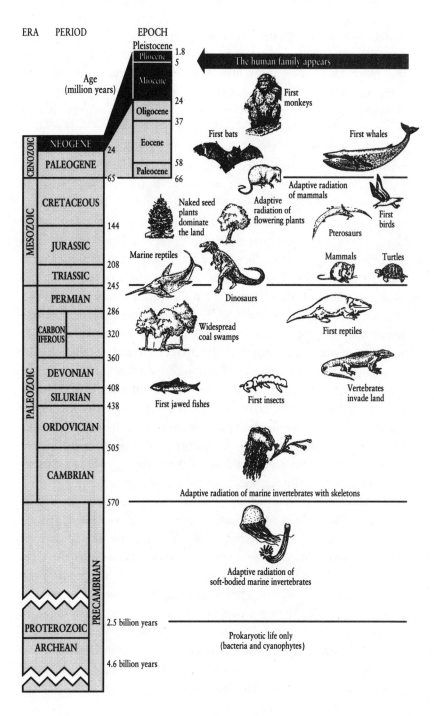

ERA   PERIOD   EPOCH

Pleistocene   1.8
                      5

Age
(million years)

The human family appears

First monkeys

First bats

First whales

Adaptive radiation of mammals

Naked seed plants dominate the land

Adaptive radiation of flowering plants

First birds

Pterosaurs

Marine reptiles

Mammals   Turtles

Dinosaurs

First reptiles

Widespread coal swamps

Vertebrates invade land

First jawed fishes   First insects

Adaptive radiation of marine invertebrates with skeletons

Adaptive radiation of soft-bodied marine invertebrates

Prokaryotic life only
(bacteria and cyanophytes)

CENOZOIC — NEOGENE 24 — PALEOGENE 65
Neogene epochs: Pliocene, Miocene 24, Oligocene 37, Eocene 58, Paleocene 66

MESOZOIC — CRETACEOUS 144 — JURASSIC 208 — TRIASSIC 245

PALEOZOIC — PERMIAN 286 — CARBONIFEROUS 320 — 360 — DEVONIAN 408 — SILURIAN 438 — ORDOVICIAN 505 — CAMBRIAN 570

PRECAMBRIAN — 2.5 billion years — PROTEROZOIC — ARCHEAN — 4.6 billion years and hind wings. Beetles are among these, but over millions of years of adaptation their forewings became highly specialized, giving them their scientific name: Coleoptera. This means sheath-winged, from the Greek *koleon,* a sheath. Over the years it is thought that the wing veins became thickened and grew harder until they developed into tough protective covers for the more delicate hind wings, the flying wings that fold underneath the body. Entomologists don't even call these forewings "wings," but "elytra," from another Greek word for sheath or case. Spread in flight, the elytra can act as stabilizers, but closed, in resting position, they give the animal that hard, armored appearance we all think about when we hear the word "beetle." These tough elytra became wing protectors, necessary for survival when beetles were new to the world. The creatures scuttled about in leaf litter and sustained themselves by eating the fungus they found there.

But up out of that litter of leaves and stems from primitive ferns, mosses, and other late Paleozoic plants that could reproduce without seeds were growing the first seed plants, the treelike cordiates, taller than ferns, with long slender stems and simple leaves. They were the earliest of what botanists call Gymnosperms, which means naked-seeded. They have no flowers in the usual sense. Their seed-producing ovaries and pollen-bearing male organs grew uncovered on the plants. The cordiates no longer grow in our world today, although there are still some Gymnosperms: pines, ginkgoes, yews, cycads, and sago palms.

As the trees developed and became more rugged, the beetles moved up into them in pursuit of food and safety. Their delicate parts protected by their elytra, they could burrow into loose bark and into woody tissue itself; they also swarmed all over the trees and, at least in some species, developed a taste for the tender parts of the plants themselves. They may even have given the competitive edge in Cretaceous times, some 135 million years ago, to plants that covered their bare sexual parts. R. A. Crowson, from the University of Glasgow, who has written the authoritative and readable *Biology of the Coleoptera,* has observed that cycad fossil plants from the early Cretaceous times show damage typical of the kind inflicted on today's plants by fruitworm and fungus beetles. He speculates that one evolutionary response to this damage may have been to enclose the flowering parts, giving the trees and other plants that protected their seeds in this way such a reproductive advantage that, botanically, they quickly took over the planet. Today these are what we call Angiosperms, the flowering plants. All seed plants that are not Gymnosperms are Angiosperms. They are the most numerous of all plants, represented by about 250,000 living species. We do not live in a Nuclear Age or an Information Technology Age. We do not live in a Post-Industrial Age, a Post–Cold War Age, or a Post-Modern Age. We do not live in an Age of Anxiety or even a New Age. We live in an Age of Flowering Plants and an Age of Beetles.

Of all those many beetles there is one family, the Coccinellidae, the ladybugs, for which we humans, as well as the Creator, have an inordinate fondness. About fifteen years ago, when I was still making vegetable gardens, I ordered ladybugs from a mail-order seed catalog in the hope that they would keep the vegetables I wanted to grow free from aphids, as it was advertised they would do. When they arrived, thousands of them neatly boxed, I followed the instructions, kept them in the refrigerator and released them, a handful at a time into my garden—and never saw them again. There weren't many destructive insects of any kind in my garden that year, but I was never sure the ladybugs had anything to do with it because they seemed to have disappeared and there was no noticeably larger population of the little beetles the following year.

I didn't order any ladybugs again, but I always wondered how they got into the box I received. It wasn't until February 1991, just after the bloom of seed catalogs, that I got around to calling the Henry Fields Company, one of the many that advertised ladybugs, and asked the man who answered the telephone, "Where do ladybugs come from?" He laughed, and explained that they were harvested from the wild in California and kindly gave me the name of several suppliers the company used. I wanted to go to a ladybug harvest, so I began to make arrangements.

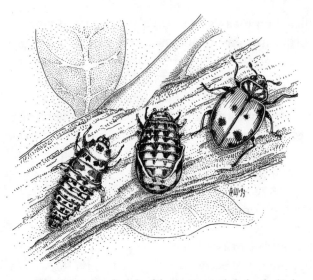

Larva, pupa, and adult of the convergent lady beetle (4x)

But the ladybugs were late in coming into the Sierra Nevadas that year. I learned that they usually begin clustering up there in May, forming big masses where they can be easily harvested. It was not until several weeks later that they began to be seen. They had hatched out of eggs in the early springtime down in California's Central Valley as they do every year, and had been feeding, in larval form, on aphids in the field crops there. Stuffed, the larvae had spent about a week quiet as pupae, in metamorphosis, rearranging their body parts before they emerged as adult ladybugs. The adults had come out of their pupal cases hungry, but as larvae they had done such a good job of disposing of all the available aphids that there was little left for them to eat. So they took to their wings and, riding the thermal currents created by the sun heating up the valley, flew to the mountains, where they could feed on pollen from the flowers blooming there. After fattening themselves on this diet for a week or so, they began to settle down in masses of thousands and thousands, under leaf litter and in protected places near streams, to last out the summer dry spell.

They were so late in coming to the mountains that gardeners all over the country who had ordered them were growing impatient.

"It's a real problem," said Jeanne Houston in May when I telephoned her. Jeanne manages Unique Insect Control, a beneficial-insect company owned by her and her parents, Mary and Peter Foley, who claim to be the largest ladybug suppliers in the business, one which the Foleys estimate generates three to five million dollars in annual sales. "The orders keep coming in," said Jeanne. "I've tried to talk customers into using green lacewings instead." Lacewings, common insects of several species in the genus *Chrysopa,* are about half an inch long, have four pale, pretty green wings and bright, prominent eyes. They are also known as aphid lions, being ferocious feeders on aphids. When raised in insectaries they are sold in egg form to those who order them.

"But people just insist on ladybugs, and they aren't up in the mountains yet," Jeanne went on to say. "The weather hasn't warmed up enough to drive them out of the valley fields. We usually stock them in refrigeration, so we can sell them year-round, but demand is up, and we are completely out of ladybugs."

By mid-June the temperatures in the fields in the Central Valley had risen and the ladybugs were beginning to be seen bedding down near streams, fat enough with pollen to last through summer drought and winter snows. In the autumn, rains would rouse them briefly and they would find protected sunny spots higher up in the canyons, away from floods, and then settle down to a period of dormancy. Early in the following year they would become active in their aggregations and would seek one another out to mate and on some mild day fly back down to the Central Valley, where they would feed on protein-rich aphids, lay eggs, and die.

Golden-eye lacewing (4x)

There are many species of ladybugs in the United States, and in places where insecticides don't kill them first they are good at eating the small, soft-bodied plant pests that we don't like—aphids, scale insects, mealy bugs. The commonest species is the one collected in the Sierras, *Hippodamia convergens*. They are found wild everywhere in the United States, but only in the prolonged dry spells of the Western mountains do they form aggregations big enough to harvest economically.

While still at home in Washington, I'd been given the name of a woman in her sixties who harvests ladybugs for one of the mail-order companies. But I discovered that she had recently been involved in a dispute over ladybug beds, as the aggregation sites are called, that had ended in gunfire. A competing family group of harvesters had been collecting in a bed the woman considered to be hers. She discovered them and cussed them out, and as soon as she left gunshots were fired. The family accused her of hiring someone to shoot them. She admitted that a gun had been fired but indignantly denied hiring a gunman. "If I were going to shoot somebody," she was quoted as saying, "I wouldn't send someone else to do it. I'd do it myself." But she said she hadn't. "I didn't even have a gun with me that day," she explained.

I decided I didn't want to go ladybug harvesting with a person who even might *sometimes* carry a gun, so I asked Jeanne Houston if she could arrange for me to go out with one of the pickers, as she called the harvesters.

"I wouldn't trust most of those pickers to spend the day with you back in those mountain canyons," she said, explaining that many of the pickers are a secretive lot, protective of their particular ladybug beds, their techniques, their skills, and their knowledge of the rough terrain up in the mountains, where gold used to be mined in an equally covert way. The pickers are people who, for one reason or another, like to be paid in cash, and good pickers can make a thousand dollars a day.

Many telephone calls later, Mike Lake, a Sacramento construction supervisor who has been picking ladybugs for ten years, agreed to let me go out with him. "He's our most *reliable* picker,"

44

said Jeanne, laying emphasis on the word "reliable" as if it were code.

I talked to Mike, and he firmly corrected me on the use of the word "picking" in referring to the harvest. "We call it 'bugging,' " he said, and those who go bugging, I discovered in later conversations, are called buggers. I promised Mike that I would keep the location of his beds a secret—he has discovered at least a hundred of them over the years—and also promised not to reveal the intricacies of his water technique of harvest, which he learned as an apprentice to the second generation of a family of buggers. These secrets shall not pass my lips.

Mike is a stocky young man with dark hair, and was dressed, on the day late in June when we went out, in white shorts, white T-shirt, and running shoes. He grew up in Nevada City, California, surrounded by the canyons where the ladybugs bed down, and knows them the way only a native can. He has a college background in forestry and loves the mountains where we spent the day. He also loves hang gliding and uses his flights to spot likely ladybug beds and the access roads to them. Single now, he plans later in the year to marry the daughter of Lowell Rouff, his apprentice, who joined us for the day of bugging.

Mike and I start out from Sacramento at eight in the morning in his red Toyota 4x4, loaded down with ladybug gear, including a Honda trail bike, and drive to pick up Lo.

"Lo's retired," Mike tells me. "He was going crazy for something to do, so I took him on as an apprentice. But I really like working alone better. I can go faster and make more money. Lo is pretty laid back. Sometimes he even takes a nap in the woods when he's bugging. But I was trained by guys who needed the money, and I like to work quickly."

Lo lives in a California sort of house in the Sierra foothills, with a view looking out over Lake Folsom, and he's a California sort of guy, slim, with a beard starting to turn gray, dressed in a red sweatshirt, jeans, and Birkenstocks. He offers me a cup of South American herbal tea. "Doesn't taste like anything, but it's good for what ails you," he explains. He shows me the holding room for ladybugs he's made in back of his garage. "This rock's lava cap," he says, waving to the cool gray walls of the cave room. "I just took a jackhammer to it. Carried out eight, ten loads of rubble a day before I had it big enough." He's jackhammered out rock ledges, on which he stacks the six-foot-wide chicken-wire trays to store the cloth sacks of ladybugs before he takes them down to the Foleys for processing. A couple of sacks containing his haul from yesterday, when he went bugging alone, lie on the trays.

Lo has a red 4x4 pickup, too, with his Honda already loaded into it; we'll need the trail bikes to get to at least one of the ladybug beds. We arrange to meet at the first bed, and Mike and I drive into the hills.

On the way, Mike points out a faded sign that says LADYBUG ROAD. He tells me that the ramshackle house on it was home to the first man to buy ladybugs from people in the mountains. The use of ladybugs in pest control is about a hundred years old in California.* In the early 1870s, an exotic, the cottony-cushion-scale insect, was accidentally imported into California from Australia and spread rapidly and harmfully through the citrus groves. In 1888, the scale's natural predator in Australia—the Vedalia ladybug, *Rodalia cardinalis*—was imported by orchardists and entomologists, and it quickly brought the scale under control. Significant populations of Vedalia thrived and continue to protect California citrus crops.

Impressed by this success, turn-of-the-century California entomologists began to take a look at the native ladybug, *H. convergens.* They knew it to be a voracious feeder on aphids and other insect pests, both in its larval and adult form, and, what was more, it

---

* It's older elsewhere, of course, for protecting crops with ladybugs is an ancient folk practice. In 1806, a pair of Englishmen, Kirby and Spence, recommended controlling hop aphids with the common English ladybird and added, "If we could but discover a mode of increasing these insects at will, we might not only clear our hothouses of aphides [*sic*] by their means, but render our crops of hops much more certain than they are now."

could be collected easily from big aggregations in the Sierras. So in the early years of this century the state of California began a program to gather ladybugs from the mountains. A few days after my trip with Mike and Lo, Kenneth Hagen, an entomologist with the Division of Biological Control in the Department of Entomology, University of California at Berkeley, showed me pictures of the old-time buggers, standing next to the mules they used to haul out the heavy loads of beetles. In Sacramento the ladybugs were packed, crated, and shipped to growers around the state. The results were disappointing. It didn't take long to discover that nearly all the beetles released in the fields flew away.

By the 1920s, scientific studies showed that although the ladybugs were important agricultural helpers in their natural cycle, these picked and shipped ones did not serve as any significant control on insect pests, and so the state of California got out of the business. But ladybugs, perhaps because they are so cute, the pandas of the insect world, became something of a symbol, and, with the growth of the organic gardening movement, there was a continuing demand for them countrywide—a demand, according to the Foleys, that still is growing; ladybugs outsell other more effective predators, they say.

Peeling off the blacktop up in fir country, Mike steers his way down a rutted road full of potholes and washouts. At last we stop next to a stream bank, in a grove of madrona, fir, and spruce trees, for a few minutes before Lo arrives. While we are waiting, Mike cuts some fir boughs with his pocketknife and tells me he will be showing me how they are used. After Lo drives up we unload the secret water equipment, cotton flour sacks, bungee cords, a blue plastic tub, and two five-gallon-can rims with hardware cloth wired into them. These will make sieves for separating the ladybugs from leaf litter; they look like gold miners' pans with screen bottoms. We scoop up the boughs and gear and edge our way across the fast-running stream on a partly submerged log. Not far from the creek, Mike stops and throws down his load. "There," he says, pointing to a spot on the ground under a cottonwood tree. "Ladybugs."

I see nothing but leaves. However, this is one of Mike's bugging beds, a spot to which ladybugs return each year, generation after generation. The leaf litter, he tells me, is sheltering thousands of ladybugs, and soon after the two men apply water, the ladybugs, reacting as though it were raining, begin to climb up out of the leaves, turning them orange with their numbers. Mike and Lo spread the fir boughs on top of the beetles, who climb onto them because they are dry. When the boughs are covered, the two men shake them, over the big blue plastic tub, and the beetles fall in. Mike looks up at me and laughs. "Yeah, you gotta have a Ph.D. to run these boughs," he says. Quickly, before the beetles escape over the rim of the tub, Mike and Lo dump handfuls of them onto the sieves, which they had lashed to the mouths of two of the cotton flour sacks with bungee cord, and begin swirling and shaking the beetles down through the hardware cloth while the bits of twig and debris stay on top. I am again reminded of gold panning, and ask if I can try. Mike hands me his sieve and bag and scoops up a handful of the bright orange-and-black-spotted beetles into the sieve for me. I swirl and shake, and watch the ladybugs fall through the screen. I discover that the motion, which looks so simple in expert hands, turns out to be tricky. Lo watches me. "I got tendinitis last year," he says, "until I got the knack of it."

"Sometimes we shake out scorpions," Mike says. "Scorpions like the same sorts of places ladybugs do. So do brown recluse spiders and black widows. I've even found rattlesnakes in ladybug beds." He hardly counts the poison-oak rash with which his legs and arms are covered as a problem, but today he is wearing shorts to relieve the itching; he'd brushed into poison oak last weekend, when he had been out bugging for the first time this season. He grins. "But the biggest hazard is wandering into someone's pot field. You don't want to do that."

This bed turns out to be smaller than Mike had hoped it would be. He estimates that at most he takes somewhat better than half the ladybugs from any given bed, but he's disappointed that this one only gives us a few sackfuls. We pack up, edge across the fallen log, and load the sacks onto chicken-wire shelves in the back of Mike's pickup. They are like the ones Lo has at home in his cave. Mike spreads out the sacks, distributing the ladybugs within over the chicken wire so that they won't overheat, and we shift into four-wheel drive and bump down an even worse road to get to Mike's next bed. It is on the other side of the river too, but this time there is no easy way across. The river is fast and waist-deep. Once we get to the other side, we find fresh-cut boughs strewn about, indicating that someone else has been bugging here recently. Mike scoops up half a sackful of beetles with his bare hands and wades back over the river, holding them above his head. We drive deeper into backcountry, into the old gold-mining hills.

At a sunny pulloff near one of the forks of the Yuba River, we unload the pair of trail bikes and the gear Mike has in his truck. He is going to drive it up the road into shade for the comfort of the ladybugs in the sacks. Lo follows to give him a ride back and I stand watch over the bikes and the gear: the mysterious water apparatus, the blue plastic tub, the bungees, sieves, and flour sacks. Three men carrying fishing poles walk with their dog up a path by the river toward their battered old pickup; they stop to look at me and the equipment.

"Going mining down there?" asks one man with a gray stubble of beard.

"Nope," I reply.

"That's funny," says one of his companions, lifting his cap to scratch his head. "That's *real* funny. Most folks going down that way go mining. If they ain't going fishing. And it appears you ain't going fishing."

"No," I said. "Not mining. Not fishing. That's a nice dog you got there."

We talk dogs until Mike and Lo return, park the pickup, and leap out. We load up the trail bikes. I'm going to ride behind Mike, so he makes a seat for me out of the flour sacks. We stuff everything else into the blue plastic tub and load it onto Lo's Honda, to the considerable interest of the fishermen. After the load is secure,

Lo, an environmentally concerned man who does not like to cut fresh boughs at each bed, reaches into the back of his pickup, gathers up the armload of fir boughs Mike cut in the morning, and bungees them on top of the rest of the gear. The fishermen exchange glances and are probably still talking about what they saw, or think they saw, that day. I climb on Mike's Honda and cling tightly to his waist as we bounce on down the rocky path along the Yuba. Here and there are tents. Aging refugees from the Woodstock nation still live in the California hills. Some stay there even in the winter, Mike tells me over his shoulder. "I know those people," he says. "Talk to 'em sometimes. There's miners here, too."

When we get to our destination near a creek branch, we scramble down a hillside to the bed. Mike's face falls. A big swath has been cut in the shrubby deciduous growth and a fir tree stands, mutilated, all its smaller branches ripped off. Someone has taken beetles here. "Well, there's a lot left," says Mike. "This is a big bed. He's never even worked the hill a little higher up." The whole bed is perhaps a fifty-foot square, and even I can see beetles, gleaming orange, crawling here and there, hinting at the numbers tucked into the leaf litter.

A miner wanders up from a tent nearby. Heavyset, he has a beard the color and texture of corn silk. "Any of those little fellers left?" he asks Mike, whose buddy he appears to be. "Another guy was here two—no, three—days ago."

Mike asks him what the other guy looked like, and when he hears he and Lo look at each other and nod. "I knew it was him," Mike says. "This is the way he works. I hate to see such a mess made of a place. People who like the environment are pushing ladybugs, and so far they haven't got us for disturbing the beds. This will all grow back, so it doesn't hurt much in the long run, but it's not the way I like to see a place left."

Mike and Lo settle down to business, and soon there are what appear to be easily thirty-seven zillion ladybugs spread across the hillside. The men are shaking them down into sacks quickly, before the beetles take wing, which they are likely to do as the sun, shining through the leaves, warms the air. I soon notice the distinctive odor of ladybugs: a musty fragrance, something like wet earth and leaves but more than that—pungent, ancient. There are ladybugs everywhere. Climbing a gnarly moss-covered oak, dotting it with flashes of orange. On the green boughs. Every stalk of grass is studded with them. They are crawling up the insides of my jeans, creeping across my midriff, tickling my neck, nipping, ever so lightly, my arms. A big black butterfly, a red admiral, its wings edged in orange, a variation upon today's theme, flies in and out of the sunbeams. Today, in this Sierra canyon, enveloped in the scent and feel of ladybugs, I remember Haldane and smile.

Before long, the sun will disappear from this canyon: the afternoon, at least here, is ending. Even though I've not been working as hard as the two men, I'm weary. I find a stone to sit on, and watch them climbing up and down the slope, shaking ladybugs from the boughs into the blue plastic tub and sifting them into the sacks. The sacks are lined up on the ground—five, six, seven—each with several gallons of beetles in them. The sweat is streaming from Mike's face.

Lo climbs the hill to the rock where I am sitting.

"You know, sometimes I feel like I'm losing power," he says, "and I think maybe the ladybugs are getting me."

"Yeah, I know," I replied. "Ever since I turned fifty, I've been losing power steadily."

"I'm pushing sixty, though," says Lo.

"So am I. So am I," I tell him, and we look each other in the eyes and smile. We both know about losing power and know that ladybugs have nothing to do with it.

Mike is still a young horse, however, and even after the sun disappears behind the ridge he is reluctant to quit until he has every last harvestable ladybug in his bag. But by a quarter to six there is a chill in the air in the shade of the canyon evening; we have filled nine sacks, and Mike calls it a day.

We pack the gear on the trail bikes. Lacking the mules of the old days, the two men tie the sacks together in bundles of four and five each and I help them put the bundles around their necks after they are on their bikes. Then I climb on behind Mike, and we make our way up the rocky trail to the pickup.

It is nearly dark even in the lowlands by the time we get to Lo's garage, where, using a one-gallon scoop, we portion out the ladybugs into cloth bags. Our harvest for the day totals thirty-one gallons. At 75,000 ladybugs to a gallon, the official estimate, the haul has amounted to 2,325,000 beetles. Pete Foley had told me that he pays $15 to $20 a gallon for them. Mike often makes $1,000 a day bugging, but today he will fall far short of that.

I spend one day with Mary and Pete Foley at their processing building, along with their daughter, Jeanne Houston. Pete, a man with dark-rimmed glasses and an outgoing manner, retired from his job as a chainsaw salesman ten years ago, when he and Mary bought the business. They had hoped that it would provide them with employment a couple of days a week. "But now," says Mary, a comfortable, motherly-looking woman, laughing, "we work ten days a week on it." Jeanne is crisp, positive, efficient, with business-school training. Blonde, with hazel eyes, she is well-organized, and says "Exactly!" often enough to inspire confidence. None of the family have an entomological background, but have picked up their knowledge on the job. The Foleys' processing building is behind their home in Citrus Heights, a tidy, middle-class Sacramento suburb of well-tended houses. Their van doesn't fit into the garage in front of their house because the space for it has been taken over by stacks of chicken-wire ladybug trays and a big walk-in refrigerator. Ladybugs that can't be held here are taken in the van to cold storage, some fifteen miles distant. These will make up the stock that allows the Foleys to sell ladybugs year round to commercial greenhouses long after the two harvest periods, the present summer one and a winter one, when lack of snow permits the buggers to get up into the hills to collect beetles before they fly back to the Central Valley.

In the Foleys' processing plant, the beetles are dumped in ten-gallon lots into a plastic tub with a chalk line on the inside. The chalk line is the beetle version of a cattle guard: The chalk granules are so slippery that the beetles will not crawl across. Instead they sit quietly in their tub and await being scooped out in measured amounts (the company sells in volume lots ranging from half a pint to a gallon) by Pete and today also by a part-time assistant, a young woman named Marie. They are scooped into tight-weave cotton sacks containing wood shavings for them to crawl on, and passed on to Jeanne, who packs them into cartons previously folded by her grandmother, who lives with the Foleys. She also inserts an information sheet and staples the cartons closed. Her mother, Mary, addresses each carton. Today they are filling drop-ship orders for Burpee customers. The Foleys receive orders from sixty seed and garden-supply companies for drop shipments, and also have their own direct customers. In addition they sell whole-sale to a number of other ladybug suppliers. On a normal day, they ship six hundred to seven hundred orders but, on a busy one, may send out three or four times that number. They all take turns answering the telephone, which is ringing constantly, for this very day *The New York Times* has published a gardening story about beneficial insects and has listed Unique Insect Control as a supplier.

"When we bought this company," Jeanne says, "our sales were only about $35,000 annually. The first year, we lost money, the second year, we broke even, and the third year, we showed a profit. The business has been expanding ever since."

The processing room is a cheerful place, well lighted, well laid out, its walls painted white. Today Marie has left her children at home with her mother, but sometimes she brings them to work and the Foleys' son's child, a toddler named Cameron, busily wheels a plastic wheelbarrow around the workers. Marie laughs as he rolls it across her foot and says, "Sometimes we call this place Foleys' Bugs and Babies." By evening, but perhaps not until nine o'clock, they will finish packing orders and will load the van and take them to Sacramento's twenty-four-hour post office, to be shipped to customers across the country.

Although ladybugs are their chief business, the Foleys supply other garden predators, too: lacewings, nematodes (a kind of worm), trichogramma wasps. Jeanne shows me a clutch of praying-mantis egg cases in the refrigerator. "Now, we don't make any claims at all for these," she says, "but people want them. We sell 50,000 a year." She shows me a packet of beneficial nematodes, a new product for them this year. I ask her how they select a new item, and whether they keep track of its effectiveness.

"Well, we get lots of letters back from customers," she tells me, "but we don't do any testing or anything like that. We'll try something that sounds interesting, and if we get reorders we'll continue it. I even tried gardening gloves once. We sell what people want. And people *do* want ladybugs."

The Division of Biological Control in the Department of Entomology of the University of California at Berkeley has its laboratory on the woodsy grounds of Berkeley's Agricultural Experiment Station in Albany, near the Berkeley campus. Kenneth Hagen, a tall, mild-mannered man, and his colleagues have their offices in a one-story, putty-colored building there. Ken is the acknowledged authority on *H. convergens;* while I was reading up on ladybugs I frequently saw his work referred to, and his papers have been published in entomological journals here and abroad. In the scientific community he is Mr. Ladybug. His office, cluttered with books and filing cabinets, is next to a laboratory, where he shows me vials of lady beetles—as he prefers to call them —in all their instars, or development stages. He also pulls out trays of artificial lady-beetle feed he is working on ("So far we're still missing the mysterious Vitamin X that will meet their needs."). He shows me a small wasp that parasitizes lady beetles, *Perilitus coccinellae.* Ken and his researchers discovered that approximately 10 percent of overwintered beetles contain wasp parasites, which adversely affect flight ability, feeding, and mating. Infested beetles are less likely to fly, and, once put out by gardeners, are more likely to stay near the release spot, fooling the person who bought them into thinking he has a population of hardworking, aphid-eating lady beetles on hand. They will feed but not reproduce, and shipping them only serves to spread the parasites. Healthy beetles collected during the winter will usually fly away quickly unless they are released into a greenhouse or other enclosed space, particularly if the temperature is 65° F. or higher, because they are already starved from their hibernation; they are ready to eat and invariably fly off before they do so. As Ken puts it, "Fly first, eat later."

I ask what would happen to the beetles I had watched Mike and Lo collect, which by now are probably on their way to a gardener. These summer-collected beetles behave quite differently, he tells me. Aroused from their summer slumber, they usually do not disperse over any great distance, because, plump with stored fat from feeding on mountain pollens, they are in a resting stage. They will probably fly up briefly, gather again, and settle down in some covered spot. They might drink a little water, but they will not eat great numbers of insect pests.

H. convergens, Ken explains to me, is found all over the country, though elsewhere on the continent the species' rhythms are different, for the rains in many places continue through the spring, summer, and autumn. In other parts of the continent, there are aphids enough and the beetles do not undergo any summer dormancy period but continue to feed, converting aphids to fat until late in the season, before bedding down at the approach of winter. They have no need to make long flights, such as the western *H. convergens* do from the hot fields to the cool mountains, for they have a steadier food supply. The long flights and the summer dormancy in aggregations, which make them easy to harvest, Ken explains, are an adaptive response of the beetles to Western weather conditions. Individual lady beetles may eat as many as five thousand aphids in their lifetime and are effective predators when allowed their natural life cycle in their natural surroundings, but Ken regards *H. convergens* gathered from aggregations in the Sierras as ineffectual predators. "Green lacewings," he tells me, "are much better. They'll eat everything a lady beetle does and more pest species as well."

With the growing unease about pesticides, Ken and his colleagues worry that too many lady beetles are being senselessly collected in the Sierras. "Of course, in some years," he says over lunch with several other researchers and me, "there are actually too many lady beetles, and they crowd their own food supply, so it doesn't hurt to collect them. But in other years I'm not sure what the long-term effect may be of taking so many beetles from their habitat." Generations of lady beetles fly back and forth from the same locations in the Central Valley and the mountains each year, and Ken observes that harvesting them in great numbers from certain easily accessible mountain beds may create a "shadow" in the agricultural fields in the valley, a place where few lady beetles return. Growers may need to resort to insecticides to kill the aphids they would have eaten.

Ken Hagen and his colleagues are working with what he describes as classic biological control: In order to avoid the misuse and overuse of pesticides, they study a particular pest species that has been introduced into an area and try to match it with its natural predator. There is another species of lady beetle, the mealybug destroyer, *Cryptolaemus montrouzieri,* that insectaries are now raising on mealybug-infested potato sprouts; it is a good predator, but its usefulness is limited because it only eats mealybugs. Insectaries could also raise *H. convergens* if researchers could develop a food for them. And so the practice of harvesting and selling wild ladybugs continues.

I tell Ken and the other researchers about a commercial lady beetle supplier whose methods were described to me by Jeanne Houston: this man packs handfuls of the beetles into little coarse-mesh bags and sells them from racks in hardware stores and similar retail outlets. The floor underneath the racks would be black with tiny specks. The customers, if they noticed the specks at all, would probably not know that they were the lower parts of the beetles' legs, which catch in the mesh and tear loose. When those crippled beetles left alive are released, they could no longer crawl, much less hunt aphids. Mike Lake knew about this supplier, too, and refused to sell to him.

The researchers shake their heads sadly. One tells me he had recently been talking to a California fruit grower who routinely orders large quantities of lady beetles. "I tried to tell him he was simply throwing his money away," he says. "But he claimed he had a surefire method: He put them in a big black plastic garbage bag and laid it out in the sun until the ladybugs got really hot. He said it made them so mad that when they flew out they'd attack just about anything."

Ken is dismayed. He is a man in his seventies and has spent a good part of his academic lifetime studying *H. convergens* and trying to explain its biology and behavior to a wider public. "But you just can't say a word against ladybugs," he remarks with a sigh.

The truth is that people *like* ladybugs, and there are few insects that they do. Ladybugs look as if they were designed by a children's-book illustrator, and they make us smile. The Foleys have started selling them to schools and community groups for release on Earth Day or other Green occasions instead of helium balloons. One species of ladybug, *Coccinella novemnotata,* is the New York State insect. The ladybug is a design motif in toys, fashion, jewelry, pottery. Our relationship with the cheerful-looking little beetle is long and affectionate. Ladybug. Lady beetle. Ladybird. *Bête de la Vierge. Marienkäfer.* In many languages, it is the Lady's (the Virgin Mary's) animal, and European folklore has it that if you harm a ladybug the Virgin will punish you for nine days.

> Ladybird, ladybird
> Fly away home,
> Your house is on fire
> And your children all gone;
> All except one
> And that's little Ann
> And she has crept under
> The warming pan.

Of all the puzzling rhymes in Mother Goose, this is one of the darkest and most peculiar. What is the meaning of the house on fire? And who is Ann? Is she St. Anne, the mother of the Virgin Mary? She also shows up in a German rhyme about another kind of beetle. Translated it reads: "Goldchafer, fly to your high tree. Fly to your mother Ann, who will give you cheese and bread. It is better than bitter death." There is yet another German ladybug rhyme similar to our Mother Goose one, and similarly ominous: "*Marienkäferchen,* fly away. Your little house is burning. Your little mother is crying and your father sits on the doorstep. Fly away to heaven, away from hell."

Some German folklorists believe that the ladybug rhymes may have their roots in beliefs about the scarab, the sacred beetle of Egypt whose name is derived from the same root as the word "become" and was associated with the fiery orange of the sun. The nursery-rhyme authorities Iona and Peter Opie explain that the verse may be "a charm to speed the sun across the dangers of sunset, the house on fire symbolizing the red evening sky." Others have suggested that the rhyme referred to the burning of hop vines in England, a practice that may have killed many ladybugs. The Opies also point out that a good way to get rid of witches is to tell them that their house is on fire, but since ladybugs are so universally linked with good luck and happiness (wedding days are often alluded to), the Opies are reluctant to consider the pretty little beetles as witches' familiars. In the end, the Opies are as puzzled about the rhyme as anyone else and can only conclude that it "is undoubtedly a relic of something once possessed of an aweful significance."

A waitress in a Sacramento restaurant asked what I was doing in town. When I told her I was taking in the ladybug harvest up in the mountains, "Ooooooooh! Ladybugs!" she said happily, her face opening up in a smile. "I just love seeing 'em in my garden. What are they supposed to do, anyway?"

CHAPTER IV

ORDER OPILIONES: DADDY LONGLEGS

One sunny afternoon late in the summer of 1985, I was watching a daddy longlegs striding across the side of an old shed. I cupped my fingers around him and put him on the back of my hand. He sped across it and onto the other hand. I kept placing one hand beside the other, giving his passage a futile, treadmill-like quality. He apparently sensed this for after a bit he stopped and began pumping his oval body up and down rapidly, using his long jointed legs as levers. I had recently read a speculative, unpublished paper about his species by a graduate student of entomology, Wolfgang Schroeter, who held that such pumping is male mating-display behavior, also seen when the male is in a novel or stressful situation, a kind of displacement activity.

My daddy longlegs having thus identified himself, if one is to believe Schroeter, as male and bewildered, I put him down on a small bush, taking care lest his fragile legs be harmed, and watched him speed away, confused and stressed no longer.

Those eight long legs of his are delicate and break off easily at the first joint nearest the body, either side of which is studded with sensory organs that let him know where there is stress on his legs. Unlike spiders, who are only distant cousins, daddy longlegs can't actually regenerate missing legs, but the loss of even several both-ers them very little and serves as a defense against predators. The muscles in the separated legs continue to contract for some time, twitching the shed limb in a way that is distracting to the animal that has grabbed one. However, the second pair of legs, which are longer than the others, are more important. They contain sense organs that tell the daddy longlegs about food, danger, and other things of which we humans may have no understanding. If he were to lose a single one of them he could still get by, but the loss of both would make him so vulnerable that he would not live long. Theodore Savory, a British arachnologist, reported that he once had a captive pair, a male who had lost his right second leg and a female who had lost her left second leg. When they met they attempted to mate, taking the usual stance facing each other, but because their second legs were missing from the same side, they were unable to copulate.

Those easily detachable legs have been noticed by generations of unpleasant children, who have caught daddy longlegs and pulled off their legs one by one. An eighteenth-century English children's rhyme runs:

> Old father Long-Legs
> Wouldn't say his prayers:
> Take him by the left leg;
> And throw him downstairs.
> And when he's at the bottom,
> Before he long has lain
> Take him by the right leg,
> And throw him up again.

Although they do not recite the rhyme, here in the Ozarks country boys still enjoy pulling off those long legs and throwing the helpless bodies downstairs. They also claim that intact daddy longlegs (called granddaddy longlegs here) make superior fish bait, and that they are stinky little bugs, smelling just like a copperhead snake does before it is going to strike. Anyone who is old enough to remember the open range recollects that the best way to find a lost cow is to look for a daddy longlegs and see which way his second legs are pointing, because that is where the cow will be—a centuries-old belief reflected in the ancient name for the daddy longlegs: shepherd spider. In summertime I often find them in great numbers, their legs entwined, between the inner and outer covers of my beehives; the bees ignore them. And I sometimes stoop to watch single daddy longlegs speeding along the ground, and try to figure out how they can glide so rapidly through thick tangles of grass and twigs without being tripped up.

When I realized I had seen daddy longlegs all my life but knew practically nothing about them, I began to ask friends and neighbors what they knew about the creatures. I discovered that, for all their commonness, no one else knows much about them, either. Most people are aware that they are not exactly spiders, though they are not sure what they might be; that they are everywhere during the summer, sometimes in big bunches; that their legs come off easily; that they don't seem to hurt anything; and that they smell funny. The odor is responsible for a bit of feed-store biology, which has it that some of them lay their eggs on bats and that these eggs hatch out into bedbugs, "proof" of which is that mashed daddy longlegs smell just like bedbugs. I also heard that you can wish on one and it will bring you good luck, and that if one walks over your clothes, you will soon get new ones. Alternatively, if a daddy longlegs walks on your shoulder, you will die. All this is entertaining but has more to do with us than it does with the biology of daddy longlegs, so when I had a chance later that year to spend time finding out more about them, I was happy to take it.

The animals we commonly call daddy longlegs or harvestmen belong to several different species of the order Opiliones, sometimes named Phalangida. This order is not in the class Insecta, despite the fact that we usually call them bugs, along with insects. Insects have six legs, antennae, and segmented bodies that come in three parts: head, thorax, and abdomen. Daddy longlegs and their kin—scorpions, mites, ticks, spiders, and the like—all belong to the class Arachnida, and members of that class, all its various

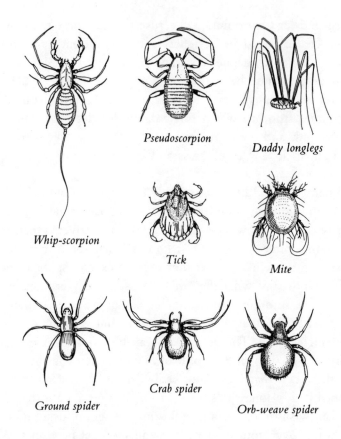

Pseudoscorpion

Daddy longlegs

Whip-scorpion

Tick

Mite

Ground spider

Crab spider

Orb-weave spider

orders, lack antennae, have eight legs and a two-part body, with head and thorax fused together into a cephalothorax. For all their outward similarity to spiders, daddy longlegs are considered by arachnologists to be more closely related to the Acari—the mites and ticks—than they are to the spiders, the Araneae. Unlike spiders, their abdomen and cephalothorax are broadly joined, so that they seem to have no waists. Their lives are quite different from those of spiders, and they do not spin webs. In addition, there are many short-legged species of Opiliones that look nothing at all like spiders, or even like daddy longlegs.

The grouping we call by that name belong to a number of different species. *Mitopus morio,* one of the commonest and most widespread, is readily distinguishable from others by a black stripe on the forward part of the top of the cephalothorax. Various species of the genus *Leiobunum* can be identified only by microscope, but members of the genus are common and widespread. They are notable because many are big and all have extremely long legs, the second leg sometimes being fifteen times the body length. *Phalangium opilio,* a smaller species, is one of the most noticed and most studied. Named by Linnaeus himself, *P. opilio* is often seen around houses, for it is less fussy about a specialized habitat and more tolerant of places that may be disturbed by man than are some other species. "Indeed, it appears to be man's closest phalangid fellow traveler," wrote Arlan Edgar, who has been quietly publishing elegant papers on the biology and behavior of daddy longlegs for an academic lifetime.

After some preliminary reading, I realized I needed more firsthand observation than I could get from chance encounters. By then it was early autumn, and the daddy longlegs population, which peaks in summer, was ebbing, but I decided to capture a few. I set up a screen-wire cage and lined the bottom with sand and dead leaves to make it as homelike as possible. Into the sand I sank a shallow jar cap of fresh water, because I knew that water is critical for daddy longlegs and that they need it constantly. The ratio of body surface to mass on these leggy creatures is high. Often nocturnal, they do not like direct sun, and dry out rapidly. They prefer humid places. Without water they become sluggish and torpid, and eventually die.

Food, I believed, would not be a problem, for I had read that daddy longlegs eat a variety of things, plant and animal. Edgar had even fed them marshmallows, that unusual but favorite food of animals in captivity. Unlike spiders, they are not forced to take their food in liquid form, because they are equipped with forceplike jaws that can rip off solid morsels. In this they are aided by a pair of pedipalps, jointed leglike appendages above the jaws in front of the first pair of legs, which hold the food in place. They are also scavengers. An invertebrate biologist friend once told me about watching a daddy longlegs picking his way through a spider's web with great agility, eating up the leftovers from the spider's dinner as he went. But they are also capable of taking live prey. M. Roters, a British arachnologist, wrote of a dramatic encounter involving a live moth he had put into a cage with a daddy longlegs. The latter first touched the moth with his second pair of legs, then ran forward quickly, surrounded his victim with a cage of legs and, when the moth tried to escape, raised his body and dropped it down onto the moth like a pile driver. The daddy longlegs then ate the moths' body, continuing to hold the wings in place with his legs.

The pair I captured, an easily identifiable *M. morio* and a larger one of another species that I could not identify but which I came to think of as female since she appeared gravid, lived in apparent contentment with me until the end of their lives, thriving on a diet of overripe persimmons, cornmeal, bacon fat, and an occasional dead fly. During this time I spent more hours than I should like to admit watching them eating, drinking, and preening, the last a favorite activity. One leg at a time, the animal would thread its leg through its mouth, holding it in place with its pedipalps and working along the entire length until it reached the tip, when the leg would comically spring back into place. The process not only cleans the important sensory receptors on the legs (daddy longlegs are scrupulously clean creatures), but may also help prevent dessication.

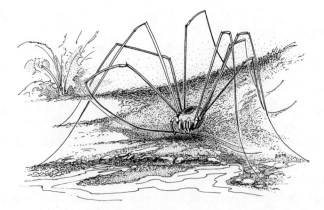

Daddy longlegs preens by grasping the top of each leg between its jaws and pulling the leg along its entire length (life-size).

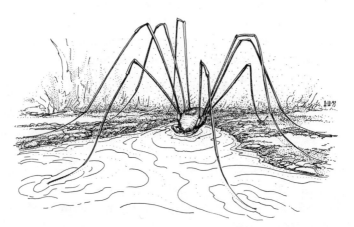

Daddy longlegs drinks by immersing its jaws in water while resting pedipalps and one or more legs on water's surface.

I had read about large groupings of daddy longlegs in the vicinity of egg hatches in the springtime, and also mating aggregations later in the season, when sexually mature males will even attempt to mate with females of other species, but I still had no explanation for the thick congregations within my beehives, so I was interested to see what my captives would do. Their interaction was of an entirely negative sort. They probably could not see each other, for their vision is said to be poor. They can distinguish light from dark and can detect motion, but little else. Yet in some way my pair were always aware of each other, for they divided up the space in the cage, and kept as much distance between themselves as they could. Only twice, in the process of expeditions to the water, did I see the female blunder into the smaller *M. morio,* which I came to regard as male for no good reason. Each time, as soon as she touched him with her second legs, she withdrew as if she had received an electric shock and scurried away.

I had captured my pair toward the end of their natural life spans. In the springtime, baby daddy longlegs of most species, tiny creatures, hatch from eggs laid at summer's end the previous year. They are aided in their escape from the egg by an "egg tooth," which disappears after the first molt. The metamorphosis is a simple one: They grow discontinuously by molting, splitting the old outer body covering and stepping out of it in a larger but similar form. Their first molt often takes place just hours after hatch; they will molt six more times until they are fully grown and sexually mature. Then they mate, oviposit, and die. In temperate climates most go through this entire cycle in one season, although some overwinter in the last immature instar and experience final molt the following springtime.

After several weeks, the *M. morio,* who had been the more sprightly of my two daddy longlegs, became lethargic. He was old. Climbing the sides of the cage was too much for him. He did not preen, and was not interested in food or water. In the wild he would have been picked off by a predator, a bobwhite, perhaps, but I sat and watched him die. Afterward I took him from the cage and clumsily, with the aid of a hand lens and a pin as a probe, determined his sex. Male daddy longlegs, unlike spiders, have an intromittent penis, and by pressing against his abdomen with the pin I had read that I would be able to force its extension if he was indeed a male. He was.

During mating, male daddy longlegs seek out females. Sometimes the latter are not ready for mating and will run away, but if they are receptive, the male faces and grasps the female, who assists in the transfer of sperm to her underside genital opening by grasping the male's penis in her pedipalps and jaws. Her eggs mature over a period of time, so repeated copulations may be necessary for fertile eggs. Daddy longlegs are famous for their enthusiastic and frequent matings. In his laboratory Arlan Edgar once watched two *Leiobunum longipes* (now known as *L. aldrichi*) pair twenty-nine times in the course of two and a half hours. After copulation is completed, the male stands over the female, his legs forming a canopy over her, defending her from other males until she lays the eggs he has fertilized. Females prefer to lay their eggs in damp soil or cracks and crevices of decaying wood, where they insert their eggs as deeply as the length of their oviposter will allow.

There is competition among males during peak mating activity.

This is when Schroeter noted frenzies of pumping among males, and there are often battles, males tussling with one another, grabbing and attempting to break off the legs of their rivals. Sometimes during these free-for-alls, smaller, even disabled males with legs missing are able to sneak in and mate with willing females, thus avoiding competition entirely.

In my clumsy attempt to sex my newly dead *M. morio* I had applied enough pressure to his body to release the contents of his scent glands and got a full whiff of their fetid odor. The paired glands, at the sides between the first and second legs, contain a fluid that is generally considered to be one of the animal's main defenses against predators. Many invertebrates—ants, for instance —do not eat daddy longlegs, presumably because they are squirted with this fluid when they attempt to do so. There are also reports of vertebrate predators—certain birds and frogs, for instance— who seize one and then drop it, wiping beak or mouth afterward as though trying to rid themselves of the disgusting taste. But the defense is not perfect, because other birds, frogs, certain snakes, and a variety of animals eat them with relish. I began to wonder what was currently known about the scent-gland secretions.

There is little money available for academic research on daddy longlegs, and only a few investigators here or abroad work on them. In the mid-eighties, James C. Cokendolpher, a young researcher at Texas Tech University in Lubbock, was one of them. His specialty is Palpatores, the suborder that includes daddy longlegs, and he was in the process of revising the classification and collecting and identifying new species from Alaska to South America. When I talked to him he was working on the defensive behavior of a Panamanian species, a more aggressive animal than our peaceable daddy longlegs. "It's really exciting . . . well, to me it is," he said, with a laugh. I asked him what he knew about the scent-gland secretions. Despite their being called defensive or repugnatory, Cokendolpher was not sure that this was their purpose, or at least their only purpose. He had found, for instance, that in one South American species the fluid is a fungicide, and fungal growths are common among them. He has coauthored a paper reporting on the analysis of the chemical components of the secretions in several species. The authors concluded: "From the limited chemical data available . . . it is clear that these chemical characters can be useful in understanding phylogenetic relationships. Species-specific characteristics can be found in the chemical components." Couched in words of scientific caution, the authors were saying that each species may be chemically different.

I knew that Arlan Edgar had done some work on those scent-gland secretions and I wondered what he could tell me. He has spent an academic lifetime teaching at a small liberal arts school in Michigan, Alma College, in the town of the same name, and studying daddy longlegs, principally those found in the Middle West. When I telephoned him for an appointment, he agreed to spend some time with me the following week.

Just before I was to leave I noticed that my remaining daddy longlegs was behaving as the *M. morio* had before he died. She was slowing down and growing weaker by the moment. I count a number of entomologists among my friends, and know that there is no better present for one than a specimen taken from a location different from his own. From a scientific standpoint, a specimen should be taken while still alive, but this specimen had been my companion for weeks, and even though she was moribund I felt cruel as I plunged her into a 70 percent alcohol solution, where she twitched a few times and died.

"You can think of it as euthanasia," said Arlan after I had explained my qualms about pickling her. Under the microscope we discovered she was indeed female, and she turned out to be *Leiobunun ventricosum* (Wood). Arlan invited me to look through the microscope at the fungus that had begun to spread on her body, and assured me she had been on the point of death. She was very old; no later specimen had ever been collected at my latitude, and the ones in his area in central Michigan had died months before.

Since we are dealing with serious biologists now, I should say something at this point about the name of the animals they are studying. "Shepherd spider," the early common name, is reflected in the name Linnaeus selected that came to be used for the order.

"Opiliones" is derived from the Latin word for shepherd. But harvest time was when numbers of them were most noticed in northern Europe, and so in England "harvest spider" or "harvestman" had by the early nineteenth century gradually replaced "shepherd spider" or the even older "father longlegs" in common speech. To add to the confusion, "father longlegs" was also used as the name for the crane fly, an insect with six long legs that looks something like an exaggerated mosquito. But it was "father longlegs" that crossed the Atlantic and in our demotic speech became "daddy longlegs," or, in the more expansive West, which added a generation, "granddaddy longlegs." Mark Twain betrayed his Midwestern origins when he wrote, "The learned and aged Lord Grand-Daddy Longlegs has been sitting in deep study with his slender limbs crossed." But Twain's grandniece, Jean Webster, an Easterner and Vassar graduate, hence daintier in her speech, called her successful novel, written in 1912, *Daddy Longlegs*. It became a popular play and movie.

Entomologists are embarrassed by either American name and prefer the British "harvestman." But I am not.

Arlan Edgar has a quick smile and shows every sign of being a man who enjoys life. He sits in an office, surrounded by the trophies of a successful teaching career. On his wall is the Michigan Academy Citation for Scholarly Achievement, a plaque awarded for excellence. Students and colleagues in and out of his office show him affection and respect. He was department head at Alma for a number of years, but has stepped down and is preparing to take early retirement next year so that he can devote himself to research. In a small college where there are no graduate students it is easy enough for a popular teacher to let research go and create an easy niche for himself, but Edgar has continued with investigations begun when he was a doctoral student at the University of Michigan and has published regularly; he says he enjoys the intellectually enlivening process of research.

Edgar is so expert that he can identify different species of daddy longlegs by smelling them, and I asked him about the scent-gland secretions. He told me that he suspects each species produces a unique fluid, but cautioned that laboratory tests are still inconclusive. He handed me a paper he had co-authored with Murray S. Blum from the University of Georgia. The men found that secretions in the species studied were chemically identical to the alarm pheromone of some ants, and observed, ". . . it is not unlikely that many compounds now utilized as volatile information-bearing agents by social arthropods originated from products which had been employed as defensive secretions by more primitive arthropods." But, Edgar tells me, whether the secretion serves harvestmen as a pheromone, providing them with chemical information about one another within their own species, is not yet known.

In addition to his ongoing research with Blum, Edgar wants to look at several other aspects of harvestman biology in his retirement. He wonders if behavior can be correlated to leg length, for instance. He also has observed changes in the behavior of the animals at various points in their lives and suspects that these changes may be tied to reproductive hormone levels within their bodies. He suggested to me, apologizing for his "anthropomorphism," that the reason my *L. ventricosum* had withdrawn so decisively from contact with the *M. morio* was because, at the end of her life, with her hormone level low, she had concluded that contact with him was "inappropriate." He has observed the reluctance of females to mate and oviposit, and believes this to be tied to hormone levels. Vision may be better, and in general the animal may be at a physiological peak, when hormone levels are high.

I asked Edgar about the aggregations of daddy longlegs I had found between my beehive covers. He says they were "seeking habitat." The upper reaches of beehives in the summer are filled with humid air from the moisture that the bees evaporate (by the movement of their wings) from nectar as they make honey, and would be a comfortable spot for the moisture-loving daddy longlegs. There are reports of two species of *Leiobunum* found in the Southwest in caves, under eaves, and in the forks of cacti—they form thick daytime clusters, with their legs interlocked, presumably to minimize water loss. The daddy longlegs in my hives have perhaps found a benign spot to live, but Edgar cautions in good scientist fashion that no one really knows for sure what makes them aggregate.

Arlan and I start talking in his office at nine in the morning and we are both having so much fun that he cancels his one afternoon appointment and we talk the day through. At six in the evening we are both high on daddy longlegs and decide to wrap up the day at a bar in town, where we go on with daddy longlegs talk over our drinks. I have found answers to some of my questions, but not enough is currently known about daddy longlegs to answer others, and after talking to him and Cokendolpher I had new ones:

• A shepherd spider, or an air-crab, as he called it, was one of the creatures that Robert Hooke slipped under his wonderful newly acquired microscope in 1665. Hooke's astonishment at what he saw is reflected in his *Micrographia,* where he wrote:

> . . . these long Leavers (as I may so call them) of legs . . . must necessarily require a vast strength to move them, and keep the body ballanc'd and suspended, in so much, that if we should suppose a man's body suspended by such a contrivance, an hundred and fifty times the strength of a man would not keep the body from falling on the breast. To supply therefore each of these leggs with its proper strength, Nature has allow'd each a large Chest or Cell, in which is included a very large and strong Muscle, and thereby this little Animal is not onely able to suspend its body upon less than these eight, but to move it very swiftly over the tops of grass and leaves.

Daddy longlegs spend most of their time in a resting position, with their bodies suspended from their knees, as it were, one third of the way below the top of the arch made by their legs. Presumably their muscles are in a state of equilibrium at this point, but no research has addressed itself to Hooke's curiosity about the musculature and locomotion of the animals. They move rapidly on their fragile legs through obstacle-covered terrain, and no one knows quite how they do it. The mechanics of the process has not been studied, and Edgar hopes that engineers working on robotics and walking computers will take an interest in them.

• In 1845, nearly two hundred years after Hooke published his *Micrographia,* Alfred Tulk published in England the first thorough dissection of *P. opilio.* Little is known of Tulk except that he was a surgeon with a wide-ranging and lively intellect; in addition to his paper on *P. opilio,* he translated scholarly writings in a number of fields. Although some of the conclusions he·drew about the anatomy of *P. opilio* turned out to be wrong (he thought that the scent glands were a second pair of eyes, for instance), his descriptions were careful and his drawings lovingly made. He observed:

> The most striking peculiarity connected with the nervous system of the *Phalangia* is the presence of several large transversely striated muscular fasciculi which radiate from the sides of the thoracic ganglion, where they are attached by short tendons. Their arrangement is such, that, according as either one or the other set of fibres act, they will draw the nervous mass either forwards or backwards, horizontally or in the vertical direction. I am not aware that this voluntary power of moving the nervous centres exists in any of the other Articulata.

Edgar knows of no one who has followed up on this extraordinary observation about a possibly *movable* nervous system.

• There are reports now and then that some species of daddy longlegs can reproduce parthenogenetically, but Edgar knows of no one who has investigated this matter, either.

• Anyone who has captured several daddy longlegs and put them in a jar to carry home has noticed an odd phenomenon. After scuttling about for a few moments as any animals will do when trapped, they collapse as though in a dead faint and remain that way until they are released into more spacious accommodations, where they recover immediately. Some years ago, before much had been done on the nature of the scent-gland secretions, the theory was that their fetid odor produced something of a locker-room effect when they were shut up together in close quarters, and this has been frequently repeated in the literature. Neither Cokendolpher nor Edgar believe this to be true; they simply don't know why harvestmen have a narcotic effect upon their own kind, even though, collectors that they are, both have observed it.

• The interaction of daddy longlegs with other animals and the rest of their world is poorly understood. The published list of their prey and predators is diverse and often contradictory. Cokendolpher carried out investigations with other entomologists among several species in the Maine woods in an attempt to determine whether or not they might be significant predators on spruce budworm eggs, since the larvae of spruce budworms are a severe economic problem in those forests. The results were suggestive but inconclusive, and daddy longlegs' role as predators is largely unknown.

These and all the other questions to which Cokendolpher, Arlan Edgar, and the few other investigators were addressing themselves could keep many hatches of graduate students busy through all their professional instars if there were grants enough to support them. But despite the evidence that science continues to give us that ours is not the only game in town, we humans still continue to act as though we are the focus of everything that is interesting and important. Animals such as daddy longlegs, even though they are ubiquitous and easily observable, do not have an obvious relationship to us, and therefore are of little interest or importance to grant givers. If anything is to be learned about them it will be by people like Hooke or Tulk, who enjoy astonishment; like Cokendolpher, who can confess that his work is "really exciting"; like Arlan, who carries out his research on his own time and with considerable glee.

The sign on Edgar's door read:

DR. ARLAN L. EDGAR
BIG DADDY LONGLEGS

CHAPTER V

ORDER DIPTERA: BLACK FLIES

It is hard to find any human being who has a good word to say about black flies. Black flies are Bad Bugs. At least the adult females of about forty of the 1,554 known and described species of black flies are Bad Bugs. The adult males of *all* species and both sexes of the other species do nothing bad, for they merely sip nectar and help pollinate flowers. It should also be said that a number of animals don't regard *any* adult black flies as bad but as dinner. Among these are insectivorous bats and birds, a number of other flies, certain wasps, and dragonflies. A host of tiny parasites—mites, fungi, protozoans, nematodes, and such creatures—simply couldn't do without black flies, to whom they represent opportunity for life. But we are not nematodes or birds, and since we are the ones who label them, black flies are Bad Bugs.

Residents of the northern states and Canada have had to learn to make some kind of accommodation with black flies in order to be able to go outdoors during the late spring and early summer, which is the season when the adult females bite. Visitors go canoeing in the Boundary Waters of Minnesota, fishing in Ontario, and hiking in New Hampshire during those months armed with bug dope and fortitude. Many, after scratching their bites for weeks, vow never to return—a loss to those on the serving end of

the tourist business. Cattlemen in
Canada know that the flies
torment their stock,
and during particularly
severe outbreaks the
cattle lose weight,
sicken, and may even die.
One researcher in the
cattle-raising area of
Saskatchewan, studying a
black-fly plague year during
the 1980s, estimated that if the

Simulium venustum *Say*
(= reptans L.), female
North America (3x)

cattle were left untreated in another such year, losses to dairy and
beef ranchers could run as high as $2.9 million.

As serious as all this sounds, however, it is a mere nuisance
compared to the human misery caused by certain species of black
flies in the tropics of Africa and Latin America, where they are
vectors for a disease named onchocerciasis or, more ominously in
English, river blindness. There, some of the black flies carry
within their bodies the larvae of parasitic worms, filarial nematodes called *Onchocerca volvulus*. When the black flies bite a human
being, the larvae are passed on in the process, grow, and reproduce
a progeny of tiny microfilariae that develop within the victim,
producing nodules on the skin that itch intolerably, and lesions in
the eyes that can cause blindness. Although the infestation is not
fatal per se, there are areas, such as West Africa, where in the
recent past 30 percent of adult men were blinded from it, and as a
result their life expectancy was reduced by thirteen years from that
of a sighted man. Families were destroyed, and fertile lands and
villages near places where black flies were abundant were aban-
doned. Agriculture suffered.

The social and economic problems caused were severe enough
for the World Bank, in the early 1970s, to back a huge black-fly
scheme, the Onchocerciasis Control Program, known as OCP,
administered by the World Health Organization. This has resulted
in funds being made available for applied and basic research on

black flies, and as a consequence, many black-fly entomologists have published a lot of information on the animals. Every year in the last decade there have been, on the average, 300 papers added to the scientific literature about black flies. It may be hard to get money to support a graduate student wanting to study the basic biology of daddy longlegs, but it is not nearly so difficult to get funding to support a student specializing in black flies. The result is that a good deal more is known about black flies, their biology, their behavior, and how they fit into the world than is known about many other insects of less economic importance.

With all this in mind I assumed that there must be someone at the University of Maine working on them. There was. K. Elizabeth Gibbs is an aquatic entomologist at the University of Maine in Orono. Her own graduate specialty was mayflies, but she has done important work on black-fly control and kindly agreed to talk to me about it. Before our appointment she gave me the titles of several books and research papers, which she suggested I read in order to gain some background on the subject.

Although black flies are also members of the two-winged order, they are quite different from the Diptera of Chapter II, the midges and gnats, although they are not much bigger. Instead of being

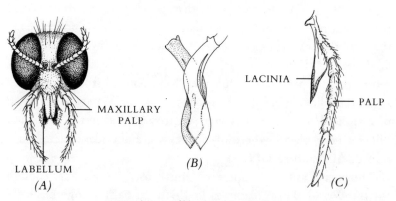

Mouthparts of blood-sucking Diptera
(A) Simulium *(Simuliidae) head and mouthparts, front view;*
(B) Simulium *mandibles, crossed in scissorlike position;*
(C) Simulium, *maxilla*

slender and fragile, they are squat, compact flies with powerful wings. Most of the species of black flies belong to the family Simuliidae, which means "little snub-nosed beings." Of those 1,554 described species, roughly 10 percent—that is 150—are known to suck blood from man or domestic animals. And of those 150, fewer than forty are the subject of most of the research, because they are the ones who cause the most trouble.

Although all black flies are water animals during the first part of their lives and live and feed similarly to some of their other fly cousins, once they emerge from the water different species grow into adults with quite different ways of getting on in the world. Some species have fed well enough as larvae that they need to eat nothing more for the rest of their lives. In this respect they are rather like the nonbiting midges, and their brief adult lives are spent in coming out of the water, mating, and laying eggs. In other species, in fact in *most* species, the adults need only the nectar from flowers to feed upon, both to fuel their flight muscles and lay their eggs. Others may be able to lay a first batch of eggs if they have had an adequate diet as larvae, but need a protein-rich blood meal before they can lay additional batches. Among the remaining species, the females need a blood meal before they can lay any eggs at all. None of the males of any species ever need a blood meal. They don't even have mouths that are able to bite. It is always the females that bite us or other animals. No black-fly female feeds exclusively on human blood, and some never bite us at all, preferring other animals. One species, for instance, *Simulium euryadmin-iculum,* is so specialized that its members feed only on the blood of loons and would scorn a human being if one was offered.

Perhaps this reluctance to take human blood (hard as that may be to believe for someone walking along a stream in Maine on a Memorial Day weekend) is because human beings are such a recent addition to the black-fly world that they are not sure we will work out to be a dependable protein source. The fossil record shows that black flies are conservative, successful insects, which have been around, in pretty much unchanged form, since the middle of the Jurassic Era, some 180 million years ago. Their form worked so well for them that there was no reason to modify it. Why fiddle with what works? In those 180 million years, different species have managed to thrive in a variety of water conditions in their larval stages and to specialize in a variety of foods in their adult lives.

Generally the adult female black fly lays her eggs in the late afternoon or dusk, in damp seeps at a stream edge, on leaves trailing in the water, or other such moist spots, depending upon the species—where her progeny will do best. From them hatch out larvae that can spin a kind of silk which they will use to attach themselves to some solid object in the water such as a rock, twig, the surface of a waterfall. Seven African species, including *S. neavei* and *S. woodi,* which transmit onchocerciasis, even attach themselves to river crabs, hitching a ride to wherever the crab takes them. Their point of attachment to the silken pad is a hooked false foot, known as a proleg, on their hinder end. These larvae, tiny little animals a quarter inch or so in length, are vase-shaped, and bend and reach for floating particles of food in the flow of

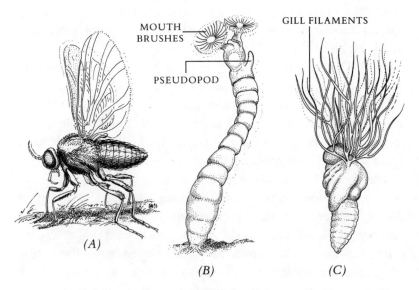

MOUTH
BRUSHES

PSEUDOPOD

GILL FILAMENTS

(A)

(B)   *(C)*

Simulium
(A) Adult (4x); (B) larva (10x); (C) pupa (5x), with spiracular gills

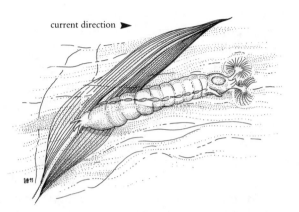

current direction ▶

A Simulium vittatum complex *larva in typical filtering stance with body twisted and the opened cephalic fans facing upward.*

water. (Researchers call their food FPOMs, that is, Fine Particulate Organic Matter.) They are aided in their feeding by a pair of structures, called fans, growing from their heads—these sweep particles into their mouths.

"Fan" does not quite give an accurate picture of these structures. Scanning Electron Microscope (SEM) photographs show them to be beautiful, long-curved filaments, not joined like a lady's fan, but floating freely in a coordinated manner, rather like a flexible leaf rake but more graceful. The larvae, attached to their silken pads, can spin a long thread that allows them to venture safely and securely out into the current if necessary. They can even change to a safer, better, richer feeding spot by throwing down a new silken pad and "walking" to it on an additional proleg on their thorax.

Black-fly larvae of all species feed in the water and live inno-cently, harming us not at all, clearing our streams of organic de-bris. In addition, they also serve as an important source of food for many other animals: the larvae of certain insects, such as drag-onflies, dobsonflies, hellgrammites, and caddis flies; they are also a food source for a number of fish, including commercially valuable ones such as salmon and trout. Larvae of different species inhabit fresh water all over the globe, from tropical rivers in Guatemala to the lips of mountain waterfalls to trickles in the Arctic tundra.

Most species prefer clear, fast water, but there are some that thrive in sluggish, even polluted water.

The larva, fed to a sufficiency, turns into a pupa, also attached to a solid substrate with silk. Inside the pupal case, the larva transforms itself into a winged adult fly. When ready to emerge, a bubble of air forms around the new black fly, which bursts from the case and rides in its protection to the water's surface, where, safe and dry, it flies away, finds a mate, and begins the cycle all over again. It is at this point that we begin to have trouble with those black flies that are looking for a blood meal. Terrible trouble they can be, too, for they are purposeful and unrelenting in their hunt. Louis Agassiz, writing from the northeastern shore of Lake Superior in midsummer 1859, says of the black flies he encountered there:

> . . . neither the love of the picturesque, nor the interests of science could tempt us into the woods, so terrible were the black flies. This pest of flies, which all the way hither had confined our ramblings on shore pretty close to the rocks and the beach, and had been growing constantly worse and worse, here reached its climax. . . . One whom scientific ardour tempted up the river, after waterplants, came back a frightful spectacle, with blood red rings round his eyes, his face bloody and covered with punctures. The next morning his head and neck were swollen as if from an attack of erysipelas.

Some people are more bothered by black flies than others. The supersensitive can become feverish and suffer from a stiff neck after an encounter. But Stewart Edward White, that turn-of-the-century writer on the north woods, was not one of them. He boasted in *The Forest* (1903) that he minded black flies less than mosquitoes for, he said, the black fly has a recommendation

> . . . that he holds still to be killed. No frantic slaps, no waving of arms, no muffled curses. You just place your finger calmly and firmly on the spot. You get him every time. In this is great, heart-lifting joy. It may be unholy joy, perhaps even vengeful, but it leaves the spirit ecstatic. The satisfaction of *murdering* the beast that has had the nerve to light on you just as you are reeling in almost counterbalances the pain . . .

Various bug dopes have been used to repel black flies: pork fat, kerosene, pine tar, pennyroyal, oil of cloves, castor oil, a host of modern chemicals, and smudge fires. But adult flies are elusive, thinly spread, and good fliers, and so what entomologists usually mean today when they talk about black-fly control is killing the larvae where they are concentrated in close, dense masses in streams and rivers. As early as 1944, field trials in Guatemala showed that DDT applied to streams would kill black-fly larvae. The 1952 *Yearbook of Agriculture* from the USDA is devoted to insects (their killing, that is). It suggests draining and filling streams to control black-fly larvae and the application of chemicals that now, a scant forty years later, sound appalling: DDT, TDE, chlordane, methoxychlor, and benzene hexachloride. Toxaphene, the *Yearbook* notes, should be used with caution because it will kill fish. Of these DDT is recommended as being the safest. Of course, today we know that DDT is not safe at all.

When I was in California for the ladybug harvest, I met a researcher at the Beneficial Insects Lab who was both a medical doctor and an entomologist. He had worked on black-fly control programs in the early days in the tropics, and said that river life systems had been badly disrupted by dumping larvicides into them. "We go about it the wrong way," he said. "We shouldn't be killing black flies. Our research should be concentrated on discovering treatments for onchocerciasis and its prevention."

Dr. Elizabeth Gibbs does not entirely agree. I asked her whether she thought that research should focus on treatment and prevention of river blindness rather than better ways to get rid of black flies. "Well, that's a difficult decision to make from up here, away from the tropics," she said. "I'm a mother, and river blindness is a terrible disease. I wouldn't want to condemn my child or anyone else's to it if we had the means available for black-fly control."

Some progress has been made on the treatment and diagnosis of onchocerciasis. Recent reports indicate that scientists working together from several research institutions have developed a new, simple technique to diagnose the disease before the symptoms appear. Also, in the late 1980s, ivermectin began to be used to kill the microfilariae in infested humans. That drug is familiar to American dog owners, who use a formulation of it, sold under the name Heartgard by their veterinarians, to control heartworms in dogs. New drugs are being tested to kill the adult worms in humans too, but so far no vaccine has been developed as a preventative against onchocerciasis.

Parallel with the medical research, entomologists have been working on new and safer ways to kill black-fly larvae without causing as much harm to other animals or the water as the earlier generations of insecticides did. They have developed a number of biological controls, including the naturally occurring black-fly enemies: viruses, protozoa, and fungi. But the most successful so far has turned out to be a natural, unengineered bacterium, discovered in 1977 from samples of sand gathered in the Negev Desert. Its full name is *Bacillus thuringiensis* var. *israelensis* (serotype H-14), but nearly everyone calls it Bti. The first two words of the scientific name will be familiar to many organic gardeners who have used varieties of *B. thuringiensis,* purchased from garden-supply companies, to keep cabbage loopers, corn borers, and other lepidopteran pests from their gardens. It is also the commonest spray used today for gypsy-moth control. Bti, a different strain, is also sold through garden catalogs and is similar in some respects in that it is also a spore-forming bacterium that produces protein crystals. Those crystals, when eaten by a black-fly larva, begin a chemical reaction inside the gut that produces a stomach poison, which kills it quickly. Bti does not cause any infectious diseases, and extensive testing both in the tropics and in the north shows that it is toxic only to the larvae of black flies, mosquitoes, and a few midges (including the innocent, nonbiting Chironomidae). Fish, at least in the long term, and mammals are not affected.

Applied in liquid form, Bti results can be seen almost immediately; laboratory researchers report that the larvae begin to die within fifteen minutes. In the field, the temperature of the water, its speed, depth, and a variety of other conditions affect the results, but (oversimplifying a bit) in general something like 95 percent of black-fly larvae are usually killed within six to twelve hours down-water after the application of recommended doses of Bti.

Bti was welcomed in the tropics, where in places black-fly larvae were beginning to develop a resistance to some of the chemical insecticides, and it is applied there as an alternative or in alternation with chemical larvicides. Costs for treatment also compare favorably with insecticides. When a treatment program in upstate New York that had been spending $5,000 per square mile for aerial applications of insecticide in the early 1980s switched to Bti, its costs were reduced to $800 per square mile. For a variety of technical and biological reasons, most authorities believe that Bti resistance in black flies will be slow to develop, although only time can prove or disprove this.* These results interest applied entomologists: Bti seems to be a cheap, fast, and safe way to snuff out a Bad Bug, a medically dangerous insect in the tropics.

Are there any biological risks if we use the same treatment to kill the pesty, annoying black flies in the north? Do we have the capability of eliminating black flies from the earth? And is there any harm in doing so if we can? These were the questions I wanted to ask Dr. Gibbs the day I went to talk to her.

Cassie Gibbs, as she calls herself, is Canadian born and educated and has been teaching graduate and undergraduate students at the University of Maine for many years. Those years have been kind to her ("I tell my graduate students I love my job," she says). She is gray-haired, her eyes are set far apart, and she has a good, open face and a kindly, motherly manner. When I put my questions to her, she began her reply by asking me a question of her own. "Did you know that the Endangered Species Act gives no protection to insects we regard as pests?"

---

* According to a recent report in *Scientific American*, by the mid-1980s some pest insects, such as the Colorado potato beetle, the tobacco budworm, and diamond-back moths, began to show they were developing resistance to the regular Bt used in agriculture since the 1950s.

No, I hadn't known that. But a reading of the act, passed in December 1973, shows it to be the case. The act says:

> The term "endangered species" means any species which is in danger of extinction throughout all or a significant portion of its range other than a species of the Class Insecta determined by the Secretary to constitute a pest whose protection under the provisions of this Act would present an overwhelming and overriding risk to man.

Not only do we have a way to kill black flies, an undoubted pest species, that is cheap, fast, and safe; it is also legal. The language of the act reflects a way of looking at the world that will strike some readers as perfectly reasonable: If we can, it's fine to get rid of pieces of the world that are in competition with us for our blood. That's what life is like at the top of the food chain—or as Harold Ross, the phrase-bending editor of *The New Yorker*, is supposed to have put it, that is "nature, red in claw and tooth." Other readers will find it arrogant. The reasonableness or arrogance of this world view is a good thing to ponder, but is in the end an ethical question, not a biological, empirical one.

Cassie Gibbs's research, in particular one project that involved the testing of Bti on a stream that ran near a golf course where black flies had been bothersome to its members, showed that they could be neatly and dramatically eliminated with no ill effects on other invertebrates, although since black-fly larvae made up 25 percent of the diet of brook trout, she recommended further study should be made of them in Bti-treated streams. Maine rates its streams and rivers A through D, and allows nothing foreign to be put in the higher-classed ones except for experimental insecticides of this sort, so there was no question of being able to set up a long-term treatment program in Maine to see what the effects might be. But Cassie Gibbs did not even think it was as good idea. "I'm old enough to remember the use of DDT," she said. "It was considered good for just the reasons it is considered bad today: It is long-lasting and it has a wide kill spectrum. Over the years I've seen a pattern: A new treatment comes along, it sounds good, but all of its effects are not yet widely known. We praise it and use it, find out its hazards, and move on to the next new thing. We should be more skeptical. We should consider the effects of altering interacting relationships. I also wonder if we are justified in acting as though we have a *right* to live in an insect-free world. I think there's a different set of attitudes for people who live in the country and people who live in cities. Actually, we've found that people in Maine are surprisingly tolerant of black flies. They get used to them, dress appropriately, and plan their outdoor activities around the black flies' presence or absence. I get bitten a lot because of my field work. I work in areas where you can get 2,000 black flies in a ten-minute sweep. I cover my head with a scarf, wear a long-sleeved shirt, dab Avon Skin-So-Soft [the universal bug dope of country people everywhere] on my bare skin, and get on with my research."

Outside the tropics, Cassie told me, there have been a few rivers treated with Bti for several years, and entomologists have studied its effects. The two people whose work she recommended in particular were Richard Merritt and Daniel Molloy. She gave me the titles of some of their papers, and suggested I look them up.

Daniel P. Molloy, a black-fly specialist with the New York State Museum, has studied the relationship of black flies to other organisms in their environment, their predators, and their parasites, and the effect on some of these organisms when black flies are eliminated. "Are Black Flies a Critically Important Element in the Food Web of a Trout Stream?" is the title of one of the papers he presented at a Summer 1990 New York Natural History Conference. The paper discusses his recent research, which shows no decrease in numbers of fish or catastrophic changes in the insect populations. Significant change was found among only three dipteran taxa, ones that were not present in great numbers anyway: A few species of midges and dance flies (so called because their mating swarms seem to dance up and down in the air) actually increased, and a few species of midges decreased in the two-year study. Says Molloy:

Since black flies were a major component of the riffle insect community, it would be naive to think that their elimination did not actually cause density shifts in other riffle insects. Yet only three statistically significant changes were detected. This was probably due to the modest levels of precision inherent in such benthic [bottom of the water] insect studies, where, due to sampling variability, statistically significant changes are recorded only when major changes in density occur. The lack of major detectable impacts, however, challenges the hypothesis that black flies are a critically important component of stream ecosystems and provide further confidence of the low risk of environmental disruption caused by Bti as a black-fly larvicide.

Richard Merritt, an entomologist at Michigan State University, is one of the biggest names in black-fly research in the United States. He has coedited one of the standard textbooks on the insect, and is the author of enormously interesting research on black flies and how they interact with other parts of their world. He has examined the disruption to the food chain caused by the sudden and nearly complete removal of black-fly larvae after the application of Bti. In particular, he addresses himself to the problem that turns up over and over again when we humans step in to eliminate populations of animals that we consider pests: There is a natural check on those populations, for other animals eat them. When the dinners of those predator animals are taken away from a place, the predators will also be reduced in number, and so when the pesty animal once again increases because it has become resistant to whatever we have used to kill it or because new individuals have moved back into the place, the naturally occurring predators will no longer be there and the pest problem will actually become worse. Additional or stronger methods will be needed to deal with it, and a whole new escalating cycle will have begun.

Merritt set up an experiment to examine an aspect of this problem by investigating the changes in feeding habits of two stream predators and a detritivore ("detritivore" is what animals are called who eat detritus—i.e., dead animals, bits and pieces of this and that). The report of his research was published in the January/

February 1991 issue of *Canadian Entomologist*. The conclusion of his discussion is so interesting that I quote it in full:

> The accelerated transformation of live to dead prey biomass following *B.t.i.* application will most likely influence the habits of some stream insects including *Acroneuria* [the commonest genus of stoneflies, mostly predators] and *Prostoia* [stonefly detritivore] nymphs. The predators will lose an abundant food resource and the detritivores will have a new, but short-term, resource provided. We observed dead black flies still attached to substrates for over a week following *B.t.i.* application. As *B.t.i.* treatment can significantly reduce the presence of live black fly larvae for several months, the indirect effect on the feeding habits of predators and detritivores therefore may be considerable. The predators must switch to new sources of prey and, if these are in short supply, this could promote interference competition which is known to reduce attack rate . . . and thus affect the growth and survival of predators. This would be critical when black fly larvae reappear if these predators are important natural control agents. Peckarsky . . . concluded that Plecoptera [the stonefly order] and Megaloptera [suborder for fishflies and dobsonflies] fed on all types of prey within the size range they could handle, so the probability of a specific predator-prey association being broken is unlikely unless black flies comprise a major percentage of prey biomass. Nevertheless, we have seen that, although nontarget organisms are not directly affected by *B.t.i.* treatment, there are secondary consequences for nontarget organisms, including predators and detritivores. As these insects are generalists, however, the effects of population suppression may be minor and the space vacated by black fly larvae may be taken up by other taxa that are suitable prey.

I telephoned Richard Merritt. He emphasized that all the studies done on Bti so far show that it has no long-term effect on other animals. Some fish, he said, show an immediate weight loss, which may be due to a short-term decrease in stream oxygen levels after Bti is applied, but they quickly regain it. He told me that Pennsylvania had used Bti extensively in black-fly control. I had read that the Pennsylvania Black Fly Suppression Effort treated about 290 stream miles of the Susquehanna River and 245 miles of the Allegheny with 93,000 gallons of Bti, at a cost of $2.9 million in 1985 and 1986, and had achieved about 90 percent reduction in black-fly populations as a result. "I was recently talking to the man doing the science on the project, Bernard Sweeney, from the Philadelphia Academy of Science," Merritt said, "and he told me there had been no ill effects. Anyway, the program is over now. It was dropped for budgetary reasons."

I asked Merritt if we are in a position to completely eliminate an insect we don't like. He chuckled. "It would be *very* hard to get rid of black flies completely," he replied. "The adults are strong fliers and can move into an area that has been treated. New larvae can drift into a stream that has been cleared and recolonize it." One hundred and eighty million years of survival, apparently, gives the insects a formidable edge in their competition with us.

In the tropics, where black-fly larvae clearing is a serious business, Bti, the experts agree, is a welcome, environmentally safer addition to chemical control of a pest species. I did not find any study of public attitudes in those places, but it stands to reason that people there would be in favor of having their chances of going blind reduced significantly. However, there is some indication of what residents of northern climates think about black-fly control. Cassie Gibbs gave me a report of a study done by her University of Maine colleagues, Stephen D. Reiling and Kevin J. Boyle, surveying the attitudes of residents of one part of Maine where black flies are a nuisance and also are suspected of causing a loss of tourist dollars. The results may surprise you if you do not know Maine folks, but they make sense if you do. The study shows that 70 percent of the Maine residents surveyed thought that black flies were the most bothersome bug they knew—worse than mosquitoes, deer flies, no-see-ums, or any other flying insect. Yet nearly the same number, 65 percent, thought that there was no need to spend money on their control. In part this is because the respondents were deeply distrustful of the efficacy, safety, and cost of any control program, but also, in part, because they said they had learned to live with the nuisance. When Cassie Gibbs gave me the report, she said she had talked with a Maine resort owner who neatly put into words a point of view that she has heard from others. "I'm not interested in black-fly control," the resort owner, a woman, told her. "I prefer my clients to be the sort of people who can accept the out-of-doors the way it really is. If a guest is someone who can't handle black flies, he'll also want a lot of other things I can't or don't want to provide."

I turned up no suggestions to help Liddy and Brian, whose questions started all of this, get through black-fly season while I was talking to the researchers or reading their papers. However, recently I went to Guatemala to investigate killer bees, and this provided one solution, at least. For my trip I packed a regular cotton bee suit—a zippered coverall—so that I would be able to work closely with the bees. But I also took along a nylon bee suit, for cotton, some of the experts warned me, did not have a weave dense enough to protect me from killer-bee stings. I didn't need the nylon suit. The ferocity of the bees had been overstated, and the cotton one was adequate. But I remembered that Liddy and Brian had once tried cotton bee suits against black flies and had reported that the flies bit right through the fabric, so after I came back I gave them the nylon suit and asked them to test it. That June, Brian told me that killer-bee regalia—nylon suit and the rest of a full bee kit, including zippered veil and cowhide gloves—was just right for black-fly season. The nylon suit proved stout enough to keep the black flies from biting in most cases, and it now allows them to work outdoors during May and June in comfort. That, I think, is a good, Maine-like solution.

CHAPTER VI

ORDER HYMENOPTERA: BRAVO BEES

 I first laid eyes on the honeybees that headline writers like to call "killer bees" in February 1991, after I had arrived in Guatemala and was walking around the Mayan ruins of Tikal, in the northeastern jungle department of Petén. I was listening to a guide talk about the remains of this pre-conquest culture—some of what he was telling us may even have been true—when I became distracted by a sound familiar to any beekeeper: the industrious hum of bees at work. I dropped to my knees to watch them gathering golden pollen from the small yellow flowers all around our feet. They looked just like the honeybees in my hives back home in Missouri—perhaps a bit smaller, but it was hard to judge. One of the other Americans in the group asked me what I was doing. "These are killer bees," I told her. "They have replaced other honeybees in Guatemala and I want a closer look."

The Americans reacted with alarm, apparently expecting the bees to rise up in wrath from their flowers and sting them to death. They didn't. Any bee, even a killer bee, will not sting while happily collecting pollen or nectar unless she is stepped on or otherwise attacked. She can only sting once and dies afterward, so she will reserve that suicidal gesture for the defense of her home—her hive, its honey, and her sister bees.

Stinging is one of the things—probably the main thing—that people know bees do, and as soon as someone finds out I am a beekeeper he usually asks me about it. Most people are surprised to learn that a bee's stinger is pulled from her body when she stings, eviscerating her in the process, and are curious about such a sacrifice. Bees' biology is so different from our own that it is hard and sometimes confusing to use our words to describe their lives and their ways of ordering them.

Lots of insects group together in big companionable bunches. March flies, gnats, and midges form mating swarms. Ladybugs make their trek to the mountains en masse, but few people have any trouble picking out the individual bug in those aggregations. At other times they will go off by themselves and get on with their lives, eat, grow up, and reproduce. The individual is rather like us in this respect. It is this one here, that one there, or even that one over there. But all the ants and some of the bees and wasps, as well as the termites, are more sociable. They don't merely come together at certain times of their lives; they live together in a group of their sisters and brothers all of the time, and die if they become separated. Members of the colony become specialists in one or another of life's problems—getting food, nurturing larvae, defending the colony, or reproducing, for example—and in many cases one set of specialists, or, in entomological terms, caste members, are incapable of doing the job of the others. We are used to thinking of one individual, this one here, that one walking around over there, as a generalist, capable, within the limits of sexual dimorphism when that applies, of doing all of life's tasks, so the organization of insects of this sort makes us a little dizzy if we think about it too long.

Some writers, starting with Maurice Maeterlinck, went so far as to suggest that each bee, each ant, is a cell in the body of the colony which itself is the real individual, a superorganism. This is playing with words, and again tells more about our own categorizing minds than it does about bees or ants. Entomologists don't much like the superorganism idea; instead they call such enormously clubby insects "eusocial." *Eu-* is a Greek intensifying prefix, so the word means that these insects are well and truly social. Thinking about them this way suggests an answer to the question I'm so often asked when someone learns that a bee dies after she has stung: "What's in it for the bee?" The question is really about biological altruism. Why should a bee sting to defend the colony or protect the stores of her sisters when she herself will die in the act? The answer is that as long as the colony survives, many of her genes will be passed on for the members of the colony—her siblings, or at least step-siblings (the queen bee, mother to all members of the colony, mates with eight, ten, or more male bees)—will, to the last remaining bee, defend the queen, the reproductive "cell" of this "body" which will pass on many of the genes of the kamikaze bee. In recent years, we have come to think that the action takes place at the gene level. Grown-up organisms we see —you, me, a dog, the oak tree outside the window, the ladybug who flew from the Central Valley to the Sierras—are simply the package that genes make to replicate themselves. The idea is not brand-new. Samuel Butler was hinting at a similar notion back in 1877 when he wrote, "A hen is only an egg's way of making another egg." But the idea has been reformulated, and a good deal of interesting, helpful, and important work has been done with it that has given us an understanding of behaviors that have seemed puzzling. And this is why, now and again, it is good to give the kaleidoscope another twist to rearrange the colored stones, get a new picture of what words like "individual" or "organism" mean. But we must remember that they are just classificatory words into which we stuff bits of reality. Such labels are tools, the categories we humans need in order to think about the world.

I once entered into a world without categories and found it interesting but unworkable. Along with two other people, I took mescaline, and for the hours that the drug acted on our brains everything we saw appeared the same, equal, lacking classification. Perspective held, but figure and ground did not; *all* elements were significant. Selectivity of perception had been lost; thought was impossible. We went for a walk in the woods, and when we sat down on some pine needles it was as if we had discovered

A portion of a colony of honey bees. In the upper righthand corner the queen is surrounded by attendants. The capped cells contain developing workers. The open cells contain eggs, larvae in various stages of development, pollen, and honey. Near the center, a worker is taking nectar from a sister. At the lower right, another worker begins to drag a drone away by its wings; the drone will soon be killed or driven from the nest. One of the royal cells at the bottom has been cut open to show the queen larva. (Based on a drawing by Sarah Landry.)

pinecones for the first time. The light brought out colors we had never noticed; the shadow revealed their surfaces in a way we had never seen. We sat there sopping up pineconeishness but also sopping up pine needles, our hands, the pine's boughs, the texture of the earth, the blood pulsing in our temples, the warmth and pleasure of our companionship, all equal and all equally scattered because we were unable to focus on any element. There were no elements, in fact, only aspects of a whole. We were immersed in a warm oatmeal of perception. It was enlightening in several respects, but not much could be done with it.

That evening at Tikal, over dinner, several Americans asked me what I knew about killer bees and what could be expected of them when they reached the United States. I had not yet worked with them in their hives, as I was to do in the following weeks, and all I could tell them was what I had gleaned from reading beekeeping magazines over the twenty years I have kept bees and what I had learned more recently from entomologists in preparation for my trip.

What's in a name? Chances are that thrill movies like *The Swarm,* featuring major death by bee sting, would not have been made had those bees been called anything but killer bees. In Portuguese the bees were known as *Abelhas assassinas:* killer bees, the media call them. *Las Africanas:* Africanized bees, the scientists and those taught by them say. *Abejas bravas:* bravo or fierce bees, that's the Spanish name for them among some South American beekeepers. I prefer to call them "bravo bees," and will henceforth use that term. It turns out that it is not even politically correct to call them killer bees. Roger Morse, professor emeritus at Cornell University and the grand old man of American beekeeping, has worked with Warwick E. Kerr, the university professor in Brazil who first introduced these bees back in 1956 from South Africa, where they were (and are) used widely and successfully for commercial honey production. The Brazilian Ministry of Agriculture had requested Kerr's help to bolster beekeeping in the warmer parts of Brazil, where other subspecies of honeybees had not thrived. Morse tells the story in the second edition of his book, *Bees and Beekeeping:*

> On April 1, 1964, military forces took over the government in Brazil. Professor Kerr, who had introduced the African bees, was a

well-known scientist in Brazil and represented his country at many international meetings; in this regard he was badly needed by the government. Kerr was also critical of the military government and there was conflict between him and the local military commander. Kerr was jailed twice by the military, the first time in 1964 when he protested that a group of local railway workers were being mal-treated, and a second time in 1969 for protesting the torture of a Catholic nun. In an effort to discredit Kerr as a scientist, the mili-tary played upon the fear that many people have of stinging insects. Since most people do not know the difference between bees and wasps, any stinging incident, many of which were caused by wasps, was blamed on Professor Kerr. The bees were called killer bees. So far as I can determine, the first mention of the words "killer bees" in the United States was in *Time* magazine in the September 24, 1965, issue that picked up one of these military press releases. Much the same story was repeated in a second article in the same magazine in the April 12, 1968, issue. Those stories prompted others to write in this same vein, and the term and the Brazilian association with "killer bees" was firmly established.

There are several species of bugs we call honeybees: *Apis melli-fera, A. dorsata, A. florea,* and *A. indica.* The last three are not in the Western Hemisphere, and you can forget about them for the pur-poses of this chapter. But not even *A. mellifera* was in the Americas until the colonists brought them when they settled here. The bee they introduced, a subspecies, *A. mellifera mellifera,* is small, dark, and extremely ill-tempered: the German bee, by common name. For 200 years it stung people a lot but provided honey for those willing to destroy its hives to get some.

In the late 1800s, with the invention of better beekeeping equip-ment, people began to import other subspecies from around the world in the interests of getting a more productive, gentler bee. The record suggests, but does not absolutely prove, that one of those subspecies may have been *A. m. scutellata,* the same bee that Kerr later imported from Africa. Thus its genes may already be present in our American honeybees. The most successful of the imports, however, were various central and southern Euro-pean subspecies, particularly the Italian bee, *A. m. ligustica,* a bee with a happy Mediterranean disposition. Queen-bee breeders have used it, along with some of the other European races, to produce hybrid honeybees so gentle that beekeeping has become a backyard hobby. These bees are as near to tame as an insect can be.

Lurking in tree cavities and other wild places, however, descendants of the German bees have lived on and continue to interbreed with hive bees. Sometimes they are captured and kept by bee hunters in my Ozark home country, where they are known as Mean Little Suckers, or something very like. The daughter bees of Mean Little Suckers crossed with gentle Italians can be hot-tempered and quick to sting, running rapidly on the comb when it is removed, and generally hard to work with. Like other commercial beekeepers, I have learned to deal with bees that have a hair-trigger temper. I wear protective clothing, a veil, and gloves; I pour soothing smoke from a bee smoker on them when I open their hives, and I treat them gently and politely, especially in inclement weather, when they are quicker to take offense than on warm, sunny days.

About forty people die each year in the United States from the stings of venomous insects. Of these deaths, ordinary European honeybees are responsible for about half. They can also kill animals. About fifteen years ago a horse in my own Missouri town, tethered too near some hives, was stung to death. Also in Missouri, in 1981, a woman who was reported as already having health problems was stung to death by bees. They were identified as German bees that had been disturbed by her husband's tractor. It was a death every bit as horrible as those in any of the stories I have read about "killer bees." Many of these stories, incidentally, check out to be untrue, the product of the fevered imaginations of journalists unfamiliar with bees.

My driver, interpreter and, after a week's work together, friend in Guatemala was a young man named Jorge Ibarra, a professional with a small beekeeping program associated with Moscomed, a project funded by the United States, Guatemala, and Mexico to check the spread of the Mediterranean fruitfly. Jorge is a veteran beekeeper who had kept 2,000 hives of bees in Costa Rica. He told

me that after his bees became Africanized, an American TV producer wanted to film them for a story. He allowed the producer to
accompany him on his bee rounds, but when the bees showed no
evidence of ferocity, the producer offered him two hundred dollars
to stir them up so that he "could take back a good story." Jorge
refused.

When I first began reading about bravo bees, their reported
behavior reminded me very much of German bees. I asked all the
scientists I talked to if they had compared the two subspecies.
None had; none had ever worked with German bees at all. Bret
Adee, co-owner with his father, Richard, of the largest commercial honey-producing operation in North America, Adee Honey
Farms in South Dakota, mentioned this lack when I talked to him
by telephone. He had just returned from a trip to Mexico and
Belize to study bravo bees firsthand, and thought their "aggressiveness" had been oversold by scientists, who had made their
comparisons with bees gentler than those commercial beekeepers
are already used to handling. He reported that the Central American beekeepers he talked to preferred bravo bees, finding them
more productive and disease-free than the ones they had used before. "The scientists," complained Adee, "are interested in research, not practical beekeeping."

In fairness, the spread of the bravo bee is, biologically speaking,
an interesting event—the rapid genetic takeover and replacement
of one subspecies by another—and there has been a scramble for
limited research funds to study it. Much of the scientific work that
has been done relates to identification of the bees. Since they look
so much alike, how do you know when you have a bravo bee?
Researchers have catalogued some suggestive differences in size,
weight, and wing structure, and some genetic variations. But these
don't always correlate with aggressive or placid behavior, says
R. L. Hellmich II, a researcher at the U.S. Agricultural Service of
the federal Baton Rouge Honey Bee Laboratory in Louisiana, describing research work done by Marla Spivak from the University
of Arizona. And mildness or feistiness is what interests people
working with the bees on a day-to-day basis. In Latin America the

rule is: If they sting a lot, they are *las Africanas*. As Hellmich explained it to me, this is the Sandal Test. Researchers in Argentina studying the southward spread of the bee concluded that bravo bees had arrived in any place where they could no longer wear sandals while studying them.

Once the bravo bees had escaped the confines of Warwick Kerr's research apiary, they spread rapidly, partly because they could outbreed the European stocks already present. Virgin queen bees and males, or drones, mate free, high in the air. Each queen, who will head up a new colony, may mate with eight to seventeen drones. Because of their generally aggressive mating habits, the bravo drones are better breeders than the Europeans, and so although the first-generation cross of European and African drones may represent a genetic heritage that is 50-50, in subsequent generations the African genes will tend increasingly to dominate until the stock gradually reverts to a more nearly *A.m. scutellata* pattern. Thus, as they migrated northward, the bravo bees genetically took over local bees.

But bravo bees also have other behavioral characteristics that give them a competitive edge. The queens lay more eggs that develop into adult bees sooner than European bees, and thus can dominate food sources. They also go to work earlier. A Guatemalan beekeeper told me that *las Africanas* are out on the flowers before dawn, almost an hour earlier than the Europeans. They seem to be remarkably disease resistant, and, possibly, mite resistant (disease and mites are a terrible bother to North America's refined, overbred bees). They swarm more frequently than do European bees, which has accounted for their spread northward at the average rate of two hundred miles a year. Our docile hive bees, bred for temperate regions, have adapted to working furiously during the months of flowers, gathering nectar that they turn into honey. They store it and feed upon it during the winter, and will meekly starve to death after their stores are gone unless a kindly beekeeper feeds them some sugar syrup. Not so the bravo bees. Having evolved in tropical Africa, they have made their way differently; when blossoms cease flowering in one area, they move on to another, flying many miles to find new nectar sources, leaving their old hives behind. Beekeepers call this "absconding," and in Latin America they have had to learn to feed sugar syrup as soon as blossoms disappear in their area in order to keep their bees. But the keepers have also discovered that as soon as flowers begin to bloom again, they often need only set out an empty hive and an absconding swarm may come to live in it. Acquiring new bees is easy.

Beekeepers south of our border have had to change their methods in other ways, too. Used to lazy, tropical temperatures, their former bees had been of such mild disposition that they could be placed near houses, and keepers could work without protective clothing or the smoke that North Americans use to quiet bees before they open hives. They often used to keep their bees in rows on common stands, for the gentle bees did not become aggravated if the hive was jiggled by someone working another on the same stand. Bravo bees *do* become aggravated, and rapidly recruit their sisters to investigate and defend against this perceived threat. They must be kept on individual stands well away from animals and houses, and their keepers have learned to wear protective clothing and carry jumbo-sized bee smokers.

In the years I have been reading beekeeping magazines, I have followed the spread of bravo bees northward and have noticed a pattern. The first bees to cross a country's boundary caused few problems, for they interbred and became gentle, but within a few years, as the African genes reasserted themselves, honey production in that country would fall as beekeepers unwilling or unable to change their methods went out of business. The price of honey would then rise, and new beekeepers, unacquainted with any other bees, would learn how to handle the bravo bees and do better than their predecessors. Brazil, for instance, ranked forty-seventh in world honey production before Kerr brought over the African bees. A generation has passed, the new beekeeping methods have been learned, and today Brazil ranks seventh. Much of the crop is exported elsewhere, but in the years 1985–88, Brazil exported three thousand metric tons of honey to United States honey pack-ers, so the chances are the honey you have found on the supermarket shelves is "killer-bee" honey.

Back in 1986, as bravo bees were heading northward, the U.S. Department of Agriculture proposed an $8 million project to build a sort of Maginot Line, consisting of traplines and scientists, in southern Mexico to stop them. It was called the Bee Regulated Zone, or BRZ. This caused some merriment in certain parts of the beekeeping community; anyone who has worked with bees has had to learn that they cannot be forced to do anything or prevented from doing anything. The best beekeepers learn to accommodate themselves to the bees. The BRZ, funded at a lesser level, did not hold, of course, and the bees continued to progress northward. In October 1990, the first swarm crossed the Rio Grande into Texas. The USDA, always quick with the Flit gun, killed them.

Knowing that there would be more, I decided to travel to Guatemala, where beekeepers were still working out the problems with bravo bees that had arrived in their country in the mid-1980s and by now dominated all the feral bees to be found anywhere within it. In Guatemala City, Eduardo Diaz, manager of El Panal, the biggest commercial honey business in the country, said flatly to me, "These bees are not killers." He admitted that the company had seen a decline in honey production, but was in the process of helping beekeepers to change their methods. It had also started up a separate division to breed gentle queen bees that could be used to re-queen, and thus quiet, hives that were too difficult to handle.

But some of the beekeepers I talked to knew of incidents in which bravo bees had killed farm animals, mostly small ones like ducks and chickens. And near Coatepeque, in the department of San Marcos, I visited thirty members of a beekeeping cooperative called COOPRAM, * where one man told me about a village baby who had been killed by bees. The baby had been with her older brother and sister, who were throwing stones at the hive. Disturbed, the bees flew out and stung the children. The two older ones were able to run away. The baby was not.

* Cooperativa de Producción Apis Mellifera

Whack! Whack! Whack! One of the group of beekeepers who had
come along with Ibarra and me, presumably to protect the *gringa,*
was thumping one of the hives in an apiary near Malacatán, also
in San Marcos. The bees in this yard, I had been assured, were
highly Africanized and sometimes almost impossible to handle.
"Muy brava," the beekeeper exclaimed as, after some more thumping and a shake of the hive, the bees flew out to investigate. I was
shocked, for I would never dare disturb my own Missouri hives
that severely. I began to open hives, pull out frames of honeycomb
and young bees. Working in approved bravo bee fashion, Jorge
Mansilla, manager of this beekeeping cooperative, was using a
jumbo bee smoker, puffing smoke into the hives for me as I
worked along the row. I was wrapped up in the same protective
gear I wear in Missouri, and most of the other keepers were com-
parably dressed, although here and there a bee suit or veil showed
holes and tears. But Mansilla wore only a veil. His hands, pumping the smoker directly in front of the hive entrances, were bare.
His light cotton shirt was rolled up past his elbows, leaving his
arms unprotected. As we worked on down the row of hives, more
and more bees flew up into the air as bees from each successive
hive egged one another on into a display of defensive behavior.
Plok! Plok! They began to throw themselves against our veils, just
as German bees do. We closed the last hive and walked away. No
one was stung, including the lightly clad Mansilla, who told me
that the bees he prefers to use are bravo queens crossed with gentler European drones, because the queen bees lay so many eggs.

We visited another beeyard, where highly Africanized bees had
been moved in for the purpose of teaching students at the adjacent
trade school, near Huehuetenango in the department of the same
name. The bees in those hives, Ibarra told me, had been extremely
ill-tempered in the lowlands, but here, at an altitude of 2,000 me-
ters (6,650 feet), they were no touchier than bees I routinely handle
in Missouri, even though, just hours before, all the hives had been
moved about fifty feet to get them away from some nearby
houses, a disturbance that normally I would expect to aggravate
bees beyond telling. They may have been having a particularly

good day, for bravo bees are reported to be quirky and unpredictable, but they may also have been showing the benign effect of the cooler, drier climate at that altitude—an effect that researchers have often noted.

The altitude was lower and the climate warmer near Coatepeque, where I had earlier visited the COOPRAM apiary. That area had already been taken over by bravo bees when Ibarra, working with Rick Hellmich, began a program funded by the USDA and the Agency for International Development to teach the coop's thirty beekeepers better methods. The project made use of research that Hellmich had begun in Venezuela, which has had a particularly rough time with bravo bees (problems that now seem to be coming to an end, according to Hellmich). Hellmich's research was able to determine the number of drones of gentle stock needed to flood an area in order to overcome the natural breeding advantage of bravo bees. Ibarra and Hellmich taught these beekeepers how to raise gentler queen bees and how to introduce them into their hives to alter the behavior of the resident bees. I walked into one of their yards without a veil, protective clothing, or smoke, and opened hives there. The bees flew busily past us to the flowers they were working, taking no notice of us at all. "I prefer *las Africanas,*" one of the coop members told me, "because with the techniques we have learned we have become better beekeepers." The group's 2,000 hives are now producing an annual average honey yield of 135 pounds each (a quantity North American beekeepers would envy), more than ever before. Just a few days earlier, COOPRAM had received its first order for queen bees from a Mexican apiary. The members believe that within a year they will be self-sufficient.

At the end of my visit to Guatemala I talked with Magali Stitlemann and Steve Todhunter, two young expatriates—she Swiss, he American—who are in charge of the queen-breeding division of El Panal, near Lake Atitlán, in central Guatemala. They say that the bravo bees are hardest to work with during the rainy season in the autumn in Guatemala, but that even then they can be managed. By producing enough gentle-stock queen bees—thousands an nually is their goal—they hope to be able to furnish El Panal, and perhaps other honey producers, with queen bees that have the virtues of several races. Said Todhunter, "What we hope for is to develop, through crosses, a new kind of bee—a Guatemalan bee —that will be dependable, gentle, and productive, one that may be used in other places where Africanized bees become a problem."

How far north will these bees be a "problem"? American queen-bee breeders, who have their apiaries in the southern part of the United States, where the bees will come first, wish they knew the answer to this, and are studying Hellmich's work on the methods of maintaining the purity of breeding stock. The experts don't even agree on whether there will be a problem. Orley Taylor, professor at the University of Kansas, who has studied bravo bees for years, emphasized in conversations with me their aggressiveness, the stinging incidents, and the bees' unpredictability. Others, such as Marla Spivak, a one-time Taylor student who has studied bravo bees throughout Latin America and is coeditor of the book *The "African" Honey Bee,* says, "I guess I have an unusual point of view, but I think that the arrival of the Africanized Honey Bee may *eventually* be the best thing that ever happened to American beekeeping." Why is that? Disease resistance and, mainly, the improvement of our bee-management practices. Another researcher, David J.C. Fletcher, also a coeditor of *The "African" Honey Bee* and a Bucknell University professor who worked with *A.m. scutellata* in South Africa, believes that there may be some problems, but that the way to solve them is to import gentler bees from Africa and use them to develop new strains. Taylor strongly disagrees, holding that there are *no* gentle bees in South Africa.

The truth is that no one knows for sure how far the bravo bees will come into the United States or how they will behave when they get here. Our climate, our beekeeping practices, our huge population of sunny-dispositioned bees, their diseases and enemies, are all new to bravo bees. Even our own scientists, with their knowledge of the bees in Africa and Latin America, cannot predict how bravo bees will fare under these new circumstances. But life is unpredictable and does not come with guarantees.

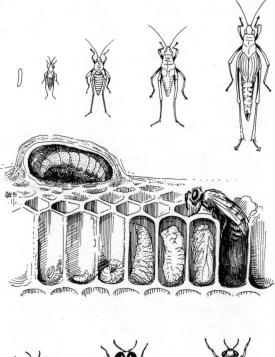

Life histories of an insect with incomplete metamorphosis (southern lubber grasshopper, upper row of drawings), and one having complete metamorphosis (honey bee, middle and lower rows). All nymphal instars of the grasshopper are not shown. In the series of comb (left to right): egg; larvae; pupa; adult; queen cell containing larva. Bottom row: Worker bee; drone; queen.

There is real danger in the world. When I left my other home in Washington, D.C., to go to Guatemala, the Persian Gulf War had just started. The house my husband and I share is one street away from that of the Israeli ambassador to the United States. Guards with rifles protected his house and the Secret Service patrolled our street. Our house was, in government parlance, "co-located" and we might become "collateral damage"—that is, dead —in a terrorist attack. On the flight to Guatemala City, security was tight and thorough, conducted by a grim-faced Israeli. In Guatemala, Ibarra and I could not drive at night because of bandits. We detoured to avoid gaps in the highway that were the result of bridges being blown up during the civil unrest. In the mountains, Ibarra pointed out the debris from a volcano that had erupted two months previously, killing thirty-eight people. On the penultimate night of my stay, I was awakened by a small earthquake. While visiting the queen-breeders near Santiago Atitlán, where the Guatemalan army had killed fourteen unarmed Indian villagers the previous December, I heard bursts of gunfire in the hills. As dangers go, I'll take "killer bees" any day.

CHAPTER VII

ORDER HEMIPTERA: WATER STRIDERS

If water striders, those skinny, leggy skitterers upon ponds and rivers, didn't exist and we were set the task of designing a new bug, I don't believe we would ever come up with this one. They are about as unlikely a form of life, at least to our thinking, as could be. Take the particular environmental niche in which they live, for instance: the surface film of water, puddles, creeks, ponds, even the salty oceans. They live on water, not in it. They live in two dimensions. In some places they are called Jesus bugs, because they can walk upon water. In others they are skaters or pond skimmers. By any name they are odd and different bugs.

Differentness is what made me fall in love with bugs in the first place. I can remember the exact moment I was smitten. It was shortly after my first husband and I had started our commercial beekeeping business in the Ozarks. I had pretty much forgotten the entomology I had learned twenty years earlier in college and, my interest sharpened by the need to make a living, I was reading everything I could about bees. The day I became an entomophile I was studying insect circulatory systems. The insect body, I read, is filled with hemolymph, free and unconstrained by vessels or arteries, except for a single long one that runs along the insect's back or dorsum. The business part of this vessel is called a heart,

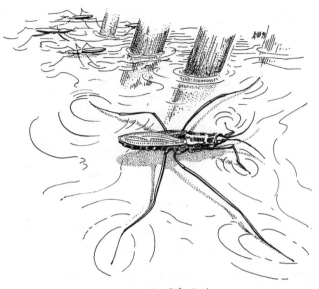

Water strider (life-size)

and it pumps the hemolymph forward to bathe the organs in the head. The undulating movements of an abdominal, or ventral, diaphragm help move the hemolymph backward, so that it can continue its good work of carrying nutrients and hormones, helping in the regulation of body temperature, and carrying away wastes. On the heart's diastole, the hemolymph is drawn back into the dorsal vessel through tiny holes called ostia.

This is a different way of solving some of the basic problems with which life presents its various forms, a solution that differs from the one we and other vertebrates have developed. Although considering how insects outnumber us, perhaps it is more accurate to say that it is we who are different, with our red, oxygen-rich blood neatly enclosed in arteries and veins, and that bugs represent the standard plan. However, here we are, so let us call it *their* difference. Their way seemed to me to be elegant and efficient, at least for animals up to a certain size. I knew it had been working well for hundreds of millions of years. I was hooked. I wanted to know everything about bugs and how they had managed to survive so successfully.

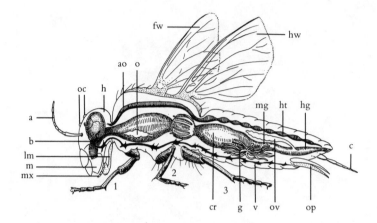

General organization of a winged insect:
a, *antenna;* ao, *aorta;* c, *cercus;* cr, *crop;* fw, *forewing;* g, *gizzard;*
hg, *hind gut;* ht, *heart;* hw, *hind wing;* lm, *labium;* m, *mandible;*
mg, *mid gut;* mx, *maxilla;* o, *oesophagus;* oc, *ocelli;* op, *ovipositor;*
ov, *ovary;* v, *ventral nerve cord;* 1, 2, 3, *fore, mid, and hind legs*

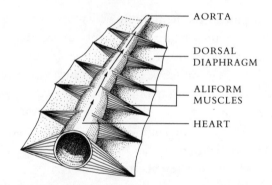

Dorsal vessel of a Coleopteran, ventral view
Arrows show direction of blood flow

But even in the general context of buggish difference, water
striders are bizarre. I had occasion to think about this one April
day in Missouri, when I was walking down to my mailbox, a little
more than a mile from my farm. It was a sunny, crisp day and I
had cut through an old field edged with scraggly growth to keep
out of the wind. Spring had been unusual, and the wild flowering
trees had all bloomed at once: quince, redbud, dogwood, wild

108

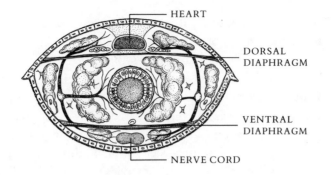

Schematic transverse section of an insect abdomen to show circulatory system

peach, wild plum. I had walked through Dutchman's-breeches, wild phlox, Johnny-jump-ups, and other violets of many species. Rain had left temporary puddles in truck tracks and potholes on the field, and floating in them were gelatinous egg masses, promises of frogs to come. On the surface of one muddy puddle, water striders, half-inchers, were skimming about fussily. I squatted down to take a closer look. I could feel the warm sun on the back of my neck, and the air was sweet with the scent of blossoms. There was sex and springtime everywhere. A little earlier these ruts and holes had been filled with snow. In a few more weeks they would dry up completely, yet the water striders sported as though they had lived there always and would be there forever. Where had they come from? How did they get there? What were they feeding on? How did they stay on top of the water? What were they up to?

I was looking at one species or another of the Gerridae, the family to which most water striders belong. As with others of their kind, they have short forelegs, a long, gangly pair of middle ones that touch the water at the very tip end, and a medium-long set of hind legs. Water striders are bugs. I have been using the word "bug" in this book the way most of us do, including most entomologists when they are being informal, to mean all those little animals that creep, jump, and fly about, including insects— that is, members of the class Insecta—but also spiders, daddy longlegs, ticks, and mites, which are in the class Arachnida, as well as the terrestrial order Isopoda, the sow bugs, and centipedes and millipedes, too, both of which have their own classes. People who aren't entomologists sometimes think that the word "bug" is a little slangy, not latinate enough to be a scientific term, but it is. Water striders, the Gerridae, are among what entomologists call true bugs—that is, members of the order Hemiptera. And when entomologists want to be strict they use the word "bug" to mean an insect grouped in this order. But (and this is the confusing part) not every insect whose name includes the word "bug" is a member of the order Hemiptera, the true bugs. A ladybug is not a bug, (which is why Ken Hagen was so careful to call it "lady beetle") but a member of the order Coleoptera.

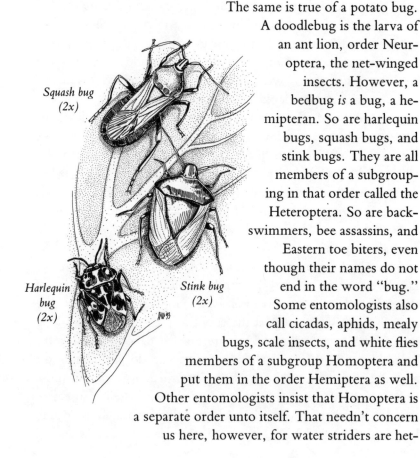

Squash bug
(2x)

Harlequin
bug
(2x)

Stink bug
(2x)

The same is true of a potato bug. A doodlebug is the larva of an ant lion, order Neuroptera, the net-winged insects. However, a bedbug *is* a bug, a hemipteran. So are harlequin bugs, squash bugs, and stink bugs. They are all members of a subgrouping in that order called the Heteroptera. So are backswimmers, bee assassins, and Eastern toe biters, even though their names do not end in the word "bug." Some entomologists also call cicadas, aphids, mealy bugs, scale insects, and white flies members of a subgroup Homoptera and put them in the order Hemiptera as well. Other entomologists insist that Homoptera is a separate order unto itself. That needn't concern us here, however, for water striders are het-

110

eropterans, and so no matter the classificatory scheme, they live tidily in the order Hemiptera, the true bugs. Thus they are bugs in the loose sense that you and I use the word, and in the sense that entomologists, speaking both strictly and informally, use it too.

Hemiptera means "half-winged" and was selected for this order because many of the insects in it have forewings that are divided in halves: the first, or basal, part thickened and leathery looking, but with delicately membranous tips. However, this characteristic is not the defining one. Some of the bugs in the order have uniformly thickened forewings, and some—the water striders, for instance—rarely have any wings at all. Instead, the order, despite its name, is defined by the long piercing mouthparts, which are arranged in a beak that allow Hemiptera to suck up juices from a plant or animal.

The particular juices that water striders suck up are those of mosquito larvae that float up to the water's surface, or other insects, spiders, or such small prey which have had the ill luck to fall onto the water. Sometimes water striders even eat one another. When they feed, they hold their prey tightly with their two short front legs and pierce it with a pair of long, strawlike stylets extending from their beaks. These stylets secrete an enzyme, which dissolves the insides of their victim into a beautiful soup.

I've spent unconscionable amounts of time in my sixty years crouched over puddles, ponds, and streams watching water striders skitter about. On a sunny day, in clear, shallow water, you can see a dimple of shadow around each slim foot, a depression in the unbroken film of the water's surface. How come they don't sink, these Jesus bugs? Water striders are covered with a velvety layer of waxy, many-branched hairs, which trap air and are what entomologists call hydrofuge in character. This is a two-bit word that means air is trapped among the tangle of hairs and holds water away from the water strider. Snug and dry inside this coat of air, water striders slide about and carry on life's business, oaring along with their second pair of legs and steering with the hinder ones.

José Rollin de la Torre-Bueno (1871–1948) was a great and

111

graceful writer on aquatic Hemiptera—that is, not only the water striders but also all the other species of bugs (upward of 400 in the freshwaters of North America alone, among them water boatmen, marsh treaders, and water scorpions) that live in, on, or along the edges of water. In 1917, in a paper entitled "Life-history and Habits of the Larger Waterstrider, *Gerris remigis* Say (Hem.)," he wrote, "Of all the bugs I know, I can think of none so amorous as our common large waterstrider . . ." Later researchers have also mentioned the generally zesty mating habits of water striders. One, R. Stimson Wilcox, in his 1972 paper "Communication by Surface Waves," observed a single male copulating five times in an hour, thrice with the same female.

Wilcox makes it clear that everything in water striders' lives, including courtship, relates to the thin surface film on which they live. Males set up a seductive tattoo upon it, creating wavelets of a certain periodicity in order to attract females to them at good oviposition sites. Receptive females answer in the same way. After copulation, the males' further wave-making stimulates the females to lay their eggs. During their wooing, males also send aggressive messages through waves of different frequencies, as a warning signal to other males. If the warnings are ignored, fights lasting several minutes can take place.

The mated female lays her eggs on plants trailing in the water, and the nymphs (very like the adult water striders in appearance, but smaller) hatch in a week or ten days under the surface. They may struggle for an hour or two before they can pierce the surface film of the water from below and clamber up onto it. Those unable to do so die, for they cannot live under the surface.

Many, if not most, insects have wings. Water striders—at least the freshwater ones—sometimes have them. Entomologists have a phrase for this that rolls off the tongue beautifully: alary polymorphism. *Alary* comes from the Latin word for wing, and *polymorphism* means "of many forms." Within the same species of water striders—even within the same population—some individuals are born with wings and some without. Obviously, winged water striders are the ones who colonize new bodies of water, even such temporary ones as the chuck holes and ruts I found them in that April day on my walk to the mailbox.

In the same paper quoted above, Torre-Bueno writes:

> The possession of wings always causes a change in the structure of the thorax to accommodate the much enlarged muscles which the use of organs of flight requires. These winged adults are generally found solitary in the most unlikely places—isolated little pools, springs, rockholes, beach drift, far from the favorite haunts of this stream-loving bug.

There is one genus of the Gerridae that those who have studied them say have no wings at all. These are the *Halobates,* who live on what seems to be the most inhospitable water of all for a bug, the salt ocean. *Halobates* are ocean water striders of many species; some of them hug the shores, while others skate about far from land in the open sea.

If water striders are unlikely bugs, the sea skaters, as *Halobates* are commonly called, are the oddest of the odd. If the surface film of water appears an improbable habitat, the surface film of salt water is even more improbable, and yet there are more than forty species of *Halobates* for whom it is home. The majority hug the shores of islands or mangrove swamps, bays, or coral-reef-protected lagoons. They are thought to have originated in the warm waters off the coast of Southeast Asia. None of the coastal species has been found in the Atlantic. However, at least five species have colonized the open seas, and can be found in the warm areas of the Pacific, Indian, and Atlantic oceans, where they seem to defy all the rules for a calm, sensible bug. There they lack fresh water; they are splashed continually by drying salt and are buffeted by ocean storms. Their food supply is chancy—the occasional floating dead insect, zooplankton, and one another. Oviposition sites are scarce: *Halobates* must lay their eggs on something that floats: cork, seaweed, or other flotsam. Despite living in vast open oceans, they have somehow managed to sort themselves out into separate species that do not interbreed. They were observed by seafarers long

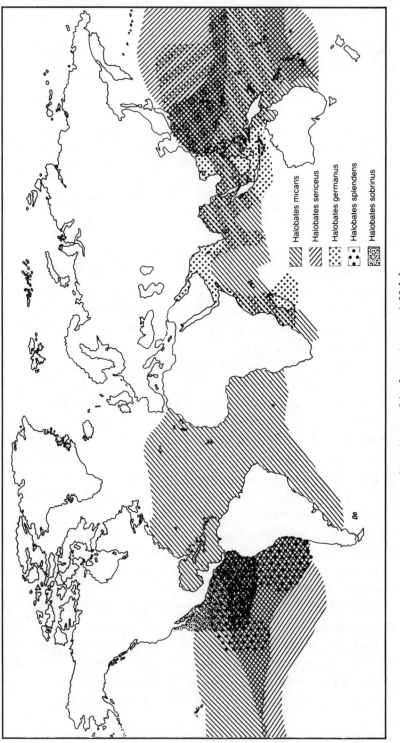

Ranges of distribution of the five major oceanic Halobates spp.
(Lanna Cheng, "Biology of Halobates," *Annual Review of Entomology, 1985*)

Halobates micans
Halobates sericeus
Halobates germanus
Halobates splendens
Halobates sobrinus

before they were studied. Wrote one such, a man named Robert McLachlan, in 1871:

Long before crossing the line, on the outward voyage, I was struck by small whitish creatures which often appeared coursing with great rapidity over the surface of the oceans; at length one was captured, and I well remember my astonishment on finding it was a spider-like insect. . . . If these notes should be read by any one of those "who go down to the sea in ships," I would remind him that, if he can throw any light upon the life history of this most wonderful insect . . . he will confer the utmost benefit upon natural science.

When I talked to Ken Hagen about ladybugs, he asked me what other bugs I was interested in. When I mentioned water striders, he smiled. "You must talk to Lanna Cheng down at Scripps," he said. "She's done wonderful work on ocean water striders and brought them to everyone's attention. Before she started publishing, most people just assumed salt water was too hostile an environment for insects. Some entomologists knew there were some out there, mostly along the edges [1,400 known species of insects can be found in various marine habitats], but her sea skaters are the only ones that are found out in the open ocean, and no one had done work on them until she came along." He scribbled down her telephone number and handed it to me.

Dr. Cheng is a woman in her fifties, who was born in Singapore and educated there before she went to Oxford, where she studied water striders of Malaysia and Singapore. Today she is at the Scripps Institution of Oceanography in California. I telephoned her and found her to be a gracious woman with a warm and mellifluous voice that has just a hint of Singapore in it. She told me about work that had been done by John Spence, John Treherne, and William Foster on the biology and behavior of *Halobates,* and agreed to send me several of her own recent papers, including a summary of one scheduled for publication. I asked her about current research on sea skaters. "The great puzzle," she said, "is how the separate species are established. Remember, not only

115

do these animals lack wings, but there are no natural barriers to their spread. There are many other questions, too, but we are most interested in learning about speciation among them." I told her I was not far from the University of Kansas, which I knew had acquired the great collection of aquatic Hemiptera made by Torre-Bueno. "Oh! There is a wealth of treasure there," she said, sounding pleased that I intended to make a pilgrimage to Lawrence to see it. "And, yes, there are some specimens of *Halobates* in it."

For obvious reasons, the open-ocean *Halobates* have been less studied than those that hug the coasts. Even among the latter there appear to be more questions than answers, but what is known about them is fascinating. They are solitary hunters, who dart about, quartering the water surface that is their hunting ground to find a morsel of prey from which they can suck the juices. However, the males and mating pairs form big rafts, called flotillas, a two-dimensional version of a gnat mating swarm. Members of the flotillas orient themselves to a particular mangrove root or lava promontory, staying close to it while the tide goes out, but loosening and dispersing to feed when it comes in and they are in no danger of being swept out to sea. Aside from the opportunity for mating that it gives, their massing is protective, not only because the tangle of bugs in and of itself confuses predators, but also because the group becomes its own early-warning system. This alarm factor was noted and named the "Trafalgar Effect" by J.E. Treherne and W. A. Foster, Cambridge entomologists who studied *Halobates* in the Galápagos. They found that the bugs in the flotillas are often touching one another, and as sea skaters at the outer edges spot a predator, they begin to dart about, spreading the news of an enemy at a speed so fast that it exceeds his approach. For those of us whose recollection of Nelson's famous battle is a bit dim, Treherne and Foster, in their 1981 paper on the subject, "Group Transmission of Predator Avoidance Behaviour in a Marine Insect: The Trafalgar Effect," write that they so named the effect because "of its similarity to the series of signals that were transmitted along the chain of frigates and ships of the line to the H.M.S. *Victory* before the Battle of Trafalgar, and which informed

Admiral Viscount Nelson that the combined French and Spanish
Fleet was leaving Cadiz, even though it was far beyond the hori-
zon of his flagship."

Once the alarming news of the enemy's approach has spread
throughout the flotilla, the bugs dash about rapidly and randomly,
reflecting light from their bodies, confusing and bewildering the
predator, serving to protect most of their companions, who would
be easier pickings if isolated.

Robert Brooks is the collections manager at the Snow Entomological Museum at the University of Kansas, a hilltop building
that also houses classrooms and offices. He is a young man, with
light-brown hair and beard. His office is a pleasant clutter of bugs
in jars and boxes, lab equipment, and books. The day I visited
him, a student was sitting at a computer making labels for insects
that were entering the collection. He got me a cup of coffee and
we settled down at his desk for a talk.

"Insect collections here and elsewhere," Rob told me, "are
made to study biodiversity, species range, and species types. You
can think of these specimens as a sort of library for scholars to use
as a reference source." Specimens are loaned out to entomologists
around the world for work and study. He showed me boxes of
carefully preserved, boxed specimens; these will be cushioned and
packed into cartons for shipping. "Insect collections at any institution always reflect the interests and specialties of the directors,"
he continued. "The Torre-Bueno collection was purchased in 1948
by Herbert Hungerford, who was department head at the time.
He was an armchair scientist himself, not a collector, but his specialty was aquatic Hemiptera, which of course include the water
striders. He built up the collection in that field. Before his time it
was leafhoppers, and today we concentrate on beetles and bees.
The whole collection contains somewhere between three-and-a-
half to four million pinned specimens, and that doesn't include
those unprocessed or preserved in alcohol. We have the second-
best collection of aquatic Hemiptera in the world. The best belongs to John T. Polhemus, a private collector, and we wish he
would leave it to us." He paused and laughed. "Then we would

117

have both the first *and* second best collections. Right now we have about 26,000 water striders, among them those of Torre-Bueno. His specimens include a number of Types." Type specimens are the individual insects from which the description of the species has been written.

When Rob tells me that he has just returned from a collecting expedition to South America, I ask him if he could describe how insects are prepared for the museum. "In the wild," he says, "insects are trapped and dropped into a mixture of 50 percent antifreeze, which kills them quickly. They are transferred to plastic bags and brought back to the museum in alcohol. Here they are worked over. The ones not needed are sent off in trade to other collectors. The ones we want to keep are air dried and pinned or glued to pins, and given data labels that not only identify them, but tell where they were collected. Then they are pinned into white Styrofoam in boxes inside glass-covered drawers." Each drawer includes a container of moth crystals as fumigant to keep the specimens free of the live insects that otherwise would soon infest, eat, and destroy the dead, preserved ones.

"There is no reason," Rob tells me as we walk downstairs to look at the water striders, "that, once they are mounted, specimens can't be useful for all time. When I was in London not long ago, I saw specimens 250 years old from Linnaeus's own collection, and the Type specimens were still good. One of the big problems for a collection is humidity. Our weather here in Kansas is more humid than in many places, and Snow Hall was air-conditioned very early, in 1960, not for the people, but for the insect collection. It was air-conditioned even before the chancellor's office was."

The big metal cabinets containing the collections fill the rooms below Rob Brooks's office and overflow out into the hallways, which are redolent of mothballs. The collection has no master index; it does not need one, for it is arranged phylogenetically, and Rob can go to the specimens wanted simply through his knowledge of the classification scheme. The water striders are in the hallway. "The Torre-Bueno collection is integrated into the main collection," he tells me, pulling out drawers, "although it wasn't, completely, when I came here. I finished putting it together. You can tell which ones were his because they are labeled on yellow paper. It was not a 'pretty' collection. His labels were not precise and informative. For instance, where a more exacting collector would give all the details of where he'd found the bug, he would simply write 'Thailand' and let it go at that. But Hungerford was eager to get it because of the fame of the collector."

Each metal cabinet contains sixty-five glass-covered drawers of beautiful golden oak, polished and neatly mitred. The Gerridae in the collection run from *Amemboa brevifasciata Miyamoto,* a water strider from Sumatra, to *Xenobates seminulum* (Esaki), from New Guinea. Yellow Torre-Bueno labels twinkle throughout the drawers. There are no nymphs—that is, immature specimens—in the collections, and no eggs, although there is a dish of spare legs in one drawer. Nymphs that come in among collected specimens are thrown out, Rob tells me. "The collection is not strong in *Halobates,*" he says apologetically as we come to their drawers. However, it includes one of the biggest water striders I have ever seen, maybe a couple of inches long, and one of the smallest, a mere speck of a sea skater. I put on my glasses and peer at it.

Before I began reading up on water striders I had not known about the winged forms, and to my knowledge I had never seen one. I ask Rob about them. He shows me a specimen with wings so tightly folded across its skinny back that I would not have known there were wings there at all unless he had pointed them out. I ask him what the current thinking is about alary polymorphism, showing off the phrase I had just learned. "They are born this way, you know," he says. "They don't shed their wings, either. Once winged, the same individual stays that way. The current theory is that the buildup of population density may be the trigger that causes winged individuals to be born. They migrate to a new spot where the numbers are fewer, and then the next generation has no wings. But that's only theory, and someone has to work on it to see if it's true."

I tell Rob I am interested in learning more about Torre-Bueno

and how his collection came to Snow Hall. We decide to talk about
it over lunch, but seated in a dim booth at a comfortable off-
campus café, I discover that Rob is a beekeeper. He began keeping
them when he was eight years old, and it was this passion that
brought him to entomology as a profession. Educated in California, where he was born, he took his graduate degrees at Kansas
and came to work here because of the good academic research
currently being done on bees at the university. He knows all the
players in the bravo bee games and we talk about this, gossiping
spiritedly while we eat and drink.

We only return to Torre-Buneo on the drive back to campus.
José Rollin de la Torre-Bueno was born in Lima, Peru, but came
to the United States with his family when he was only fourteen
years old. He was said to speak English in "bell-like tones," with
only the slightest of accents. Like many another immigrant who
has learned a new tongue, he was fascinated with words, and in
addition to becoming an outstanding collector of insects, he was
also a linguist, writer, and editor. Sitting on my desk, I have a gift
from my cousin Asher, the 1989 edition of *The Torre-Bueno Glossary of Entomology,* a revision of the dictionary of entomological
terms which he published in 1937. A glossary-dictionary is necessary for anyone who hopes to be able to read and enjoy the stories
prized from bugs that entomologists have to tell. All arcane bodies
of knowledge, be they political theory or prosody, have their own
vocabularies. It is an exquisite way to keep the initiate inside the
magic circle and the uninitiate out. But there is an additional reason for the special vocabulary of entomology that becomes such
an impenetrable and thorny barrier to the nonentomologist's understanding. Torre-Bueno, himself an entomological writer of
great accessibility, even elegance, made the following point in his
introduction to his glossary:

> The entomologist of the early days was the closet naturalist *par
> excellence.* He was a distinguisher and namer of things not hereto-
> fore discriminated. In consequence, an undue value was set on the
> bare description of species and the higher categories. The natural

result flowed from this: a new technical vocabulary came into being; and since so much of the work done was independent and so much on very limited groups, practically each investigator invented new terms for his group, or improved on those of his predecessors, or by misinterpretation mis-named structures already recognized and named. But this condition naturally made any explanation of terms refer practically to nothing other than those structures employed in entomography or descriptive entomology.

In addition, Torre-Bueno revived the publication *Entomologica Americana* and was the enlivener of one of the most famous and productive of groups interested in insects, the Brooklyn Entomological Society. After a meeting, he wrote in 1948, members often

> . . . adjourned to a German biergarten nearby the place of meeting, going into the back room by the Family Entrance, where they were served sauerfleisch and other hearty Teutonic food and delicacies washed down with foaming steins of "echt bier"—none of the feeble latter-day imitations or "ersatz."

Torre-Bueno's portrait shows him to be a mustachioed man, dashing in appearance. He was educated at the School of Mines, Columbia University, and made his living as an editor at the General Chemical Company in New York. He and his wife had seven children, whom he is reported to have adored. In his biographical sketch of Torre-Bueno in *American Entomologists,* Arnold Mallis writes: "Although of mild disposition, he was a man of independent spirit who would not tolerate anything unjust or unscrupulous."

I asked Rob if he thought there was anyone still around the university entomology department who had ever met Torre-Bueno. "George Byers, the retired director, might have met him," he said, so we went to visit Byers in the office he still maintains in Snow Hall. Byers, who has a lively interest in the history of entomology, said he had not met him, but he remembers the collection when it came to the university.

"It had been damaged by water," he said. "Torre-Bueno and his wife had moved out to Tucson and the collection had been stored in a basement there when a flash flood came through. Hungerford brought it back to the university, and a lot of work needed to be done on it. Some of the specimens had fallen off the paper points and that sort of thing. I did the work on it myself. There should be some letters over at the archives if you want to know more about it. Hungerford really went after it."

I had already asked Rob if he knew what the university had paid for the Torre-Bueno collection. I wondered about the worth of a bunch of bugs that wasn't "pretty," yet was celebrated and important. Rob had not known; curiosity piqued, he decided to join me in my rummage through the university archives. The archivist sounded dubious when we asked him about it. "A collection of insects?" he asked. "You think we paid *money* for it?" He showed us a stack of boxes and we started going through the yellowing correspondence inside, finding nothing. Rob told the archivist that this was a very important collection that was probably expensive. "Well . . ." The archivist hesitated, sighed, and then said in a voice which suggested that he found this hard to believe, "if it was *very* important, there may be copies of letters in the chancellor's file." He pulled out a folder for 1948 containing only two letters. They were both about the Torre-Bueno collection. Rob and I looked at each other and grinned. The letters were from Hungerford, asking for funds to buy the collection and, once that was approved, for additional travel money to go to Tucson and pick it up. Here are some pertinent excerpts from his first letter, dated April 13, 1948:

> I spent four very busy days in Tucson, Arizona, going over the Bueno collection of Hemiptera. . . . The collection . . . which he has been accumulating for forty-seven years, contains exotic species, much of it genotypic which is exceedingly valuable in our own taxonomic work. In North American material it contains about 300 species that would be new to our collections. Most of the terrestrial species of the exotics would be new. His collection of aquatic Hemiptera is large and contains a number of types which we need. . . .

The only figure Mr. Bueno ever mentioned as a possible valuation of his collection is $5000.00. However, the collection suffered some water damage in a flash flood some years ago and I do not think it is worth $5000.00. I request that $3000.00 be set aside for the purchase of this collection. . . . Since Mr. Bueno must move in a week or two to a small house, he is anxious to place his collection somewhere, so we may be able to get it even though he thinks it worth more money. I have always hoped that some day we might add the Bueno collection to our own.

That 1948 asking price of $5,000 would be in the neighborhood of $30,000 today, and the price paid, $3,000, would amount to something like $18,000.

Rob shook his head, impressed. In a voice with just a tinge of yearning in it, he said, "We'd never be able to buy a collection like that today."

CHAPTER VIII

ORDER THYSANURA: SILVERFISH

We all know that silverfish, those spindle-shaped, shiny, wingless little animals that sometimes vanish into the crack of the shelf when we remove a book from it, are not fish. But what are they? They look metallic, but if you squish one, all that is left is a smear like a dusting of graphite.

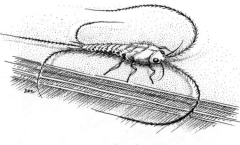

Silverfish (2x)

They seem too soft and powdery to be insects; they resemble almost-insects, those creatures we could, in a broad sense, call bugs—something on the fringes of bugdom like spiders, or sow bugs, which curl up in little balls when we lift the stones they are hiding under, or millipedes, which look like worms with legs, or even the outrageous centipedes.

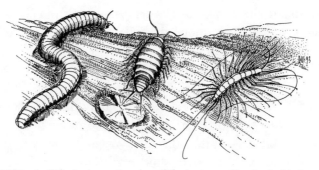

Millipede (life-size)   Sow bug (life-size)   Centipede (⅓x)

In fact, however, silverfish are proper members of the Class Insecta, although I have a paper written more than a hundred years ago, in 1873, by an English natural historian, John Lubbock, in which he debated whether or not this was true. Silverfish have the usual defining characteristics of insects: six legs and a segmented body that is divided into three parts, head, thorax, and abdomen.

Most insects have wings. Entomologists, following the remnants of a scheme begun by Linnaeus, call them the Pterygota, a fancy way of saying "have wings." The grouping includes even those insects that you and I in our common-sense way would point out *don't* have wings: water striders (ah! but they *sometimes* have wings) or fleas (ah! but the study of their thoracic structure reveals that they are evolved from insects that *did* have them, and that they just lost them on the way to their present form). But silverfish and a few other insects have never had wings. Therefore they are called the Apterygota, the wingless, and are considered by entomologists to be a primitive sort of insect. But primitive doesn't mean simple, clumsy, tentative, experimental, or that the silverfish slipping behind books on shelves are the ancestors of butterflies. What it does mean is that, a very long time ago, there were animals rather like today's silverfish which evolved into an effective, practical form that enabled them to get on in the world. They developed this form back in the Beginning of Insects, as it were, and it was so suited to the changes and challenges the world has offered in the millions of years that followed that they had no need to make any more major alterations to themselves in order to continue to get along well. They are among the real conservatives of life; they are also among its successes.

The oldest insect fossil yet found is a silverfish cousin. Silverfish are members of the order Thysanura, which means "tassel tail." Silverfish, family Lepismatidae, prefer to live in cool, damp places. Firebrats, another of their cousins in the order, look a lot like them, but are darker; they thrive in warm, dry places, such as the back of a furnace. Silverfishes' other cousins, a little more distant, are the bristletails, similar in many respects, and copper-colored. Their family name is Machilidae, and they are usually found outside, under bark or stones. The fossil that Conrad C. Labandeira, a paleobotanist at the University of Chicago, found a couple of years ago in a chunk of ancient mudstone is very like a modern bristletail, but smaller. The mudstone, taken from the north shore of Quebec's Gaspé Bay, exquisitely preserved the head and much of the thorax of the insect, which is believed to have lived 390 million years ago, its form and structure already complex, the result even then of millions of years of adaptation. So animals very like modern Thysanurans have been around for something like 400 million years.

By comparison, humankind is only a couple of million years old. Geologists call the era in which the Thysanurans developed the Devonian, and tell us that it was an ocean sort of time: fine fishes swimming about and corals busily building reefs. On land, plants and some animals, in a cozy, mutual coevolution, had begun to develop from those that had made their first tentative invasions from the seas. They had to work out the problems that resulted from living outside that moist, hospitable environment. The first simple low plants had established a hold along the ancient shores, and provided a benign humid home for the first terrestrial animals—buggish sorts, modified worms, entomologists suggest, who still lacked the waxy coating their successors would develop to keep themselves from drying out. Those first plants also provided food for the animals, but the act of eating them would provoke, in turn, the development and evolution of defenses against being eaten. The plants toughened their fibers, protected their spores, and formed whatever structures were necessary to survive and spread.

Over millions of years a few plants and animals managed so well that they were able to survive one of those great mass extinctions which come now and again in the history of life on the planet. This particular one, possibly caused by cooling, extinguished many ocean animals and is used as a marker for the end of the Devonian period some 360 million years ago. Thysanurans were among those who survived the cooling, and they also managed to survive other mass extinctions, such as the one that put an end to the dinosaurs.

Thysanurans have stayed flexible, taking food and shelter whenever and wherever they could through the changing geographic and climatic conditions the world has had to offer them. Most of the 550 known and described contemporary species live concealed in the soil, in rotting wood, under stones or leaf litter. Many still wait to be described. Asher told me recently that in his younger days he used to collect silverfish and bristletails for Pedro W. Wygodzinsky. Wygodzinsky, who died in 1987, was curator of entomology at the American Museum of Natural History, and specialized in assassin bugs, but he also wrote some of the few recent papers on silverfish and their kin. Where did he find specimens to send Wygodzinsky, I asked. "Oh, in the bathtub sometimes," Asher said, chuckling. "But mostly under stones along the edge of the road. Wygodzinsky told me that nearly anything I found in this country would prove to be a new species."

It was Wygodzinsky who first described a rare Thysanuran, sometimes called the primitive bristletail, an example of the sort of animal that newspaper writers like to call "living fossils," for it closely resembles those of its kin preserved for millions of years in sedimentary rock. It belongs to the family Lepidotrichidae, was named *Tricholepidon gertschi,* and was found scuttling about under the bark of a fallen Douglas fir in northern California. In his 1961 paper, Wygodzinsky wrote that it is characterized by many primitive features, most of them highly technical, but one of which, a lack of scales, would distinguish the yellow-gray animal for even an amateur. Other members of the order, including the familiar silverfish, all have scales.

Indeed, it is the scales which give the silverfish its metallic appearance (the English sometimes call them silver ladies), and serve to protect it, for they slip off easily in a predator's grasp and allow the insect to escape. It is the greased pig of bugdom. This primitive bristletail, lacking those scales, has other means of defense. Wygodzinsky wrote that when the animal was exposed, it would either run away rapidly or raise its body high on the tips of its claws and lash its three-part tail aggressively from side to side. Stomach analysis revealed it to be a vegetable feeder, and specimens were kept alive in the laboratory on a diet of rolled oats, dry yeast, and small pieces of wood covered with algae.

Sizing up the main chance, making the best of whatever food sources come along, has obviously contributed to the success of Thysanurans. Some species of silverfish have taken up with ants, others with termites, and live in their nests. And some species, as we know, have discovered humans, for we are a good food source for them. They like last winter's oatmeal, still stored undisturbed on the kitchen shelf, or that half-used bag of flour. They like house dust. In 1940, Eder Lindsay, an Australian entomologist, published a thorough study of the silverfish's eating habits. She analyzed, for instance, the contents of house dust, finding it to contain crumbs, small cellulose fibers, woody fragments, insect legs, feelers, and claws, pieces of leaves and dried grass, string, and sawdust. These would be nutritious chow for silverfish. But the members of the commonest species that live with us, *Lepisma saccharina* (the name means, literally, sugar-taker), especially like the starch we have about us, starch which they can convert to useful sugars. They find it in paste that holds wallpaper to walls, in the glues that bind covers to our books, in the sizings of paper and fabric. A couple of human generations ago, when men wore stiffly starched, detachable collars and stored them in drawers, reports indicate that silverfish were a terrible household problem. This may explain why much of the published work on silverfish (and there is not a lot) is more than fifty years old.

Silverfish are gregarious, sociable animals, liking their own company so much that they often eat one another. Their bodies are flattened, which allows them to find cover in the merest slivers of space. They run quickly, on legs that are attached in such a way as to move horizontally, giving them a rowing gait. They not only shed their shimmering scales easily in a predator's claws, but can also quickly regenerate antennae and other sensing organs lost through misadventure. Researchers say they lack the ability to hear airborne sound and that their eyesight is not keen. They can only tell dark, which they prefer, from light, which they avoid. But they make up for these sensory lacks by an array of chemical and tactile sensitivities so varied and precise that we, who are so inept about such matters, can have no real understanding of what a silverfish's world is like. Even the slightest change in an air current is enough to set off the sensory hairs on their bodies.

Eleanor Slifer, a Pennsylvania researcher who published a paper in 1970 on the silverfish's senses, wrote: "The many tactile hairs on the body and appendages must be very useful to an animal that spends most of its time in narrow passages or crevices." According to Slifer, their antennae contain at least six different kinds of sense receptors, some that allow them, at the very least, to touch their world and recognize its shape and features, and others that are also chemoreceptors, which give them information about the constituent nature of that world. They also probably tell them many other things that are unknown to us in our largely visual and aural world. Silverfish also have an additional set of similar sensory receptors at their nether end, located on a triad of "filaments" that extend, taillike, from their abdomen. The two shorter filaments splay out sideways and are called cerci.

Many other insects and arthropods have cerci. They are sensory, but are sometimes used by insects to hold partners during copulation, so they are also called "claspers." The middle filament, longer than the cerci and extending straight out from the tip of the abdomen, is similar to the telson or terminal segment of a lobster. It is given the lumbering, ponderous name "median terminal filament," or worse, "medium caudal filament" (caudal means tail). *Hmmmmm . . . Tazzie looked up at me with her soft brown eyes and wagged her caudal filament . . . her terminal filament. No, it won't fly. Tail.*

These silverfish tails are stuffed with sensory cells, too. But whereas a silverfish runs about with antennae in constant motion, flicking them this way and that to learn its world, the tail drags along the ground, kenning what is underfoot. This is the same sort of tail Pedro Wygodzinsky tells us a primitive bristletail thrashed so extravagantly at him when he had the temerity to lift up a piece of bark to look at it, so the tail is obviously used in other ways. It is also wagged lasciviously in courtship. I had no idea that back behind the books there was such tempestuousness. This tail-wagging is called a love dance, and was closely studied by Von H. Sturm, a German entomologist who described it in twelve pages of Teutonic detail in his 1965 paper *Die Paarung beim Silberfischen.* It is a lusty, indirect, probably primitive sort of pairing. When a male and female silverfish in mating condition meet each other, they face their future partner and exchange erotic messages through quivering, trembling antennae, backing off sometimes as though the intensity were too great, coming together, vibrating antennae again, twisting, whirling their abdomens, running away, returning. This part of the dance may last for as long as half an hour, until the male, overcome, breaks away and runs from the female, who pursues him until she comes to rest at his side, head to tail. He vibrates his tail, with all its sensory capabilities, against her. The pair break away only to repeat this side-to-side, tail-touching phase of their lovemaking over and over with growing intensity until the male, increasingly aroused, comes to a climax in which he spins threads from his aedeagus, or phallus tip, at the end of his abdomen. This thread is studded with sperm encased in spermatophore. A final touch from the male makes the female walk forward, entangle herself in the threads, and, ovipositor bent downward, straddle the spermatophore, which she takes up into her body to store and use to fertilize the eggs she will soon lay.

The female silverfish lays these eggs in batches of six or so in cracks or crevices, but sometimes even in the open. If they are laid in damp, hospitable places, silverfish youngsters, which look almost exactly like their parents, but smaller, hatch. But if the air is too dry, the young insect becomes so stressed and stunted that he can only partially break out of the egg and will die before he can escape. Young silverfish grow slowly over their lifetimes, which last several years, molting dozens of times in the process. Each instar is so similar to the one before and after it, and the molts are so frequent, that even entomologists sometimes have a hard time telling which stage the animal is in. When the silverfish is about to molt, he grows quiet, arches his body, and expands and contracts his abdomen until a split appears along his back. Gradually undulating his new body, he pulls himself through the crack headfirst.

Silverfish, it will be remembered, are eager cannibals, and so they often feed on one another during molt, when they are quiet, vulnerable, and trying to extricate themselves from the confines of their old cuticles. In addition, just as when they are hatching, a certain number simply die, unable to escape through the slit in their former backs. Considering how perilous this often-repeated process is, it is a wonder any silverfish grow to maturity. The number of molts a silverfish goes through varies, depending upon species and environmental conditions, but they are many: from seventeen to sixty-six under laboratory conditions. That is a lot, considering that many insects make do with ten or fewer. The silverfish is only a few instars old when rudiments of sexual organs begin to appear, and after perhaps ten more molts he is sexually mature. Unlike many other insects, who do not mature sexually until their final form, silverfish continue to molt even after mating. And since the females lose any spermatozoa they have acquired at mating when they shed the lining of their own spermatheca in which it is stored during the molt, they need to mate again in each adult instar in order to lay fertile eggs. A silverfish's life is molt and mate, molt and mate, molt and mate.

If they do not succumb to death while hatching or molting, and escape becoming dinner to their own kind or some other predator or parasite, silverfish prove to be enduring animals. Given adequate food, decent moisture (which they take up into their body through their anus), and a protective cranny, they can live for a long time. Depending upon species, lifetimes of eighteen months to four years have been recorded under laboratory conditions, and claims are made that they may live even longer. Some of this time can be spent without food. Even without their bit of wallpaper paste, plant spore, or leaf fragment, they seem to get on remarkably well, everything considered. Silverfish in laboratory starvation experiments have lived nearly a year without food and can live astonishingly long on the most meager of diets. Eder Lindsay kept adult silverfish (youngsters need better food) alive for nearly two years, even though she fed them only scraps of filter paper. J.W. Cornwall, a doctor stationed in India, conducted longevity experiments on silverfish—which he called, Anglo-Indian style, "fish insects"—in 1915, and noted that a few days before death from starvation, the animal's abdomen suddenly shortened by one third—it had absorbed all its own connective and fatty tissue in order to stay alive.

I know of no one with a good word for silverfish. Whenever I mentioned that I was reading up on them, friends and neighbors responded by telling me stories about silverfish destructiveness—of the holes they chewed in stored linens, the books they ruined, the files they made useless. Silverfish are so tough and can shelter in such small, tight spaces that toxic sprays cannot harm or reach them. The usual advice for countering the damage they cause is to seal off their hiding places, reduce the humidity, replace decayed building materials, and store food and clothing carefully.

But if a bug could be allowed a point of view, silverfish would regard humans tenderly, as something of a treat. For them we are a young, trial species that has come into the world in benign climatic times, a species with the ability to alter its environment modestly, thus allowing our kind to increase to ridiculous numbers for the express purpose of creating habitat and food for a few species of *their* kind. Good but probably not dependable providers. Will very likely disappear in the next mass extinction. Better not get accustomed to them.

CHAPTER IX

ORDER ORTHOPTERA: KATYDIDS

I love to hear thine earnest voice,
    Wherever thou art hid,
Thou testy little dogmatist,
    Thou pretty Katydid!
          —OLIVER WENDELL HOLMES

The green insect known in the U'States by the
    name of sawyer or chittediddle was first heard
    to cry on the 27th of July.
          —MERIWETHER LEWIS

A huge ugly grasshopper [sic], *Deinacrida megacephala,*
    called by the Bushmen, the Sawyer.
          —EDWARD E. MORRIS,
          Australian English

. . . the Sawyer beetle [sic] is the very largest
    insect known.
          —*The Sunday Magazine,* 1890

"*Deinacrida megacephala.* Hmmmm. Let me look that up for you. Here it is. No, it's not a beetle, it's a katydid," said Dave Nickle, the federal katydid man. "Yes, I seem to remember hearing that 'sawyer' was an old name for 'katydid.' " "Katydid" is an American word that is supposed to describe the song of an eastern species. In other places they are called "bush crickets."

Growing up, as I did, east of the Mississippi, where the katydids' song matched the name, I was conned into believing, at least for a time, a fierce story told me by a fierce grandmother: She said that Katy was a little girl very like me, who had told a fib, and when she willfully and stubbornly compounded it by saying she hadn't lied, God struck her dead. Thereafter, Grandma insisted, Katy's shame lived on, for the very bugs in the trees still debate whether Katy did or Katy didn't, and if I would listen carefully I could hear that most of them said she did. And it was true: The rebuttals were not many. I suspect that the story was made up on the spot for my moral improvement.

A less fierce, but sadder and also murderous story comes from the hills of North Carolina, where a slightly older, nubile Katy fell in love with a handsome young man who scorned her and instead took to wife her prettier sister. After the honeymooning couple were found poisoned in their bed, arms entwined, the bugs began their debate as to whether Katy was the responsible party.

Any way the story goes, it is obvious that Katy is less than admirable. As if to back this up, the *Oxford English Dictionary* tells us that "katy" is an old word for "a wanton." Early American spelling seems to have been "catedid."

The first reference that the O.E.D. lists is dated 1751, when John Bartram, the naturalist-explorer, wrote, "It was fair and pleasant and the great green grasshopper began to sing (Catedidist)." Flipping to the *cate-* entry, the O.E.D. gives the intriguing bit of information that "catachesis, instruction by word of mouth," spins out from Greek origins and means to resound, to din in one's ears.

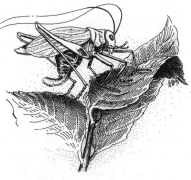

Katydid (½x)

135

(Holmes knew his Greek and may have had this derivation in mind . . . "Thou testy little dogmatist . . .")

No matter what the origins, "katydid" is a perfectly respectable, if American, common name used by entomologists for the family Tettigoniidae, which comes from the Greek word for cicada, which is not in the family at all. Cicadas belong to the family Cicadidae way over in the order Homoptera, so this doesn't make any sense, but there you are. "I've always thought," said Asher, "that *Katydididae* would make a lovely family name." The Tettigoniidae are quite distinct from grasshoppers (family Acrididae) and crickets (family Gryllidae), but they are cousins, all belonging to the order Orthoptera. Orthoptera means straight-winged, from *ortho-*, as in orthopedics, orthography, and orthodoxy.

True katydid
(½x)

The bug that carries on the debate about whether Katy did or didn't is *Pterophylla camellifolia,* the eastern katydid, sometimes called the true katydid. Dave Nickle told me this one day over lunch at a restaurant on Capitol Hill, not far from the Natural History Museum at the Smithsonian, where he has his office. The restaurant is a homey, cluttered place with eclectic furnishings and menu, and it is staffed by underemployed actors who don't mind people who stay a long time and spread papers all over the table.

Nickle, the Smithsonian's expert on Orthoptera, has specialized in katydids. A handsome young man with dark hair and mustache and expressive brown eyes, he arrived at lunch with a stack of books and papers. I emptied my briefcase of the journal articles I'd already read and had questions about. *P. camellifolia,* he told me, was only one of more than a hundred species of katydids found in the United States, all members of the family Tettigoniidae, a slim sampling of the more than 5,000 described species found worldwide, mostly in the tropics, where Dave does a major part of his research.

"Actually, although we call them katydids because of their song, a much more widespread American katydid is *Microcentrum rhombifolium*. It's found all over the United States, coast to coast, border to border. You can call it to you. Both the males and females sing, which is highly unusual; among most species the female is silent and only the male sings. It's got a common name, too, but I'd have to look that up." If it didn't sing about Katy, I wondered, what did it sing? I asked Dave and right there in the restaurant he started singing katydid—sharp, chirping sounds. I was impressed.

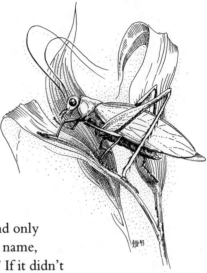

Microcentrum
rhombifolium ♂
(³⁄₄x)

Other species of katydids, I learned after listening to Dave, may sing *Ch-ch-chhhh* or even *buzzzzZZZZZ*. None of them care about our doings; they sing not of lies or murders but of their own affairs. In many species it is only the males who sing, hoping to warn away competitors or to attract a female. Katydid experts such as Dave are able to interpret these songs. The common name for *M. rhombifolium,* the species in which the female answers back, said Dave after thumbing through a reference book, is the angular-winged katydid. In 1959, D.G. Grove wrote his Ph.D. thesis at Cornell about its natural history.

Davison Greenawalt Grove, a native of Chambersburg, Pennsylvania, has spent his teaching lifetime at Wilson College there. In his thesis he writes:

My interest in this katydid stems from the bug-collecting days of childhood. Its large size, gentleness, and nocturnal activity all fascinated me. After many abortive attempts, I succeeded in rearing specimens in cages and, finally, nine years ago, in forcing early hatching of eggs. My acquaintance with them is thus more than academic, for these insects have, literally, been members of my household for a decade.

Even out-of-doors katydids can be tamed:

> Wild katydids attempt to bite when picked up in the fingers, but lose this response with repeated handling. A nip from one is painful but is seldom given with sufficient force to break the skin.

Keeping pet katydids has a long history, dating back, at least in Germany, several hundred years, for male katydids in small, colorful houses were sold by street vendors there throughout the eighteenth and nineteenth centuries. Although their song certainly draws us, conveying as it does warmth, summer, and the friend-liness of nighttime, I suspect part of their appeal is aesthetic. Katydids are beautiful. One summer day when my husband and I were walking the dogs in Washington, I found an eastern katydid, *P. camellifolia,* which had fallen clumsily and uncharacteristically from a tree. I picked him up and held him in my hand to show Arne. The Latin name means That Being Which Has Wings Like a Camellia Leaf. They are big, plump, jolly-looking bugs in nursery-bright green, a couple of inches long. Their leaflike wings press tightly against their sides, and their fat bodies are laterally compressed, ridged to an apex at their backs so that they look like animated prisms, triangles wrought in three dimensions. We both admired him, and then I put him back on his tree and watched while he crawled into the leaves and disappeared.

Although some people who are not familiar with them think of bugs as ugly, you can't be around entomologists for long before bug handsomeness becomes obvious. When I talked to Cassie Gibbs about black flies I asked her how it was she had specialized in mayflies, which appear to have wings made of isinglass. "They are such beautiful insects," she said forthrightly. But it was Asher who first introduced me to bug beauties beyond normal human

seeing. One day he invited me to inspect
a tiny moth, undistinguished and dun-
colored to the naked eye. Under the
microscope it revealed itself,
shimmering, gleaming,
golden, decked out in
mothly splendor.
A goldsmith would
have been impressed
by its exquisiteness,
and so was I. The
scanning electron
microscope opened
up a new world of
information and study
for entomologists, just
as it did for scientists in other

Mayfly

fields, but it also opened up a new
world of beauty. I have a copy of
A Scanning Electron Microscope Atlas of the Honey Bee, nearly 300
pages of SEM photos of bees, photos of surpassing loveliness of
shape, texture, and form. I know a sculptor who uses it to give
him inspiration for his work.

Other species of katydids have slightly different life histories,
but making allowances for this, the story Dr. Grove tells of
M. rhombifolium from his close observations of wild and captive
ones (sustained on such fare as elm and mulberry leaves, in season,
and ivy—occasionally smeared with peanut butter—and lettuce,
out of season) is typical of many katydids in the family. In southern Pennsylvania, *rhombifolium* eggs are laid in the wild in double
rows on twigs after the noisy nocturnal courtship that we all as-
sociate with high summer. Indoors, the females oviposited on
what was available, including, Grove writes, the painted strut of a
model airplane. The eggs overwinter and hatch out in early springtime.

139

Katydid metamorphosis is incomplete: Youngsters look rather like small adults, minus wings and sexual parts. They grow by molting, shedding their cuticles and stepping out of them tender and new, becoming larger and finer with each molt, achieving complete wings and sexual capabilities only in their last instars. During early summer they disperse, eat, grow . . . and are silent. But as they mature sexually, the males find their voices and begin to sing, or stridulate, as entomologists say, with their wings. Katydids are clumsy fliers, and reserve their hind wings for this purpose when they must, but their forewings are complex, highly evolved musical instruments. They produce their song by raising their forewings and scraping the rigid edge of the right forewing against teeth on the file vein on the underside of the other. The effect is rather

Microcentrum rhombifolium ♀
Ovipositing
(½x)

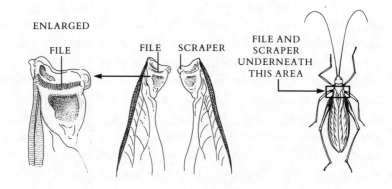

ENLARGED

FILE

FILE   SCRAPER

FILE AND
SCRAPER
UNDERNEATH
THIS AREA

A katydid's music-making parts

like drawing a fingernail along the teeth of a comb. Each species of katydid sings songs unique to it, and all are hard to put into human language. Entomologists have an understandably rough time trying to describe these songs—I found katydids' calls represented as *chirp, tschick, tsip, tap, chak,* tick, song, buzz, sound, lisp, rattle, acoustic signaling, zip, squeak, crackling, stridulatory sound, *sssst, tttk, ch-ch-cccchhhhh,* acoustic airborne signals, trill, shuffle, rustle, auditory signals, purr, *zeep, shrie-e-eek, ka ki kak,* chant, interspecific reproductive isolating mechanism, *chak,* rasp.

Grove describes the male *rhombifolium* song as *tick,* the love call, and *chirp,* the call that may warn off rival males. Unlike some of their other katydid cousins, female *rhombifolium* answer their lovers, indicating a readiness to mate. It is their soft call that can be imitated by humans to call up randy male katydids, their passions aflame, rather in the same way that hunters here in the Ozarks call up yearning turkey gobblers in the springtime by imitating the low, sexy *put-put-put* of a willing hen turkey. Writes Grove:

> Successful imitation of the female may be made in several ways, including clicking of the fingernails, compressing saliva between tongue and palate, snapping shears or scissors, or twanging a single tooth of a pocket comb. Not every male responds to all of these, but it often happens that if one does not seduce him, another will.

Like some other members of their order, such as the true crickets, katydids have the ears to hear these songs in their forelegs. Insect legs are segmented. The bottom segment, the one we would like to call the foot, is the tarsus. The segment above the tarsus is the tibia, and it is near the base of the tibia that the katydid's ears are located, a pair to each leg. They are called tympana, and consist of a delicate cuticular membrane overlying a tracheal air sac, free to vibrate when sound waves hit it. Katydids listen eagerly, using a gesture like that of a human putting his hand behind his ear to cup the sound. Grove describes it:

> After the he first response to his tick calls the male repeats the series at least 4 or 5 times, pausing between calls to catch the female's

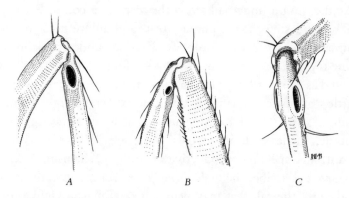

Orthopteran hearing organs: A Cricket ♂, knee; B inner side of the same; C Katydid ♂, outer side of the fore knee from the front.

response and leaning first to one side and then to the other, raising the uppermost foreleg to expose the typanum more effectively.

Guided by this sound, the two come closer and closer, the male's song softening in the process. When they are within touching distance they stroke each other's antennae, stridulating quietly all the while. They then turn end to end. The male grasps a twig or a bit of leaf with his tarsi and spreads his rear legs, while the female, rear legs supporting her, braces her first and second pair of legs against the male. He holds her abdomen with his cerci and pulls her forward and under himself. In this position he produces a spermatophore, a large jellylike blob containing not only his sperm, but also a nutritious protein snack called the spermatophyllax. He passes it to her and she secures it at, but not completely inside, her abdominal genital opening, which is just forward of her ovipositor, the curved egg-laying organ protruding from the tip of her abdomen. After mating, the *rhombifolium* couple remain close together, the male ravenously eating leaves, the female quiet, unable to move until the spermatophore hardens and dries. Over the next eighteen to twenty-four hours, her eggs become fertilized, while she slowly eats the spermatophyllax, bending herself double under her thorax to do so.

142

Grove's thesis was written twenty years before Richard Daw-kin's popular book *The Selfish Gene* brought to the attention of the general reading public a notion that today dominates biological thinking: The choosier, coyer player in the mating game is he or she who has the bigger physiological investment. Since eggs are normally larger than sperm, this is usually the female, and for the most part male katydids woo, entice, and lure females with the promise and gift of the spermatophyllax. Research has shown that the bigger the spermatophyllax, the fitter, brawnier, and more able to pass on genes the offspring produced will be. But these same courtship gifts mean that the male has a considerable phys-iological investment, too, for he must not only make the sperm as all males do, but also the protein snack that accompanies them. Recent research by W.J. Bailey, L.W. Simmons, and D.T. Gwynne has shown that among some katydids (and those other insects who produce courtship feeding gifts) hard times—famine and dearth—turn the tables. Then it is the males who become coy and the females who are the eager wooers, seeking out males not so much, it seems, for their sperm as for their nutritious sperma-tophyllax. The males sing less and become reluctant to mate.

I so enjoyed reading Grove's thesis, which was never published, that I wanted to tell him so and find out what he had been doing since 1959. I telephoned Wilson College, where the woman with whom I was connected told me that he was "a thoroughly won-derful man who had been a popular teacher" until he retired re-cently. She told me he lived nearby, so I telephoned him at his home.

"Oh, yes," Grove said. "I've gone on raising katydids. Raised them all my life. I enjoy doing it. I suppose it is a hobby, really. Right now I've got a new batch of eggs just about ready to hatch." Dr. Grove must know more about *Microcentrum rhombifolium* than anyone else in the world.

Dave Nickle said his own research on katydid behavior is mostly about how katydids keep themselves safe. "They are big, nutritious insects and they don't sting or taste bad. They are all food, so a lot of other animals eat them: monkeys, rodents, bats, birds, lizards, amphibians, spiders, wasps, ants, mantids, and other insects, too." He referred me to a paper written by his mentor, Thomas Walker, at the University of Florida, where he had done his graduate work. Walker writes about a cat—one presumes his own—who stalked katydids, locating them successfully by their song, then killing and eating them.

Winston J. Bailey, an Australian entomologist specializing in singing insects, has observed wisely, "As a general rule, it is better to mate tomorrow than be a meal today." Katydids have developed a number of ploys to help assure that they *will* be here to mate rather than end up as dinner. One of the reasons we so seldom see them and why they are so under-represented in scientific collections is that they are very good at hiding, seeming to turn themselves into something that they aren't. They are leaf-eating inhabitants of bushes and trees where, depending upon species, they mimic dead leaves, living leaves, bits of bark, or lichens. The appearance of one genus closely mimics that of wasps, presumably fooling at least some predators, which may react to them as though they had stingers. Although their song attracts mates, it also reveals their location to potential predators, so some species have tucked in their songs, singing so seldom or so high in the ultrasonic range that even bats cannot hear them. Other species have more or less forsaken their telltale audible courtship; instead, males vibrate their love, stamping and thumping on twigs to produce species-typical tremulations that undulate along a branch and are picked up by the delicate mechanoreceptors of females of their kind.

This means of communication throws into a jumble our notions about the word "sound," for our definition is based on our own narrow, clumsy, human reception of airborne audio waves. Webster defines sound as that which is heard, making reference to the stimulation of our own auditory nerves. The disturbance of air molecules, which is what this definition refers to, can be picked up by our ears and those of many insects, although even within this shared capability the ways of hearing, based as they are on different ear constructions, can be quite different. But insects can also distinguish the disturbance of molecules in solids and liquids as well as in air. This is what the water striders are doing when they communicate by ripple-making; and it is what katydids do when they vibrate twigs. Insect mechanoreceptors involve nerve endings that are excited by some disturbance of the bug's cuticle or change in position—as, for example, when delicate sensory hairs are displaced by moving molecules. There is a point at which what we call sound and what we call vibration blend and come together for bugs, and so some of the words and concepts we use so confidently, based on definitions from our human senses, begin to melt and become inadequate.

Katydids have perfectly good ears, albeit just below their knees, and they can hear airborne sound, raising one leg after another to do so more nicely, as Grove observed. In fact, the sounds they make, the nuance of messages sent, the precision of species call, and the sophistication of reception of sound and message are the stuff of much current research on katydids now that sensitive audio equipment is available to entomologists. For entomologists and nonentomologists alike, katydids are something of a disembodied voice. To most of us they may be the audible essence of a summer night, but for those studying them their song and the recording of it tells more. Because katydids are so good at concealing themselves, they have been hard to observe, catch, and put in collections. Audio-recording equipment and audio spectrographs, which give a visible record of their song, have allowed entomologists to eavesdrop on katydid courtings, to track the successes and failures of individual males and the nuances of their wooing without ever seeing or disturbing the nighttime lovers. Electronic mimics have been developed that can practice machine seduction upon female katydids or announce a male warning, thus helping us to refine our understanding of the creatures. Such gadgetry allows entomologists to study aggression, territoriality, and sexual behavior. This combination of electronic wizardry and summer-night walks in the woods sounds like enormous fun.

Each species has its own songs, so recording and analyzing them has allowed entomologists to delineate species boundaries, their overlap, and sometimes their hybridization with a precision that years of patient specimen collecting could not. This analysis has also turned up the biological phenomenon of sibling species. In the past, the close and careful study of morphology—that is, measurement of form and body parts—has been most important in the delineation of species. Bugs that were measured and found alike were put together in a species. This seemed obvious enough, and since they were of the same species, it was further assumed they would interbreed and produce like offspring. After all, that is the definition of species. But the bugs examined were dead, so no one could watch to see whether or not they actually *did* mate and reproduce their own kind.

But it turns out that in the woods and streams, in the real world, there are insects living in sexually isolated populations, sometimes in close proximity to one another, who look exactly alike or who have, at best, only a few morphological differences—differences so slight that they seem to fall well within the range of individual variation, with the result that classifiers lumped them together in museum collections. For instance, black flies show an extraordinary tendency toward sibling species, or, as the dipterists say, species complexes. Killed, the little flies all look pretty much alike, but, alive, one can distinguish differences in the season in which they breed and thrive, in their vulnerability to parasites, in the microhabitat they prefer, and in behavior. Most significantly, they do not mate with one another. Confirmation of species difference among them depends on chromosome mapping, a technique made possible by today's expensive scientific equipment. Dave Nickle told me that, when sibling species are suspected, corroboration can be had by analyzing the differences in DNA patterns and cuticular hydrocarbons. Breeding studies will show the same thing, but sometimes it is hard to breed insects in captivity, because their very captivity may distort their mating behavior.

The song variation found in the singing insects makes sibling species more easily distinguishable. Nearly thirty years ago, in 1964, Thomas Walker, the same entomologist who wrote about his cat stalking katydids, published an important paper pointing out that the study of the songs of crickets, katydids, and grasshoppers had revealed many species that were unrecognized on the basis of morphological difference. Dave said that he had been familiar with the concept of sibling species when he first came to work at the Smithsonian—he had learned of it through Walker—but found that few of his fellow entomologists took it into consideration. "But now, everyone is talking about sibling or cryptic species," he told me. I asked him how common he thought sibling species are, not just among Orthoptera and black flies, but among other insects as well. "I think they are more common than we realize," he answered, "and in the years to come we will probably discover more examples."

Katydids are big bugs; witness the 1890 quote at the head of this chapter stating, Guinness-like, that a New Zealand sawyer was the biggest insect known. To be sure, there are fossil dragonflies from Carboniferous days which had wingspreads of two feet, and even today in the tropics there are night-flying moths measuring half that, wing tip to wing tip, but both dragonflies and moths are skinny bugs with narrow bodies. For sheer massiveness katydids are right up there with the biggest of the big, rivaling the stout Goliath beetle from Africa, a five-incher with several ounces of bulk to match. In the tropics, Dave told me, there are four-inch katydids the size of sparrows, and even here in the United States three-inch katydids can be found in Florida.

Back here in this century, on this continent, on this day, Dave Nickle and I were still sitting at our table in the Washington restaurant. Most of the other diners had left and the waiter had cleared away our plates. I spread out on the table my copy of the April 9, 1991 edition of the *Weekly World News,* one of the supermarket tabloids. Screaming from its front page was the headline FARMER SHOOTS 23 LB. GRASSHOPPER! GIANT BUG IS 4 FEET LONG! The accompanying photo shows a toothy, rangy man in a feed-store cap, rifle in right hand and a generic, store-brand Orthoptera-like creature in his left. The farmer, said to be a New Zealander, is holding his trophy by the hind legs at about shoulder level, assuming the posture of a successful turkey hunter. Whoever built the creature, however, gave it only four legs instead of the standard insect issue of six. Further, its antennae, which brush the ground, look remarkably like pieces of wire. The purported "insect specialist" quoted in the inside story says ". . . this thing is damn near as big as a Labrador retriever." Perhaps it is the fabled New Zealand sawyer.

Dave laughed. "Yeah, I've got that picture taped up in my office. I think nearly every entomologist I know does, too."

"Well, what about it?" I asked him. "Is this impossible? Are there limits on insect size?"

"Well," he said, "there have been some *very* big insects . . . not twenty-three pounds, maybe, but there were those fossil dragon-flies, for instance, although since they lived a good part of their lives in water they didn't have to deal with some of the problems that large size would cause terrestrial insects. Remember, too, that the dinosaurs were bigger than reptiles living today. Animals in general seem to be getting smaller."

Entomology texts say that there are several constraints that keep insects below a certain size. One of these is respiration. Except for bloodworms, insects do not have the oxygen-rich blood or lungs

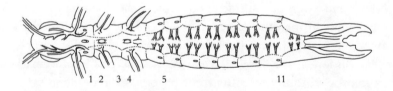

Typical insect tracheal system:
1–4: thoracic spiracles;
5, 11: abdominal spiracles

that we do. Their bodies contain a system of tubes called trachea, which open to the outside air through spiracles. Oxygen passes through them and diffuses into body tissue so effectively and efficiently that insect muscle is the most actively respiring animal tissue known. Diffusion alone is quite adequate for a small insect, but among some of the bigger, more active ones—bees, flies, beetles, locusts, and katydids—more active ventilation is necessary. The katydids, for instance, turn their abdomens into something rather like a pump, pulling and forcing air through their tracheae. Here is the way Dr. Grove describes it:

> Breathing movements are very evident in *Microcentrum*. The abdominal sterna [lower parts] are moved alternately up and down, abdominal walls folding along the dorsal-pleural groove [a line separating the insect's back from its side] to accommodate to this motion. The movement originates at the anterior end and passes, wave-like, through the posterior sterna. The rate varies with physiological condition. A resting katydid exhibiting 48 such movements per minute . . . with only the anterior end of the abdomen in obvious motion will more than double the rate and pump the whole abdomen violently if forced into sudden flight or if picked up and held, struggling, in one's fingers.

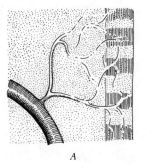 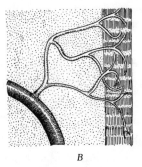

A   *B*

Tracheation of a muscle fiber:
A Muscle at rest
B Muscle fatigued, with air extending far into tracheoles

But even with this modification, oxygen must still pass along the finer-branched tracheae by diffusion, and if oxygen needs increase constantly (an assumption that has been challenged by some who study the allometry of growth), the diffusion rate of oxygen is subject to physical laws which give it a limit, and an insect may not be able to be bigger than the boundary that limit allows.

It also may be that there are engineering limitations for an animal with an exoskeleton, be it lobster or insect. There are mechanical problems, as well as advantages, connected with an outside, rigid skeleton from which the soft body parts are hung. There is a formula that expresses the resistance to bending in a solid cylinder, compared to an equivalent hollow one, which shows that insect legs—light, springy, and hollow—are three times as strong as they would be were they solid, as ours are. Thus the insect skeleton combines strength with smallness and what may seem to be insubstantiality. But there may be limits to how big a hollow tube can be before it becomes impossibly bendy and inefficient.

Because of the fixity and hardness of its cuticle, its exoskeleton, an insect must escape it to grow. Existing bugs do this either through complete metamorphosis, changing form radically—egg to larva, to pupa, to imago—as do bees, butterflies, beetles, flies, and other insects, or through a metamorphosis that is termed incomplete. Examples of the latter are katydids and water striders. A drawing showing the two kinds of metamorphosis is on page 104. In incomplete metamorphosis, youngsters hatch out of their eggs looking very much like adults, but smaller. They grow by breaking from and stepping out of their cuticle, a process called ecdysis (a term taken over in everyday language and given to strippers). They emerge, not naked as a stripper, but as a bigger model of the old instar.

The number of instars varies from species to species. Dr. Grove's katydids passed through six instars before they reached adulthood. But re-forming and renewing body parts, whether completely and radically, as in the case of butterflies, or incompletely, as in the case of katydids, is, physiologically speaking, an

150

expensive process and one during which the animal is vulnerable while its new cuticle dries and hardens. Is there some sort of risk limit or even ergonomic limit to the number of times this can be done—a point at which the cost outweighs the benefit? Could this constrain size?

"I just don't know. I'd have to think about that a very long time even to know whether it is a good question," said James Lloyd, an entomologist at the University of Florida, to whom Dave had referred me for information about size limitations on insects. "I don't even know," he went on to say on the telephone when I called him later, "whether there *are* physiological limits to arthropods that result from their having exoskeletons. Just because there aren't any big insects now, entomologists have gone about trying to prove that there can't be. But I suspect that the smaller size of insects has more to do with competition from vertebrates than it does with body design. The twenty-three-pound 'grasshopper'? Yes, I've got that picture tacked up in my lab, too. I think I could design one. It would be an engineering nightmare, but it could be done. I could put in a meshwork of struts to support it. And for respiration . . . well, we know that spiders have little pumps. Why couldn't something like that evolve among insects, too? I've got a very scientific, plausible-looking set of drawings that shows a human being evolving from a flea. I put it up for my students and they laugh. Then I ask why they're laughing. It turns out that they have accepted certain premises. But I think we should be careful about our assumptions. Is a really big insect impossible? 'Impossible' is a dangerous word in biology. There are, after all, a lot of strange tinkerings in body plans."

With the twenty-three-pound "grasshopper" photograph between us, Dave and I linger over dessert and coffee. The manager of the restaurant, an actor, a musician, and a friend, decided he would like to share his recipe for our tasty dessert.

Two Quail Restaurant
Lime Cheesecake Pie

CRUST:

    1 package graham crackers, rolled into crumbs
    2 tablespoons melted butter

FILLING:

    2 (16-ounce) packages cream cheese (2 pounds)
    1¾ cups sugar
    ¾ cup fresh lime juice
    1 cup unbeaten egg whites

TOPPING:

    1½ cups sour cream
    ¾ cup plus 1 tablespoon sugar
    2½ tablespoons fresh lime juice

Preheat oven to 350° F.

Mix cracker crumbs with melted butter and pat firmly into the bottom and partway up the sides of a lightly oiled 8- or 9-inch springform pan. In a large mixing bowl, beat together the cream cheese and sugar until smooth. Scrape down sides of bowl and add lime juice. Mix well. Add the egg whites and mix thoroughly until smooth. Pour into crust and bake 1 hour and 20 minutes. Remove from oven and cool for 10 minutes while preparing topping.

    Mix topping ingredients together and pour on top of cooled pie. Return to oven and bake 10 minutes more.

Serves 6 to 8

CHAPTER X

ORDER ODONATA: DRAGONFLIES

Arne, my husband and canoeing partner, is not here this sunny June day. If he were, I'd abandon my typewriter, load the canoe in the truck, and take it down to the river that runs by my farm. Yellow and pink columbine are blooming wherever they can find a roothold against the gray rock face of the cliffs that rise up on either side of the river. There are deep, blue-green stretches of water where the current slows, and we can drift and watch fish and water striders. The quiet places are punctuated by shallows where the current picks up, and we have to pay attention as it pulls us through. Little green herons and kingfishers, disturbed by the canoe, interrupt their fishing and fly away. Great blue herons skim on ahead, seem to lead the way. Turtles slip from logs with a splash. And everywhere there are dragonflies.

When I close my eyes and make a picture in my head of the river, it is always June, the water sparkles with sunshine, and dragonflies are soaring in the golden air. They are shimmer and sheen, bulging heads that are all eyes, glistening wings, long, slim bodies in bright metallic colors, a body-shop paint-salesman's inspiration: candy apple, seaflake, peacock fire.

I like to watch them hawk and hunt and have often wondered what they were doing in their odd, paired flight, one dragonfly

Mating posture of dragonflies

stiffly angled upward, grasping with its tail the nape of the other's neck, or sometimes doubly linked in a circle, the graspee curled back with its tail tucked under the grasper's belly. Paired bugs usually have something to do with mating, but what kind of a mating is this? And which are the sexual parts?

The name "dragonfly" makes them sound fierce, but in European languages they are named more gently. The French *demoiselle* and the Dutch *Juffer* (little miss) echo the name "damselfly," which we use for one kind of dragonfly. The Italian name is *saetta,* an arrow, and Germans, acknowledging that the animal spends most of its life under water, say *Wassernymphe.* But the Russian name is best of all, for careful observation of the insect is built into it. That language calls both a dragonfly and a flighty, lively young girl *strekosa,* which comes from a root word for a rattling, nervous noise: the chatter of a machine gun, the noise of a turning wheel on a gravel road, the *chirrr* of a bug. Dragonflies do not sing, chirp, or call, but when the air is cold their wings do make a whirring noise as they beat them rapidly to elevate their body temperature, giving their flight muscles the strength to carry them into the air. On a cool Russian morning near a lake surrounded by birches, where a group of *strekosa* have spent the night, the most noticeable sound would be the *chirrrrrr* of their warming wings.

The English "dragonfly" is justified by most authorities, who point out that in both the immature, nymphal stages, when the animal lives underwater, and the adult one, when it lives in the air, the dragonfly is a voracious feeder, snatching up gnats, mosquitoes, and even larger prey in a dragonlike way. Fish hatcheries count dragonfly nymphs as pests because they sometimes feed on the fry. The adults go after big game, too. Arthur Cleveland Bent, the father of bird-behavior studies, included the following in a 1940 Smithsonian report:

> L. T. S. Norris-Elye writes to Mr. Bent: "During the summer of 1934, James Ashdown, Jr., and his mother were walking in the woods at Kenora, Ontario, and heard a continuous rattling. Investigation showed it to be a male ruby-throated hummingbird on the ground with a huge dragonfly on the bird's back; it had seized the bird by the neck. They drove the dragonfly away, picked up the bird, and held it in the palm of the hand for several minutes, after which it flew away.

But despite these dragonish habits (actually the insect may have been trying to mate the hummingbird), the name in English probably derived equally from the dragon of myth and the dragon of fly from the Greek word for eye, *drakos*. The dragon of myth is said to have a "terrible eye," and the dragon of fly, the keenest-sighted insect, seems to be all big, bulging eye.

When I was growing up nearly sixty years ago, I was told that dragonflies were called devil's darning needles, and that if they could catch me they would sew up my mouth. It was a long time before I could look at a dragonfly and see beauty there. Fear of bugs was taught to me—and fortunately untaught. I couldn't have been more than two or three years old when, holding the hand of an adult whom memory no longer identifies, I was walked around a flower garden to be shown the flowers in bloom. In the centers of several of the roses were slim, leggy beetles that seemed to be made of dull metal. They were eating the hearts out of the blos-

155

soms, and I was told in tones of loathing by the voice above the adult hand that they were rose chafers—bad, disgusting bugs that must be killed lest they eat anything else. How could any creature want to destroy such pretty flowers? I was horror-struck, unprepared to accept that there could be such evil in the world that had up to then seemed satisfactorily benign. I hoped that the rose chafers in the garden were rare and aberrant, horrid creatures that once destroyed by a responsible adult would be gone forever. But several days later I awoke from my afternoon nap and found a rose chafer next to me on the bed. Terrified and expecting I was next on its menu, I screamed and screamed and screamed. Fortunately my father was a calm man. He comforted me, began taking me to wild places, and taught me that we are surrounded by all manner of life, plant and animal, that live differently than we do and whose stories are some of the best that can be told.

Rose chafer (2x)

My father died while I was still young. It is one of the sadnesses of my life that as an adult I never had the chance to become acquainted with him, so I've never known for sure whether he was deliberately appealing to all that was irregular and unruly in his daughter when he told me about the different ways in which life arranges itself, but he was a wise man and I like to think he understood. He must have had some hint that he had a baby anarchist on his hands, for he was the one who would come to comfort me when I awoke sobbing from my recurrent nightmare about things that were all alike. Many small children have bad dreams from which they awake crying, and none ever have words enough to be able to tell the complexity of the horror. I was no different: the only thing I could say to my father when he came to soothe me was, "It's all the same." Although I have not had that dream in nearly sixty years I still get shuddery when I remember the terror of its long, barracklike row of yellow attached houses. At precise and regular intervals in them were windows. In each window, white curtains were tied back in the same way, and directly below each window grew the same flowers, stiff red blossoms in identical attitudes over and over and over. It is not ennobling to have had my whole life shaped by what I suspect, as I write this, was a wallpaper dream, but there it is. I've spent that life turning away from repetition, uniformity, predictability, safety, and found my delight in otherness. I suspect my father understood and encouraged me.

Otherness is what I have always liked about bugs. But it is just this otherness that apparently makes many people dislike them. May Berenbaum, a professor of entomology who runs an annual Insect Fear Film Festival, told an interviewer from *The New York Times,* "Insects are so structurally different from humans that they seem like aliens. There is no point of empathy." I know of one vertebrate zoologist who always refers to them as "those damn things with legs."

Elias Canetti, the Nobel laureate, was thinking of quite a different sort of otherness, that of humankind, when he wrote

> There is nothing that man fears more than the touch of the unknown. He wants to see what is reaching towards him, and to be able to recognize or at least classify it. Man always tends to avoid physical contact with anything strange.

This sounds specious to me, but when I quoted it to a rugged, handsome college professor who once asked me if he could talk to me about his fear of bugs, he nodded his head appreciatively.

"That's it exactly," he said, and told me that he had not been able to talk about his terror of cockroaches in thirty years:

157

I see one in the kitchen and I am terrified, paralyzed, unable to speak or move. It is so small and I am so big. That is part of the horror. It is not the least afraid of me . . . it pays no attention to me at all . . . and its presence seems to fill the whole room. Kill one? That would be impossible. It is, psychically, too big to kill. When I look at it, it is everything. So huge. Besides, even if I were able to kill it, another would come, another just like it. And that is too frightening even to consider.

I have grown used to the fact that most people do not enjoy having a bee sip a drop of honey from the backs of their hands; nor do they find it fun to crouch over mud puddles watching water striders. I have had canoeing partners who didn't want to watch dragonflies for fear of losing strokes. Arne isn't one of them; that's why I married him. A recent survey by the University of Arizona showed that only a fraction of a single percent (0.7 percent) of respondents liked bugs. Nearly 90 percent said they were either acutely afraid of them or heartily disliked them. The remainder said they just tolerated them. What did surprise me, however, was that only 10 percent could recall having seen a butterfly in the past year. Vladimir Nabokov in *Speak, Memory* wrote:

> It is astonishing how little the ordinary person notices butterflies. "None," calmly replied that sturdy Swiss hiker with Camus in his rucksack when purposely asked by me for the benefit of my incredulous companion if he had seen any butterflies while descending the trail where, a moment before, you and I had been delighting in swarms of them.

The majority of bugs neither help nor harm us. They are indifferent to us and our doings, whether we like them or not. And some bugs—lacewings, ladybugs, praying mantises, dragonflies, honey bees, and syrphid flies, for instance—are beneficial to humans, giving us good things to eat or killing our enemies. Admittedly we live in the same ecological niche as some bugs, and are therefore competitors for crops, flowers, stored clothes, wooden houses, and dinner's leftovers. Those bugs who like these things as well as we do are labeled pests, but we are so powerful and have such an arsenal of weapons against them, including lethal chemicals for which we lay out $3.5 billion a year in this country, that we should feel our niche is quite secure.

Admittedly there are a couple of spiders and some insects that bite and spread disease; there are even a few that sting, and some people are allergic to the venom. Fewer than one percent are, by medical estimate, but lots more *think* they are, if the reaction I get from people who learn I keep bees is a guide. Or perhaps I have met the entire one percent. For them, bugs, at least the stinging ones, represent danger. But their numbers are so few that they cannot be responsible for the general loathing and fear of bugs. There are enough people with an abnormal fear of crane flies— leggy, harmless, insects—for psychiatrists to have given their fear a name: tipulophobia. There is another mental disorder called delusory parasitosis, in which the sufferer routinely produces bits of lint or specks scraped from his skin to prove that he is infested by bugs. Those are extremes, of course, yet when *The Silence of the Lambs,* that scary movie with the bug motif, was released, Sally Love, director of the Smithsonian's Insect Zoo and consultant on the film, commented, "It saves on script writing. Everybody has a strong reaction to insects, and most of the time that reaction is horror."

For those of us who are English speakers, entomophobia is locked into the language and reveals itself not only in names like devil's

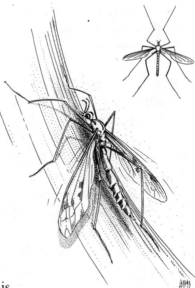

Crane fly (1½x)

159

darning needle, but in the word "bug" itself. The primary meaning lives on in "bugaboo" and "bogeyman." It comes from *bugge* or *bough*, which in the misty Anglo-Saxon past meant a terror, a ghost, a devil. Remember the creepiness of the childhood tongue twister "black bug's blood"? Reginald Scot, an English magician closer to those ancient sources, wrote in 1584:

> But you shall understand, that these bugs speciallie are spied and feared of sicke folke, children, women and cowards which through weaknesse of mind and bodie are shaken with vaine dreames and continuall feare. . . . It is a common saieng: A lion feareth no bugs. But in our childhood our mothers have so terrified us with an ouglie divell having hornes on his head, fier in his mouth, and a taile in his breech, eies like a bason, fanges like a dog, clawes like a beare . . . and a voice roring like a lion, whereby we start and are afraid when we heare one cry Bough: and they have so fraied us with bull beggers, spirits, witches, urchens, elves, hags, fairies, satyrs, pans, faunes, sylens, kit with cansticke, tritons, centaurs, dwarfes, giants, imps, calcars, conjurors, nymphes, changlings, Incubus, Robin good-fellow, the spoorne, the mare, the man in the oke, the hell waine, the fierdrake, the puckle, Tom thumbe, hobgoblin, Tom tumbler, boneles, and other such bugs, that we are afraid of our owne shadowes.

Bug loathing is not universal. In Japan, crickets, ladybugs, dragonflies, butterflies, silkworms and their moths are all admired. The Chinese consider spiders lucky. The Ashanti of Africa tell affectionate and admiring stories about Anansi, a cunning and clever spider. In many folk traditions, the creator of the world was a bug. Some of the best contemporary entomologists are British, and their writing shows a real love for their subjects. Paul Opler, an American lepidopterist, told me that in Britain insects are studied because the habitat of larger, showy animals has long since been destroyed and the animals themselves are gone. He recalled that he had once traveled to Monkswood, the national butterfly reserve in England, and told his guide how impressed he was. "In the United States," he said to the man, "people seem only interested in glamor species, whooping cranes and the like."

"In England," his guide replied, "butterflies *are* the glamour species."

Several cookbooks have been issued in this country recently that tell Americans how to cook and eat bugs. These recipes have been treated as brighteners by the news media. "If only they weren't bugs," the *Los Angeles Times* food writer lamented. Reginald Scot would have nodded. So far I have not noticed any plastic trays of mealworms in the Safeway, but in other places people recognize a good source of protein when they see it flit by. In Africa, bee-keepers sell bee larvae to be eaten along with the honey. Other insects, larvae and adults, including crickets and dragonflies, are routinely eaten in many countries. The most elegant dinner I ever attended was given thirty-five years ago by a cosmopolitan couple at their mountain retreat in Arizona. The food and wine were excellent, the company congenial. With the after-dinner coffee, my host passed a silver serving dish heaped with chocolate-dipped grasshoppers. They tasted of chocolate, but crunchier. Dragonflies are more abundant in the tropics than they are in temperate zones, and in some countries they are knocked from the air with a stick smeared with gluey lime and ground into a paste, a nutritious addition to a sparse diet. We Americans are so rich that we can indulge ourselves with food less troublesome to harvest, and can save the dragonfly for contemplation.

Perhaps because they are big and beautiful, or perhaps simply because their biology is so unusual and interesting, dragonflies have been widely studied and are the subject of an enormous number of scientific papers. They belong to the order Odonata. This name, lacking the wingish -ptera ending of many of the orders, is a relic of a classification scheme devised by Johann Christian Fabricius, an eighteenth-century Danish entomologist and some-time pupil of Linnaeus. The latter had divided all the known insects into seven orders, based on their wing characteristics; those characteristics are still considered important in classification, and many of the order names we still use are the ones Linnaeus selected: Coleoptera, Lepidoptera, Neuroptera, Diptera, Hymenoptera, Isoptera, and so on. But Fabricius believed that insect mouthparts, more specifically insect maxillae, the lower jaws, were more important than wings in distinguishing one grouping from another, and he drew up a classification scheme based on them. It was as though he picked up the kaleidoscope filled with the same colored stones that Linnaeus saw as wings, gave it a half turn, peered in, and saw jaws.

Functional insect mouths vary according to whether they suck up or chew their dinners, but in general their mouthparts are composed of some sort of tongue, an upper and lower pair of lips, and doubly paired jaws. The upper parts of the jaws are called mandibles and the lower part are called maxillae. Fabricius named beetles Eleutherata, the free-jawed. He called ants, wasps, and bees Pezata, the press-jawed. None of his names survived except for Odonata, the tooth-jawed, and it is only in this name that Fabricius's view of the world lives on. I may think of dragonflies as glittering insects flying in the sun, but if I were dragonfly prey, I might also, like Fabricius, think of their maxillae as more significant. The water-dwelling dragonfly youngsters, the nymphs who snap up mosquitos, black-fly larvae, and small fish, have extensible lower lips as well as formidable hooks and knives that turn their mouthparts into what James Needham, the great Cornell aquatic entomologist, once called "a combination of hands, carving tools, and serving table." Adult dragonflies catch their prey on the wing and their mouthparts are a little different, but their maxillae also serve as meat forks, holding and turning a captive so it can be carved by the mandibles into convenient portions.

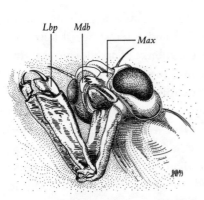

Latero-ventral view of head and mouthparts
of a dragonfly nymph: Lbp, labial pulp;
Mdb, mandible; Max, maxilla

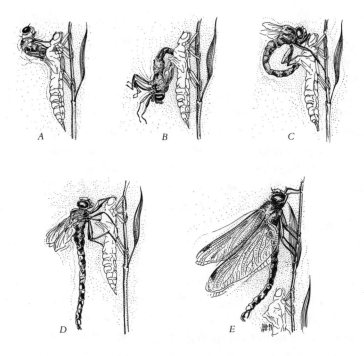

Stages in the emergence of a dragonfly (Aeshna cyanea):
A–D, emergence from the nymphal cuticicle; E, fully formed imago

Dragonfly nymphs hatch out of eggs laid in or near water and live through ten or fifteen molts in the water until they reach maturity. These drab water nymphs, sometimes called naiads, are shorter in the abdomen and stouter than adult dragonflies, but as they grow they become increasingly like the skinny adults they will finally become. Wing buds appear after the first few molts, and the insects' bulging eyes hint that they, like the imago, are sight hunters. Many species of naiads breathe and scoot about at the same time. They have gills in their rectum, suck water through it, extract the oxygen, and expel the water violently, thus moving along by jet propulsion. In their final stage they climb out of the water, shinny up a grass stem for their last ecdysis, from which they will emerge as colorful, fully winged air-breathers, then fly away to eat and mature, returning to the water's edge to mate.

Dragonflies are fast on the wing and have been clocked at speeds up to 60 mph. Superb wing and muscle design allows them to convert food energy into flight power efficiently: They are good economists in the entomological, ergonomic sense of the word. These bulging-eyed dragon bugs, these hunters-by-sight, also have vision that entomologists consider to be better than that of any other insect. On the face of it this seems to mean that the dragonfly's world is more reassuringly like ours than is, say, the world of silverfish. But insect vision is based on eyes structured so differently from our own that it must present a world we do not see and cannot really imagine. Some insects have what is called "dermal light sense." Their entire body is sensitive to light; they are, in a way, all eye. If their regular eyes are removed experimentally or taped shut, they still react to light. In addition, many insects have simple, single-lens eyes, called ocelli, in varying numbers on the tops and sides of their heads. Their functions are not clearly understood, although they may be sensitive to colors and polarized light, but entomologists agree that they complement the vision of an insect's compound eyes. These paired compound eyes are made up of what are essentially many individual eyes, facets that are capable of giving the insect many separate images. We will probably never know exactly what the insect brain does with all these separate images, but such eyes are excellent for seeing movement—one of the most important things in life if you are a bug. Flowers nodding in the breeze mean dinner to a bee; a mosquito flying means dinner to a dragonfly. A bird zooming down means death: best flit away. A toad hopping along sends the same message: best scuttle faster.

Some insects, bees for instance, have hairs growing between the facets of their compound eyes, and when these hairs are removed experimentally, the bee is unable to fly accurately, no longer able to judge the angle between the direction of the sun and the place where food is. Experiments have shown that many insects have good color vision, but see a different range of hues than we do. Their sense of color is skewed toward the ultraviolet end of the spectrum. A few insects, dragonfly nymphs among them, have red-sensitive cells in their eyes, but most do not, and so red is missing from their world. However, they can see ultraviolet, which we cannot. Flower petals that seem uniformly colored to us may have contrastingly colored pollen or nectar guides visible to the insects that feed on them. Patterns on the wings of insects or on the bodies of other animals, invisible to us, may warn them of danger or tell them where a mate is.

In bug design, the rule seems to be: the poorer the vision, the longer the antennae; the more powerful the vision, the shorter the antennae. Adult dragonflies have huge eyes, good vision, and stubby antennae. Their eyes, which they clean with a special brush built into their front legs, are so big that their heads appear to be

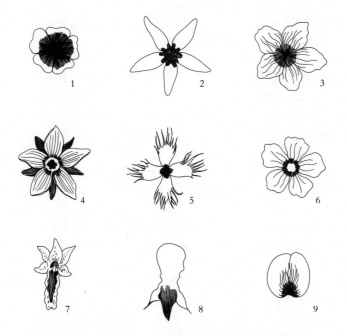

Ultraviolet marks of flowers. (1) Golden cinquefoil (Potentilla aurea); *(2) marsh felwort* (Swertia perennis); *(3) white bryony* (Bryonia dioica); *(4) borage* (Borago officinalis); *(5) pink* (Dianthus arenarius); *(6) lesser periwinkle* (Vinca minor); *(7) Jersey orchid* (Orchis laxiflora); *(8) yellow archangel* (Galeobdolon luteum); *(9) broom* (Cytisus canariensis)

165

all eye. Entomologists tell us that 80 percent of their brains are given over to analyzing what they see. They have three ocelli (simple eyes), and their single pair of compound eyes bulge out so far that they have virtually 360-degree vision. The compound eyes are divided into two regions, with a concentration of ultraviolet receptors in the upper parts. But these eyes, which allow a dragonfly to snatch up a flying mosquito with deadly accuracy, are not particularly acute when it comes to detail. A male dragonfly close to a female with whom he is attempting to mate may seize her shadow or the black spot on her wing, mistaking it for the back of her head, which is the proper focus of his lovemaking. He may also blunderingly try to seize another male or a female of a different species (perhaps even that ruby-throated hummingbird of the Bent report), but the structure of the claspers at the tip of his abdomen prevents him from compounding his mistake, for they must fit the back of the head of an appropriate female, his key to her lock, for mating to proceed.

Many species of dragonflies are territorial. Males locate a spot at stream edge, by some reeds at a lake, or a sunny cove, suitable places for the females to lay their eggs, and then defend it from other males. Nearly forty years ago Merle E. Jacobs spent a summer watching dragonflies at ponds near Bloomington, Indiana, and published his report on them in 1955. In particular, he watched the dragonflies sometimes called white tail, *Plathemis lydia*. The male, a showy creature, has a gleaming white abdomen, which he uses not to attract females (in fact, when he meets one he hides his abdomen by lowering it), but to flash at other males to warn them from his territory. If another male persists, he runs him off, darting at and sometimes even flying alongside the invader until, spooked, he leaves.

Dragonfly territories can be spatial or temporal. In other words, this patch of reeds is mine and those over there are yours, or alternatively, this patch of reeds is mine until the sun is straight overhead; you can have it afterward. Once established, territories become rendezvous spots and are visited by females in mating condition. Male dragonflies produce sperm in an organ toward the

Plathemis lydia *(½x)*

end of their abdomen, in its ninth segment. There is nothing unusual in that, but their intromittant organ, their penis, is not there,
as it is in most insects. Instead, it is at the top of the abdomen, on
its second segment—before a male dragonfly can mate, he must
bend double, curling his abdomen under himself to transfer sem-
inal fluid into an inner chamber behind his penis. The female, who
has been seized by the back of her head with the claspers at the end
of the male's abdomen, curls her abdomen forward so that her
genital opening, at its end, also in her ninth segment, meets the
male's penis. This puts the mating pair in a circle—entomologists
call it the wheel position—that makes them look as if they are tail
to head, belly to tail.

Male bugs often contrive to assure that their sperm, and theirs
alone, will fertilize the female's egg. The katydid isolates his lady
love and prevents her from mating again by distracting her with a
food gift. The daddy longlegs cages his partner with his legs until
she lays her eggs. The male parnassian butterfly fixes a chastity
belt on his mate. The male dragonfly, depending on its species,
uses several strategies to pass on his genes. In some species the

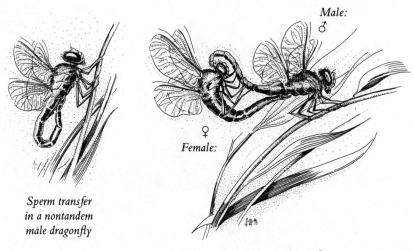

Male:
♂

Female:
♀

Sperm transfer
in a nontandem
male dragonfly

Copulation in dragonflies

male's penis is blunt and he uses it to squash down any sperm already inside the female, thus assuring his and none other's will be in the best position—on top—to fertilize the eggs. Others have a spiked, bristly penis and use it to scrape out competing sperm before replacing it with their own. Some male dragonflies keep their grasp on the back of the female's head after copulation, then guide her to an egg-laying spot, and hold her there until she has completed the task. Others simply hover over such a spot, driving away other males. Jacobs observed that in many cases the male protecting the oviposition site is driven off by one of the many other males attracted by his mate's activity. Even in the process of laying her eggs, the female is sometimes seized by one of them and mated again. Jacobs writes:

> When the female is seized, the guarding male becomes intensely active, flying toward other males and warding them from the site. In the meantime the male which seized the female copulates with her, then after replacing her on the site, guards her. The original male then dashes at the female and often catches her, then after copulation replaces her on the site. Many males may be involved in

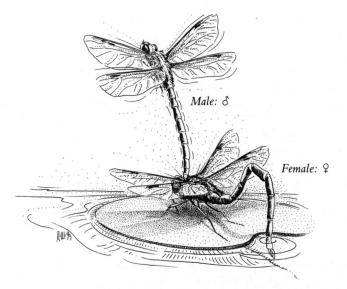

Male: ♂

Female: ♀

A male damselfly in tandem with a female during oviposition

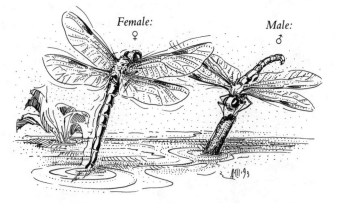

Female:
♀

Male:
♂

*A male dragonfly guarding an ovipositing female (on the wing) by
perching nearby*

this process at one site leading to a melee in which they dash at one another swiftly. . . . During one of these melees the female may perch motionless on the site whereupon the males will not seize her. (It appears they cannot see her . . .) In these cases the female, being unable to oviposit, may fly from the pond followed by many males, some of which have come from adjacent areas. Kingbirds may fly into these flocks and catch males or, more frequently, the slower-flying females.

The 5,000 known species of dragonflies have been divided by classifiers into three suborders: the Anisozygoptera, which contains only two known species, neither of them found in North America; the Anisoptera, the big, stout-bodied true dragonflies, which, when at rest, hold their dissimilarly shaped fore and hind wings outstretched; and the Zygoptera, the damselflies, which are generally slighter, with similarly shaped fore and hind wings that they hold together above their body when resting.

I don't think my family made nice distinctions among the species, or even between damsel- and dragonflies, when I was growing up. They were all lumped together by my informants and called devil's darning needles. Entomologists never call any of them devil's darning needles, although they do admit that it is one of the common names of one species in the darner family, Aeschnidae. It is the green darner, *Anax junius,* which translates splendidly to Lord of June. These are the darners, thoraxes green and abdomens varying from blue to royal purple, that I see glinting in the sunshine above the river on a summer's day. Lord of June. How I wish I had known that name when I was four years old.

Dragonfly

Damselfly

CHAPTER XI

ORDER LEPIDOPTERA: GYPSY MOTHS

 The neighborhood in which Arne and I live in Washington, D.C., prides itself on its big shade trees, oaks mostly, so householders fretted when gypsy-moth caterpillars, who like to eat oak leaves best of all, began to be seen here in the late 1980s. The moth was expanding its range, as it has been for more than a hundred years, ever since it was released accidentally in Medford, Massachusetts, just outside Boston. The newspapers in and around Washington were full of stories about the terrible things the moth larvae would do: Trees would be defoliated and die; forests would be sere and winterlike in the summer; nighttimes would be ruined by the sounds of caterpillars munching.

This should not happen, people said, so government agencies sprayed us aerially to kill the moths. They sprayed us a little with Dimilin, a persistent chemical insecticide only slightly toxic to mammals but somewhat more dangerous to crustaceans and other invertebrates. They sprayed us a lot with *Bacillus thuringiensis,* the bacterial insecticide that is cousin to the Bti used against black flies. Bt, as the former is usually called, has been used since the 1950s to control various lepidopteran pests and is generally thought to be safe for humans and other vertebrates, although it is tough on a wide variety of butterflies, moths, and some other insects.

We also got sprayed just a little with a cultured gypsy-moth virus that is supposed to hurt no one but gypsy moths. Our neighbors clubbed together and hired private sprayers, who misted the undersides of trees from pump trucks and backpack sprayers. I don't know what they were spraying, but the air smelled of chemicals afterward and I tried not to breathe. A great many neighbors also followed the advice given in the newspapers and wrapped the trunks of their oak trees in strips of folded burlap. In the course of its lifetime, a single caterpillar, feeding at night, will eat something on the order of one square yard of foliage, preferably oak; during the day it will seek refuge in a protected place—which the folds of burlap were supposed to provide. Homeowners were instructed to dump out the caterpillars thus trapped every day and kill them, but few actually bothered with this tiresome chore, so the burlap strips simply became jujus against caterpillars. One man hired a tree service to cut down his pair of one-hundred-year-old oaks in order to deprive the gypsy-moth caterpillars of food.

Despite the spraying, for a few years there were a lot of gypsy moths around the neighborhood. I often noticed the spongy-looking, tawny egg masses tucked into crevices and on tree trunks. The colorful caterpillars, an inch or more long, dark but gaily striped in yellow, were studded with paired orange and blue knobs and frosted with an untidy coat of coarse hairs that made them unpleasant to handle. Sometimes I saw them crawling along the ground or swinging from a strand of silk they had spun, being blown with the breeze from tree to tree. There were so many of them that during the night, when they were feeding, I could hear what sounded like falling rain. It was their frass, their droppings, which resembled tiny black grains, and in the mornings the sidewalks would be covered with it. I found the frail cocoons, their pupa, that they spun from a few coarse brown threads. By midsummer I saw adult moths. The females are velvety, tannish-white, sometimes spotted, with wings they cannot use. I would find them clinging to the sides of trees or buildings, looking like plush triangles. They don't see much of the world. They emerge

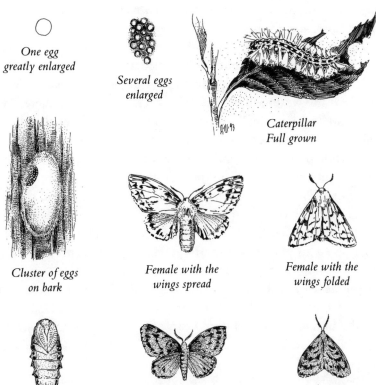

One egg
greatly enlarged

Several eggs
enlarged

Caterpillar
Full grown

Cluster of eggs
on bark

Female with the
wings spread

Female with the
wings folded

Pupa

Male with the
wings spread

Male with the
wings folded

Gypsy moth
(Note: Moths and caterpillar shown ¾ life-size)

from their pupal cases, await their suitors, mate, and creep to a protected spot to lay their eggs.

The males look and behave quite differently. They are dark, mouse-colored, and speckled. They are strong flyers, confusing predators with their dodging flight—a common name for them in France is *le zig zag*. When male and female animals of the same species look unalike, biologists say that they are "sexually dimorphic." Many of the common names for gypsy moths in other languages, as well as its scientific species name, *dispar*, reflect this disparateness. Another common French name, for instance, is *le bombyx disparate,* the dissimilar silk moth.

There was little visible leaf loss in our own neighborhood from the caterpillars' feeding, but out in the countryside the woodlands were defoliated for a couple of years running. Probably some trees, already weakened by disease or stress, did die, and there was timber loss as a result. But good healthy trees can't be killed by a defoliation or two, or even by three. In fact leaves are the most expendable part of trees, and in times of stress—drought, for instance—they will often drop them all by themselves. It is a tree's way to rein in and preserve resources. When less stressful conditions return, they will leaf out anew.

All that is past now. The woods are green and leafy again. The huge spike in the gypsy-moth population in unsprayed areas caused self-limiting starvation and provided the attractive plenty for the development of naturally occurring viruses and fungi. In areas friendlier to wildlife than northwest Washington, D.C., especially in the second and third years of the gypsy-moth invasion, there was a noticeable increase in caterpillar predators, particularly black-billed cuckoos.

The gypsy moth is here for good now. I see a few around all the time, but they no longer cause much damage. The newspapers have found new causes for horticultural alarm—dogwood die off, for instance. It has just been announced that there will be no more aerial spraying for gypsy moths. I don't know what the long-term effects are of being soaked in Dimilin, bacterial and viral insecticides, although it is probably not as bad as being soaked in Paris green, lead arsenate, and DDT, the gypsy-moth insecticides of choice in an earlier era. There aren't many butterflies left in our neighborhood, and I hardly ever see a moth anymore—except gypsy moths, of course. The sprays never kill all moths, only the most vulnerable ones. Gypsy moths, which are tougher, more resistant, live on to form the nucleus of a genetically superior (from a moth's point of view) population that settles in, endures, thrives, and, when it begins to crowd resources, moves on. Thus, as it does anywhere it is used, a spray program serves two pur-

poses. It weeds out lesser moths, becoming a pruning and invigo-
rating process for the population as a whole. It also serves to
prolong the damage done by gypsy-moth caterpillars, because a
thinned population is not only less likely to limit itself through
starvation, but is also not numerous enough to become a rich,
dense mass that will attract parasites, disease, and predators, which
are the usual mechanism of population control.

In June 1989, at the height of the Washington moth wars, we
received a neighborhood newsletter with the bold headline DEAL-
ING WITH GYPSY MOTHS. The story began: "One hundred and
twenty years ago some idiot brought the first gypsy moths to
Boston from Europe . . ."

Well, not exactly. Étienne Léopold Trouvelot, a member of the
American Academy of Arts and Sciences, the Boston Natural History Society, and the Selenographical Society of Great Britain, was
perhaps a political radical and a bit of a dreamer, but not an idiot.
Trying to turn the details of his life in the United States into a
coherent picture is like picking up clouds: they seem real enough,
but the hand that closes around them opens to reveal nothingness.
The patterns and intent I have teased from the meager information
about Trouvelot's life may be no more real than cloud shapes, but
with that warning, here is his story.

Trouvelot was born in 1827 at Guyencourt, in the French department of Aisne, which borders on Belgium. Little is known of
his schooling or early life but there are hints that he was an anti-
royalist, a republican, and that his immigration to America in 1857,
at the age of thirty, was occasioned by his opposition to the Second
Empire, which had been established five years earlier. French liberals worked hard to bring back a republic, but in 1856 a son was
born to Napoleon III and this made many of them give up in
despair, for the event seemed to guarantee the future of the royal
line. Trouvelot arrived in Boston a year later, and proved himself
both an idealistic young man and an opportunist by quickly catching silk fever, as had many other idealistic, enthusiastic, and entre-
preneurial people of his time. According to his own account, by at
least 1860 he was living at 27 Myrtle Street, Medford, Massachu-

setts, and was experimenting with the development of a better silkworm—better, that is, than the one that had been used for four thousand years, *Bombyx mori*.

I don't know what 27 Myrtle Street looked like in Trouvelot's day, but a photograph taken in 1895 shows it to be a neat, two-story clapboard house with shutters, decked out with gingerbreading along its roof edges. The house is tidily contained by a wooden picket fence, as are its neighbors. In that picture, Myrtle Street is lined with similar trig-and-trim houses, a typical street in a thrifty working-class neighborhood, where people take pride in their homes. It is shaded by huge elms and maples, the likes of which have disappeared from the streets of modern American cities, victims not of gypsy moths, but of automobile exhaust fumes, winter salt, Dutch elm disease, and road widening. By 1895, the tract of wooded land in back of Trouvelot's house, the place where he had conducted his outdoor moth experiments, had been cleared of trees. The Gypsy Moth Commission, which was appointed in 1890 to deal with what by then had become a city-wide problem, felled all the trees in the five-acre plot.

Silk culture is one of the agricultural crazes that has appeared from time to time in America, discovered over and over again by those interested in rural survival and self-sufficiency. It was the get-rich-quick project for dreamer and hustler alike, the pick-your-own-strawberry patch, the llama farm, the boutique vegetable plot, the Vietnamese pot-bellied-pig breeding scheme of our country's early history. In addition, silk had official government endorsement.

Colonial America, English authorities reasoned, would make a dandy place to establish sericulture, as silkworm raising is called. England had long wanted a piece of the worldwide silk trade and was in competition with France, where silk production thrived. But silkworms were hard to raise in England and attempts to grow them there had failed. England therefore used a combination of rewards (bounties) and punishments (fines were levied in 1619 in Virginia for *not* raising silkworms) to encourage the American colonists to succeed where English farmers had not. Silk-growing supplies were handed out for free, and an early publicist wrote a ditty to make everyone happy:

> Where Wormes and Food doe naturally abound
> A gallant Silken Trade must there be found.
> Virginia excels the World in both—
> Envie nor malice can gaine say this troth!

The project failed, but sericulture was rediscovered and patted back into shape repeatedly. At the time of the Revolution, Benjamin Franklin and others were nursing a filature—a silk factory —into healthy life in Philadelphia. After independence, state governments, with Connecticut taking the lead, resumed the bounty system to encourage silkworm raising. The following years saw booms and boomlets in domestic silk production, encouraged by state and federal departments of agriculture, right up until the discovery of artificial fibers in the twentieth century. Few worm growers made money, but land speculators did. They bought plots, cleared them of native growth, and sold them as silk plantations on which mulberry trees, silkworms' favorites, could be

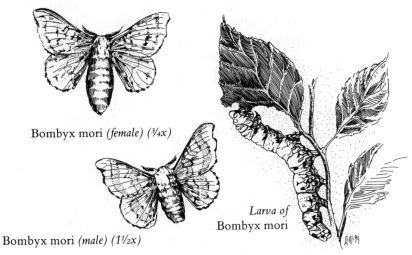

Bombyx mori *(female) (³⁄₄x)*

Bombyx mori *(male) (1¹⁄₂x)*

Larva of Bombyx mori

Silkworm

grown. The importers of mulberry trees, *Morus multicaulis,* made money, too. In Pennsylvania in the 1830s, $300,000 worth of plants were sold during a single week. Plants doubled and tripled in value in what was known at the time as Multicaulismania. Utopian communities, Fourierists, the Harmonists, Mennonites, and others all tried sericulture. The California legislature granted lavish subsidies for silk plantations. After the Civil War, silk growing was seen as a profitable occupation for freed Southern blacks, and by the turn of the century was being suggested for underemployed females of any color.

The silkworm is the larva of the moth *B. mori,* now entirely domesticated and no longer wild, which has been introduced into many parts of the world for commercial silk production. It is hardly surprising that an insect raised under artificial conditions for more than 4,000 years should be delicate and subject to disease. In the middle of the nineteenth century, a microsporidium, *Nosema bombycis,* caused the outbreak of a disease among the silkworm population called *pébrine* in France. *Pébrine* generated worldwide interest in developing a better, healthier, more disease-resistant silkworm, and there were many, besides Trouvelot, in France and elsewhere, who began importing moths from faraway places and studying them. *Pébrine*-infected silkworm larvae are darkly spotted, and they mature into moths that lay eggs which hatch either not at all or into imperfect, stunted worms, poor eaters and languid spinners of loose cocoons. Such cocoons produce inferior silken thread, not the fine abundant strands that can be unreeled from a healthy cocoon.

Initially Trouvelot worked on the assumption that some hardy native American moth might prove to be best for sericulture. In 1867 the *American Naturalist* published in three parts his report on his experiments, illustrated with his own skillful drawings; Trouvelot was also something of an artist. Prior to 1860, he wrote, he had experimented with several American moths, all classified at the time as in the same family as *B. mori,* the Bombycidae. He had studied the big, pale-green luna, the prometheus, and the eye-

spotted cecropia, but by
1860 he had settled on what
he and others called "the
American silkworm,"
the polyphemus.
Although the polyphemus
was considered difficult
to raise in captivity, its cat–
erpillar did spin itself a cocoon,
and the coarse threads it
produced could be unreeled
into commercial-grade silk.
Trouvelot hoped to solve the
problems of rearing polyphemus
so that they could be cultivated
as easily as *B. mori*. After first
recounting his difficulties,
he wrote proudly:

Cocoon of
Telea Polyphemus

The American
silkworm

It was only in 1865 that I became expert in cultivating them, and in
that year not less than a million could be seen feeding in the open
air upon bushes covered with a net; five acres of woodland were
swarming with caterpillar life.

But he discovered that there were drawbacks to his open–air cultivation:

This net, supported upon posts, was intended to protect the worms
from the depredation of the birds. The eggs were put upon the
bushes in the little hatching-box, so that after this, there seemed but
very little to do. But it was not so: over so large a space, it was
impossible to keep the net in good order, and the birds managed to
get under it; the small ones could go through the meshes, and the
larger ones through some holes in the old net, so I was obliged to
chase them all the day long, as when pursuing them on one side
they would fly to the other and quietly feed, until I reappeared.

After this experience, in 1866, he built a shed in the backyard of 27 Myrtle Street and reared part of his moth population inside it.

Today none of the moths Trouvelot experimented with are classed in the family Bombycidae. There is no clearer example of words, the insubstantial products of our brains, being taken for reality. Trouvelot, the enthusiastic but probably unschooled naturalist, seems to have been guided in his experiments by assuming that moths classed together were similar. Later, when he imported the gypsy moth, it seems likely that he did so because it was still called by many authorities *Bombyx dispar,* which would put it in the same genus as *Bombyx mori,* the silkworm. It is true that others were beginning to call the former *Ocneria dispar* or even *Porthetria dispar,* but Trouvelot may not have known this. The amateur naturalist quite reasonably could have thought that *Bombyx mori,* the silk grower, and *Bombyx dispar,* the sexually dimorphic silk moth, might have been similar in some way. He may even have thought he could crossbreed them. He certainly would have thought of them differently if the latter had been called by today's scientific name for the gypsy moth, *Lymantria dispar,* the sexually dimorphic destroyer. It is no longer even in the family Bombycidae, but is grouped with other tussock moths in the family Lymantriidae.

Hand-feeding the polyphemus caterpillars in his shed, Trouvelot was impressed with their appetite; his reflection on this carries today an unintentional irony:

> What a destruction of leaves this single species of insect could make if only a one-hundredth part of the eggs laid ever came to maturity! A few years would be sufficient for the propagation of a number large enough to devour all the leaves of our forests.

Trouvelot's experiments with raising these polyphemuses, as well as a set of hawkmoths, came to an end in November 1866, when he went to Europe. The hawkmoths, which he had kept in his cellar for three years, were eaten by rats in his absence, and his six years of note-taking on the polyphemus satisfied him that he had solved the problems connected with their cultivation. Did he bring gypsy-moth egg masses back to the United States from that winter trip? Perhaps. But perhaps he merely talked with French naturalists at that point. They would have told him about the studies undertaken by the famous Louis Pasteur to save the French silk industry from the epidemic of *pébrine*. Pasteur had been appointed the year before, in 1865, by the French government, to "elucidate" the disease. His work was certainly of interest to anyone experimenting with silkworms. Trouvelot would have understood that a person who could develop a *pébrine*-resistant silkworm would benefit sericulture around the world. What could have been more logical than to start studying a moth he thought closely related to the silkworm, a moth he knew from his native France, *le zig zag, le bombyx disparate, B. dispar*? He may even have heard about the captive breeding experiments of *le zig zag* in England, where it was known as "brown arches" or "gipsy moth." It had once thrived in England, but the population there had dwindled. Entomologists were trying unsuccessfully to reintroduce the moth, for it had become such a rarity that it was in danger of extinction from the overzealousness of English butterfly and moth collectors.

In France, Trouvelot must have known that there were periodic outbreaks of *le zig zag* that caused problems. In 1827, when he was a year old, the apple orchards in his native Aisne were stripped of their leaves by *les zig zags,* but in western Europe these outbreaks, although a nuisance, would not have given an amateur naturalist a real understanding of how devastating they could be in a place where the moth went unchecked by disease and predators. Good, knowledgeable German foresters, farther to the east, had experienced the damage caused by what they called the *Schwamm-spinner* (the fungus spinner: The egg masses resemble a spongy tree fungus) or the *Ungleicher Spinner* (the sexually dimorphic spinner). They controlled the outbreaks by protecting certain trees, wrapping their trunks in paper daubed with Raupenleim, a tanglefoot that kept the caterpillars below the band, or wrapping already infested trees with a folded cloth, just as Washingtonians were told to do in 1989, and then squashing the caterpillars trapped in it.

181

They did everything they could to encourage birds—and they also waited. They knew that once defoliated, healthy trees would leaf again and that the moths would cycle down after a year or two. The farther east one examines the record, the more serious the outbreaks were; perhaps the moth was of more recent appearance there. A devastating plague of the *Schwammspinner* occurred in 1752 in what we would now describe as southeastern Germany. A contemporary chronicler, J. C. Schaefer, wrote that all the trees of all the forests, gardens, and orchards were stripped of their leaves. After the second year, the caterpillars crawled on the ground in such numbers that people believed they came out of the earth. They had been sent, some said, by the Evil One. Others believed God had sent them as a punishment for their sins.

In 1848, when the link between eggs, caterpillars, and moths was better understood, there was a similar outbreak in Poland. A certain Count Wodzicki found all the tree trunks on his estate covered with egg masses. Removing them by hand seemed an impossible task, so great were their numbers, and he settled into a Slavic despair, assuming that his beautiful trees would be bare the following summer. But toward winter a flock of titmice and wrens came daily to the trees and ate the egg clusters. In the springtime, twenty pairs of titmice nested there, and by 1850 the birds had so cleared them of eggs that, according to Bernard Altum, a German professor who recounted the story in 1880, "he saw his trees during the entire summer in their most beautiful verdure."

In 1867, around the time Trouvelot first became interested in the gypsy moth, there was an outbreak in the provinces of Kazan, Samara, and Penza near the Black Sea of what was known as *neparniy shelkopryad,* the odd or unmatched (sexually dimorphic) silkworm. The oak and linden trees on many estates and in the forests were stripped of their leaves. By 1868 the caterpillars began dying from what today sounds like viral wilt disease; in the city of Penza the police had to be called to shovel up the putrid masses of decaying caterpillars.

Trouvelot may not have known about some of these more severe outbreaks in eastern Europe, but Nathaniel S. Shaler, the famous geologist, must have. Characterized in Jamesian by William James as a "myriad-minded and multiple-personalitied embodiment of academic and extra-academic matters," Shaler was, more simply, a scientist ahead of his time. He had broken with his mentor Agassiz over the evolution question, and was what would be described today as an environmentalist. In 1891 he would be appointed chairman of the Gypsy Moth Commission. At a meeting of the commission, he said:

> You know that about twenty years ago an interesting Frenchman brought an interesting bug to this country. His name was Trouvelot, and he brought the creature thinking to introduce it as a valuable silkworm. I begged him to destroy his specimens, and at one time he said he had. It appears, however, that they got away from him.

Trouvelot was no longer in the United States by the time the Gypsy Moth Commission was created and was not interviewed by it. Consequently there are a number of versions as to how the gypsy moth escaped Trouvelot's control, and also disagreement as to whether it happened in 1868 or 1869. One story has it that in one of those years he left egg masses on a windowsill, and that a wind came up and blew them from the unscreened window. Trouvelot hunted for the eggs in the yard below, but could not find them. Another version says that an overly tidy maid mistook the eggs for trash and threw them away when she was cleaning his room. This version has Trouvelot sorting diligently through the garbage in the town dump to try to find his household refuse, but failing to recover the eggs. A third version insists that it was caterpillars, not eggs, that escaped from one of his outdoor experiments. This may be based on a paragraph written by Edward A. Samuels in his 1870 edition of *Birds of New England:*

> Mr. Trouvelot, of Medford, Mass., who is engaged in rearing silkworms, for the production of silk, is troubled by the Robin to a degree surpassing most other birds. He has a tract of about seven

or eight acres enclosed, and mostly covered with netting. He is obliged, in self-defence, to kill the birds which penetrate into the enclosure and destroy the worms. Through the season, probably ten robins, for one of all others, thus molest him; and, of scores of these birds which he has opened and examined, none had any fruit or berries in their stomachs, nothing but insects. . . . He said that, in his opinion, if the birds were all killed off, vegetation would be entirely destroyed. To test the destructiveness of these marauders, as he regarded them, he placed on a small scrub-oak near his door two thousand of his silkworms. (These, let me say, resemble, when small, the young caterpillar of the apple-tree moth.) In a very few days they were all eaten by Cat-birds and Robins.

It is not clear in this passage whether Samuels is referring to Trouvelot's experiments with gypsy moths or his earlier ones with polyphemus. Samuels was not an entomologist, and his parenthetical description of the caterpillars looking like "apple-tree moths" is tantalizing but inexact. Polyphemus caterpillars are fat and green. Gypsy-moth caterpillars are skinny, striped, and hairy. Both would be happy to be put on a scrub-oak and both of them look a little like other caterpillars that sometimes eat apple-tree leaves. Neither of them looks anything at all like the larva of the coddling moth, a serious apple pest that is sometimes called the apple moth. I exhausted the reference sources in the Library of Congress, as well as the patience of the librarians therein and the knowledge of my favorite entomologist, and could find no reference to what, in 1870, might have been called the apple-tree moth.

All versions of the Great Gypsy Moth Escape claim that Trouvelot felt very upset about it and that he told his scientific colleagues what he had allowed to happen. Perhaps the members of the Boston Natural History Society were among these colleagues; so, perhaps, was Professor Shaler. In the twenty years that followed, however, the moths, although they spread widely, were unobtrusive and Trouvelot's story was nearly forgotten. He himself seems to have lost interest in natural history at this point. In his mid-forties he changed his profession and became an astronomer. In 1872 he was appointed to the observatory at Harvard, and

worked there for two years, producing a celebrated series of astro-
nomical drawings. The first of these were reviewed in the August
22, 1872, issue of *The New York Times*. In it Trouvelot was characterized as

> . . . an observer of great skill and experience, and with a remark-
> able gift for transmitting to others, through the medium of draw-
> ings, the results of his observation by spectroscope and telescope.
> The work upon which he is engaged must tend greatly to promote
> an accurate knowledge of science, and even to render it popular . . .

In 1875, Trouvelot published his first paper on astronomy, the
first of fifty that he was to issue during the rest of his life. There is
no record that he ever published again in the field of natural history. Four years later, in the fall of 1879, William Taylor moved
to 27 Myrtle Street, replacing Trouvelot. In the spring of 1880,
more than ten years after Trouvelot's experiments, Taylor told the
Gypsy Moth Commission:

> . . . I found the shed in the rear of his [Trouvelot's] house swarm-
> ing with caterpillars. I knew that Mr. Trouvelot had been experi-
> menting with silk-worms, but I did not know that the swarms of
> caterpillars in the shed came from the gypsy moth. The caterpillars
> were such a nuisance in and around the shed that I got permission
> to sell it, and it was taken to Mr. Harmon's on Spring Street. This
> will explain how the moth was carried into that section, and why
> the woods there became so badly infested.

From time to time the neighbors along Myrtle Street noticed
that caterpillars were nibbling the leaves on their trees, but they
blamed the damage on canker worms or tent caterpillars. By 1881,
the year that Trouvelot was elected to the American Academy of
Arts and Sciences, it has been estimated that the gypsy moth had
quietly spread throughout 400 square miles of land around Medford, but it was still not considered a real problem.

In 1882, the French republic having been reestablished for several years, Trouvelot returned to France for good to accept an

appointment on the staff of the newly built Meudon Observatory just outside Paris. He kept the position for the remainder of his life. In 1883 he was sent by the observatory to the Caroline Islands in the southwest Pacific to observe an eclipse of the sun. This was the same year that Mrs. William Belcher, who lived in the house next door to the one that had been Trouvelot's, recalled that "the caterpillars troubled us," but still no one even bothered to find out what they were, so mild was the "trouble." In fact it did not become severe until the summer of 1888, when John Stetson, a resident of South Street, nearly a mile from 27 Myrtle Street, took a specimen caterpillar, one of many that was eating the leaves off the trees in his yard, to the state board of agriculture for identification. No one there knew what it was, but sent it on to the Agriculture Experiment Station in Amherst. Charles H. Fernald, a professor at the state agriculture college, an entomologist who was the station director, was in Europe, but his wife, Maria, also an entomologist, made the identification, giving it a newer classificatory name than the one Trouvelot may have used. She called it *Ocneria dispar,* the timid, sexually dimorphic moth. When Professor Fernald returned home he consulted with his European colleagues and reported that the appearance of the gypsy moth in America was a grave matter. It might even prove a worse pest, he feared, than the potato beetle. The following year, 1889, gave him reason to believe he was right. In twenty years the moth had adapted itself to a new climate and, free of predators and diseases from its native land, the population explosion that year was vigorous.

Mrs. Belcher, the Trouvelot neighbor, testified before the Gypsy Moth Commission about that outbreak:

> My sister cried out one day, "They [the caterpillars] are marching up the street." I went to the front door and sure enough, the street was black with them, coming across from my neighbor's, Mrs. Clifford's, and heading straight for our yard. They had stripped her trees, but our trees at that time were only partially eaten.

Mrs. I. W. Hamlin, who lived up on the corner of Myrtle and Spring streets, testified:

> Our yard was overrun with caterpillars. . . . When they got their growth these caterpillars were bigger than your little finger, and would crawl very fast.

Even blocks away, toward Medford Center, D. M. Richardson told of the attack of these preternaturally large and fast caterpillars, first at Postmaster Spinney's house and then at his own:

> In 1889 the caterpillars of the gypsy moth appeared at Spinney's place on Cross Street, and after stripping the trees there started across the street. It was about five o'clock one evening that they started across the street in a great flock, and they left a plain path across the road. They struck into the first apple tree in our yard, and the next morning I took four quarts of caterpillars off of one limb.

Testimony given before this commission and others like it was for the purpose of proving that the gypsy moths so threatened good public order that public monies should be spent on getting rid of them, and of course nothing was gained by giving mild testimony or understating the problem. Nevertheless, even keeping appropriation-lust in mind, the summer of 1889 sounds just awful for the proud householders of Medford. Gypsy moths were said to be so thick on trees that they stuck together "like cold macaroni"; ladies walking along the streets had to shake their long skirts with each step to rid them of crawling caterpillars. Callers were forced to wait on house steps until the "worms" were swept away from front doors before they could be opened. Strolling down the street was like running a gauntlet, one man testified, adding that he could turn up his coat collar and sprint but still get "worms" inside his clothing. Shade trees, fruit trees, and gardens, down to the parsley, were stripped of their green leaves.

Yankee ingenuity and gossip, as neighbor told neighbor how to deal with them, played equal parts in the control methods used.

One man turned his hens on the caterpillars. Some scraped up egg masses and burned them in kerosene. Others poured scalding water over eggs and caterpillars. Running lighted candles under fence railings to burn the eggs was said to be a good control method. Householders wrapped paper around tree trunks and coated it with printers' ink, which was sticky, creating something like the Raupenleim bands European foresters used. Adopting another European method, they wrapped trees in carpet strips to trap the caterpillars, and killed them by the coal-scuttleful each day. They also sprayed their caterpillar-filled trees with an emulsion of whale-oil soap and kerosene.

In that year, 1889, the first gypsy-moth appropriation ever made in America—for $300—was authorized by the local road commission; it was used to put inked bands on trees. But the local selectmen also petitioned the general court to let the state board of agriculture exterminate the caterpillars. And in 1890, the Massachusetts legislature, working on the assumption that the gypsy moths covered a mere fifty-square-mile area, passed a bill calling for "the Extermination of the *Ocneria dispar,* or Gypsy Moth," and appropriated $25,000 for the job. The commission appointed to the work reported that the "infested territory was some sixteen times as large as first represented" and requested more funds. An additional appropriation of $25,000 was immediately granted, and during the summer of 1890 eighty-nine men were hired to scrape eggs from trees, inspect carriages leaving the town, cut down the trees in heavily infested areas (such as the woods where Trouvelot had conducted his silkworm experiments), and spray the remaining trees with Paris green, a popular and widely used insecticide, a formulation of copper acetoarsenite.

In 1891, the meeting of the commission at which Shaler told his story about Trouvelot was convened, and those attending debated the question of whether it was possible to exterminate the moth. Was control of it and its damage, the European approach, a more reasonable goal than outright extermination? The answer would determine how resources would be spent. Intensive, selective use of them could be used to limit the harm the moth caused to valuable individual trees. A more diffuse, wider use of resources, with sprays, would be required if the moth were to be eradicated completely, for the commission continued to believe that sprays could kill 100 percent of a targeted pest. Charles Fernald thought that all resources should be devoted to extermination:

> Suppose we have a tree like the elm I see yonder, and suppose we know it to be the only tree in America that is infested. I think you will all agree with me that for a small sum of money all moths on it could be destroyed. Suppose there were two,—suppose all the trees on the Common were infested. If they could be destroyed on all those trees it is only a question of time and money to eradicate them from a much larger territory.

Samuel Scudder, assistant to Agassiz, leader of the Boston Society of Natural History, an enthusiastic, kindly entomologist, one of America's greatest, was also a member of the commission.* He doubted whether the gypsy moth could be eradicated:

> . . . it does not seem likely that the thing will be exterminated, but . . . it can be held in check for many years. The reason why I don't think it can be exterminated is because we have not enough persons used to looking for the caterpillars to examine the trees and say for certain that there are none there.

At first, Charles V. Riley, a pioneer of economic entomology and head entomologist with the U.S. Department of Agriculture (a man, incidentally, who had been in favor of domestic silk culture for years), agreed with Scudder, saying:

---

* Today's entomologists remember Scudder as a man who described and classed a huge number of species, perhaps even too many, for his work has often needed revision. When told by a colleague that if one worked rapidly he was likely to make errors, Scudder is said to have replied, with emphasis, "Sure to, sure to!" and went on to become the world authority on orthoptera and an eminence in lepidoptera and insect paleontology.

Is it practicable to exterminate it or not? . . . I have serious doubts. . . . My own fears would be that it has got into the woods and on to trees that are not so easily treated. . . . I should . . . have very little hope of its ultimate extinction.

But his doubts were argued against by other commission members, except Scudder, and by the end of the meeting Riley was speaking excitedly:

Professor Shaler: I think it would be a tax of probably more than one hundred thousand dollars annually if not checked.
Professor Riley: There is no question of that, if it is allowed to take its course. That is what makes it so vitally interesting to me, and why I am so impatient of any efforts to simply check it. I have nothing to say about checking it; I speak for stamping it out.

Fernald, wise in the ways of legislatures, proposed a strategy:

. . . Professor Riley's suggestion to exterminate them in one year would be a good one if it could be accomplished; but I question whether it would be wise for us to go from this meeting to the Legislature with that proposition. If you failed to do it in one year and came back for a second appropriation you might find it difficult to get.

Riley and Shaler discussed enlisting the help of small boys, who of course like to climb trees, in the attack on the moths. In the process, they betrayed an understanding of the psychology of boys worthy of Mark Twain:

Professor Riley: I would rather offer a higher bounty to every school-boy for pointing out where the caterpillars are to be found during two weeks in June, than for gathering eggs.
Professor Shaler: I should hesitate about offering a reward for the location of the caterpillars, because there is the possibility of the school-boys planting them. A reward for eggs is much more easy, and we could probably interest the school-boys in searching for them; but it would hardly do to offer a reward which might serve to spread the plague . . .

190

Professor Riley: If the boys once learned that they could get a certain amount of money for the eggs, they would not be so interested in exterminating them, and thus cutting off future revenue.
Professor Shaler: I should state a definite reward, and not go beyond a certain time.

The meeting concluded by recommending a $100,000 appropriation for the purposes of exterminating the moth, the hiring of a team of men from the agricultural college, and the investigation of sprays that might prove better than Paris green.

The details vary, but subsequent annual commissions continued to contend that the moth could be exterminated, provided sufficient appropriation be made. To this end, fire and other methods of destruction were used, but spraying with insecticides was the most important. One economic entomologist, A. H. Kirkland, adviser to the Bowker Insecticide Company from 1894 to 1900, even became superintendent of the gypsy-moth work from 1900 to 1905.

Paris green was known to be dangerous, although in speaking to the meeting of the 1891 commission Riley is dismissive:

Professor Shaler: Have you known of any cases of poisoning in persons employed in spraying?
Professor Riley: No, I have seen none, but I have known of cases where negroes would sit on the back of a mule with spraying pumps, going through cotton fields, and carelessly allow water to fall on them. I have known them to become sore in the groin, but never knew of a fatal case.

This is troubling, because even though the carcinogenic properties of Paris green were not known at the time, its poisonous effects were, as an appendix to the massive report of the Gypsy Moth Commission, published in 1896, clearly shows. Human death and serious injury—ulceration of mucous membranes, delirium, prostration, inflammation, headaches, muscular debilitation, neuralgia, and convulsions—could be caused by contact with it. The appendix documents the cases of at least three women who needed medical treatment after the spraying in 1891. Not only was Paris green dangerous, it was ineffective. Tests soon showed that gypsy-moth caterpillars actually preferred eating leaves saturated with it to leaves left untreated. It also badly burned foliage, sometimes causing more damage and leaf drop than the caterpillars did. Yet it continued to be used for several years despite public opposition to its use. In the 1896 report, authors Charles Fernald and Edward H. Forbush, field director of the gypsy-moth work, write:

Considerable opposition to the use of Paris green for spraying was manifested by many people living in the infested towns. A mass meeting of opponents of the spraying was held in Medford. One citizen, who attempted to cut the hose attached to one of the spraying tanks, and threatened with violence the employees of the Board who had entered upon his land, was arrested and fined. Others neutralized the effects of the spraying by turning the garden hose upon trees and shrubs that had been sprayed, and washing off the solution. The opposition to spraying affected the results of the work unfavorably to a considerable extent. In June a bulletin of information was issued by the State Board of Agriculture, containing quotations from Professor Riley and other economic entomologists as to the lack of danger to man or beast attending the use of Paris green. This bulletin was distributed freely among the people of the district, but it failed to allay the popular prejudice against the spraying. . . . The prejudice against spraying in Medford and other towns was intensified by the belief that there was danger of fatal poisoning to man and animals. When the spraying was in progress, sensational reports were circulated. Statements were made in the daily press that a man had died from the effects of chewing leaves taken from trees sprayed in Medford, and that a child had been fatally poisoned by eating bread and butter on which some of the spray had fallen from the trees. On this at least one newspaper editor advised his readers to shoot at sight the workmen employed in spraying. It was reported that there was great danger from eating sprayed fruit. Several quarts of cherries which had been taken from trees and preserved in jars were analyzed, and no trace of arsenic was found. Yet even before they were analyzed, it was reported that they had been sent to Amherst and that arsenic enough had been found on them to kill a dozen people. A large portion of the cherries on these trees were stolen by boys or given away, yet no immediate mortality occurred among the juveniles of the neighborhood . . . there is a certain amount of danger from the absorption or inhalation of arsenic, and great care should be always exercised in its use. About ten per cent of the men employed in spraying suffered more or less from arsenical poisoning.

By 1896, when the report was issued under the title *The Gypsy Moth,* Trouvelot was dead, and so perhaps he never knew about the devastating results of his experiment to breed a better silkworm. He had died on April 22, 1895. *Nature Magazine* lamented his passing, writing, "Observational astronomy has lost one of its foremost workers."

By 1900, having begun to use, for the most part, a new lead arsenate spray developed by the U.S. Bureau of Entomology, Fernald was still requesting annual appropriations of $200,000 for the extermination of the moth, which he evidently still believed was possible. But damage was light in those years around the turn of the century, although the moth was actually spreading widely. It was not until 1905, when the moth covered at least 2,500 square miles of woodlands in Massachusetts, Maine, New Hampshire, and Rhode Island, that it was at last conceded that a policy of extermination would not work.★ There was an outbreak in 1905, and after it resources were devoted to learning about how gypsy-moth populations are checked in Japan and in Europe. Investigators studied the moths' predators in those places, as well as viral, fungal, and bacterial diseases. Their studies began to hint at the complexity of the relationship. In 1911, Leland O. Howard, chief of the U.S. Bureau of Entomology, wrote perceptively in his report on the importation of gypsy-moth parasites:

★ The belief in the possibility of extermination died hard. Asher tells me that when he was living in New Jersey in the 1950s, the gypsy moth experienced a population peak during several of those years and although most entomologists disagreed, a few contended that the moth could be exterminated within New Jersey borders by spraying with insecticides. Minority opinion prevailed and extermination became state policy until it failed there, as it had elsewhere.

To put it dogmatically, each species of insect in a country where the conditions are settled is subjected to a certain fixed average percentage of parasitism, which, in the vast majority of instances and in connection with numerous other controlling agencies, results in the maintenance of a perfect balance. The insect neither increases to such abundance as to be affected by disease or checked from further multiplication through lack of food, nor does it become extinct, but throughout maintains a degree of abundance in relation to other species existing in the same vicinity, which, when averaged for a long series of years, is constant.

At the time few of the parasites seemed to take hold, but in 1942 a small chalcid wasp, parasitic upon gypsy-moth caterpillars in Japan that had been released in 1908, was recaptured in the wild. It had been imported in 1908, and its population was assumed to have died out. Today it shows some promise as a natural check on gypsy moths. So does a fungus, also from Japan, *Entomophaga maimaiga*. It had been imported in 1910 and was never seen in the wild until 1989, when it was discovered in Connecticut. It, too, has interested researchers; evidently it sat there quietly percolating for eighty years, and may yet prove to help control gypsy moths in this country, as it has in Japan. Used experimentally, it has killed 95 percent of the targeted caterpillars. Currently, interesting work is being done at Pennsylvania State University on the interaction between munching gypsy-moth caterpillars and their food plants. There are hints that trees being eaten may begin secreting defensive chemicals that check caterpillar growth, suggesting a complexity of relationship never before suspected.

Chalcis flavipesi: *Adult*
(8x)

However, in the years since 1889, the first response has always been to spray gypsy moths wherever they are seen. The arsenical sprays gave way to DDT. Bacterial spray, Bt, replaced DDT, and now researchers have developed viral sprays, Gypcheck or Abby, as an alternate. More than $24 million was spent over a five-year period in the early 1980s to check gypsy-moth outbreaks. Still, despite the sprays—or perhaps because of them—the moth continues to spread at an average rate of a plodding fifteen miles a year, spreading enduringly as sprays prune, toughen, and select the population. Gypsy moths are now found over most of the northeastern United States and southern Canada. Isolated, introduced populations are found elsewhere throughout the continent. And in 1991, an Asian strain of *L. dispar* was accidentally imported into the American northwest in a shipment of grain. This has worried economic entomologists because the females of this strain, unlike the eastern gypsy-moth females, are good, strong flyers, and can therefore increase the rate of spread. The U.S. Department of Agriculture has responded with a $14.2 million eradication program, and in the spring of 1992 $10 million was earmarked for aerial spraying with Bt. The arguments presented for and against spraying were familiar; they were all eloquently and hotly debated in Medford at the various Gypsy Moth Commissions before the turn of the century.

Not long ago I was in Boston, so I drove up the Mystic River to Medford to find Trouvelot's old house on Myrtle Street. The only changes on the street are in keeping with the character it had one hundred years ago. The neighborhood still looks like a working-class one. Still trig. Still trim. The clapboards have been covered by aluminum siding that simulates clapboards. Here and there, cement blocks have replaced the old foundation bricks from the local brickyard. The wooden picket fences have been replaced by chain-link ones, but trees still shade the street. There was one change quite in keeping with the wispiness of every fact connected with Trouvelot, however: There is no longer a number 27 on Myrtle Street. The numbers skip from 25 to 29, increasing often by four, but in irregular progression.

In today's working-class neighborhoods the women are at work, too, so I had to knock on a lot of doors before I found anyone at home. But at last I found a woman who, speaking in German-accented English, told me that she had heard all the numbers had been changed on the street long ago, before she and her husband moved there in the 1950s.

Using the old 1895 photograph and the detailed map drawn by the Gypsy Moth Commission, I found Trouvelot's house; at least I am 97 percent sure I did. The position of the chimney is the same, as are the shape of the house, the attached shed, and the windows, but the pretty gingerbreading is gone. The house is sided in yellow aluminum and fitted out with aluminum storm doors, windows, and awnings. A flowering fruit tree grows in the backyard, and the householder who lives there must own an electric hedge clipper. The roses and shrubs are all trimmed squarely, as are the yews in front of the house. The yews are also wrapped in corsets of chicken wire to shape them.

I walked around the neighborhood. The railroad track, the Medford Branch line that ran in back of Trouvelot's house, has been ripped up. It may have been an avenue for the spread of gypsy moths, who hitched rides as eggs or caterpillars on its shipments. One of the reasons Medford was settled was that it was located on a fine bed of clay; brick making was an important industry, and Medford red brick was shipped throughout New England. All that remains on the railroad right-of-way is a small-boys' path through dry weeds and I walked down it. Directly in back of Trouvelot's house I picked up a little galvanized bucket that had been filled with citronella; Skeeter Beeter, it was labeled.

There must not have been mosquitoes in the old days, in Medford, for windows were opened directly to those summer breezes that may have blown gypsy-moth eggs from Number 27. One of the early recommendations made by the Gypsy Moth Commission had been for Medford residents to install window screens to keep the moths and caterpillars out of their houses. The woods in which Trouvelot raised his silkworms are gone, victims of the 1890 Gypsy Moth Commission and subsequent development. Where the trees once stood, the land is paved over, the parking lot of a steel company. Nearby is an empty, weedy space with a tired-looking FOR SALE sign on it. Beyond the steel company, the town waterworks has taken over a beautiful, free-spirited old red-brick building, constructed with a brick stepped-parapet roofline, the handiwork of someone who had bricks to spare. Most of the neighborhood still has plenty of trees, except where land has been cleared for development. August Busch has its Massachusetts corporate headquarters there, too, open and virtually treeless.

Medford seemed like a meatloaf kind of place, so I drove over a few blocks to Salem Street, and ordered it at the Towne Line Donut Shop and Restaurant. Very good meatloaf it proved to be, too, served up with frozen corn, mashed potatoes, and gravy. I stared out of the restaurant window while I ate. Across the way, in the direction of Myrtle Street, was a shopping center with a vast, treeless parking lot. At its edge, a four-lane highway, the Fellsway, sliced through Medford. In the end, a man on a bulldozer can make bigger changes than a gypsy moth ever can.

CHAPTER XII

ORDER DIPTERA: SYRPHID FLIES

While I was doing a little touch-up painting on the porch of our Washington house one day, a syrphid fly darted out of nowhere and hovered briefly in front of my face. He seemed to hang in the air as he looked me over. He satisfied some buggish curiosity about me and then flew away. I had stood still to watch him, but I have read that if you extend a finger these flies will sometimes land on it and perch for a while, so the next time I see one I want to try this. Maybe he will allow me a closer look.

I wish I could remember the first time I watched a syrphid fly, those common, big, gaily colored flies we see hovering among flowers everywhere in the summer. I must have been a child and they delight children, for they seem to be designed as toys. They are most often black or deep brown, with splotches or stripes of yellow or orange, although some species alternate the background color with green, blue, or coppery tones. They fly like helicopters, busily zooming to a place, only to wait and hover. Their wings move so fast that they can't be seen, let alone counted, but they are two in number, not four, which makes them proper Diptera, and the wings bear the identifying characteristic of the family Syrphidae, a fold or "false vein," which can be seen with the naked eye—or at least the under-forty-five-year-old naked eye. They are a pretty addition to a flower bed, where they feed on nectar; they need this source of sugary carbohydrate to fuel the muscles that power their tight, hovering flight. Curiously, their sucking mouthparts are neither as developed nor as efficient for this way of life as are those of bees, butterflies, and moths, who also visit our flowerbeds. Some syrphid flies buzz rather like bees, and some of the species are patterned in yellow and black and so resemble bees that people are often frightened of them, but they have no stingers and can do no harm. In fact they are beneficial insects: They help pollinate flowers and flowering crops, and in larval forms, depending upon the species, eat aphids or help hasten the process of decay and regeneration.

Even if you can't count their wings in flight, a closer look reveals that their antennae are not as long as a bee's, but stubby like a fly's, and their waists are not pinched-in, beelike fashion. In fact, they are stout-looking bugs. Their flight gives them away, too. A honeybee flies straight and smoothly. A syrphid fly bustles up to flowers in a highly controlled angular pattern rather like a hummingbird. Zoom, hover, and zoom again.

But though I can't remember the first time I saw a syrphid fly, I do remember the first time I watched one and wondered about its bright colors. It was more than ten years ago; I was looking at the flowers outside the windows at my farm in Missouri and a bright yellow-and-black insect flew into them. It was patterned so like a honeybee that even though I had been working with my own hives that very morning it fooled me at first. But it was one of the beelike syrphid flies. I watched it take nectar from a blossom and wondered how it helped the fly to so resemble a stinging insect in appearance when it had no hive to defend and when it led a life so different from the animal it seemed to imitate. Didn't predators with eyesight good enough to notice colors and patterns—birds, for instance—eat bees anyway? I remembered seeing phoebes and swallows chasing bees outside my honey-house door at harvest-time, when extra bees hovered there trying vainly to get to the fragrant honey within. Martins, I knew, were serious enemies of bees, and I always tried to set up my bee yards away from farms where the owner had put up a martin house.

Most animals do not live out their life spans. They starve to death, weakened from parasites, or meet with accidents. Many, if not most, are killed by other animals for life-sustaining food. It is useful to consider what animals do and what they look like in terms of how such behavior or appearance helps them cheat death long enough to pass on their genes to the next generation. Some animals avoid attention. They are dull in color or camouflaged to blend in with the place where they live—like the katydids—and they are furtive in habit, so they live on to breed. But others are just the opposite. Those with powerful defenses advertise them-selves. A skunk's white stripe makes him visible when he is hunt-ing at night, and he avoids a lot of trouble by declaring his presence.

The bright flash of danger, called by zoologists "aposematic coloration," is common among insects. Several of the butterflies —the monarchs, the cabbage butterflies, and Ernest Williams's *gillettii*—are aposematic. They strut themselves in front of birds, advertising that they have sequestered awful-tasting stuff in their flesh from the plants they fed on as caterpillars, and that if a bird dares eat them he will regret it—may even get sick. The orange and black of both the *gillettii* and the monarchs is a very common aposematic color pairing. The bright orange-and-black ladybugs I watched being harvested in the Sierras, for instance, are similarly distasteful. Some stinging wasps are orange and black. It makes good economical sense for different species to be similarly colored, for it reinforces the message and generalizes it. The message as read by birds becomes "Yuck! That black-and-orange bit of flying food tasted terrible. So did the other one, even though it looked a little different. And that one hurt me. Guess I'll lay off orange-and-black flying-food bits."

Birds, as a matter of fact, are very conservative about accepting aposematic prey; scientists believe, however, that their wariness is not innate but must be learned. Researchers have found only one case in which aversion is instinctive: Naïve six-week-old starlings reject aposematically colored dummies, but even among starlings, the rejection has to be reinforced with later unpleasant experiences or it fades as they grow older. Since most birds are not born with this aversion to bugs of any color, each new generation must learn to avoid those that taste bad or hurt by having a bad experience with a few of them. Insects, even unrelated ones, that have evolved the same advertising are less likely to be killed—it takes fewer sacrificed individuals of any one species to give the unschooled birds their brief but necessary misery. A nineteenth-century German zoologist, Fritz Müller, was the first to write about this, and so the term "Müllerian mimicry" has come to refer to the similarities that make separate bad-tasting species look like one another.

But bugs are good liars. In fact, lying is one of the things they do best—it's a way they keep from being killed and thus pass along their genes. Their exuberant, built-in, biological lying earns the admiration and respect of those of us who have to make up our paltry falsehoods consciously and laboriously with whatever scraps we can gather. Consider the walking-stick insect, which looks like a twig; the tufted bird-dropping moth, which has wings colored in such a way that at rest it looks like a dollop of bird manure; the treehopper, which sits motionless on an armed branch and can't be distinguished from the thorns. Such lying means survival, and as circumstances change new lies are told.

A stunning and well-known example of this provides an illustration of how adaptive change may work. Before the Industrial Revolution in England, the peppered moth, *Biston betularia,* was a white moth with black melanic specks that allowed it to match the bark of the birch trees to which it liked to cling. As the coal fires of the new age spread a pall of soot over the land in and around cities, the tree bark became grimy with it and the light-colored moths no longer blended in but became visible to birds, who ate them. Once again, Winston Bailey's principle applies: "As a general rule, it is better to mate tomorrow than be a meal today." Moths which had even a few more black speckles survived in greater numbers and were able to pass on their genes. Within seventy-five years melanic, closely speckled moths clung to darkened trees, blending in so well that they were safe from sharp-eyed birds. At the same time, out in the countryside, away from air pollution, lighter-colored peppered moths were still seen.

So when it comes to mimicry, it is not surprising that bugs have also proved to be skilled liars. There are several small spiders (*Synemosyna formica* is a common one in this country), members of the class Arachnida, which carry their lies across class lines, imitating, as their name implies, the form and movement of ants, which are members of the class Insecta. These spiders so resemble ants that though they themselves are edible, they live among the insects protected from those predators who find the formic acid in ants distasteful. Henry Bates, a nineteenth-century English naturalist and friend of Alfred Wallace, observed that sometimes butterflies that taste bad to birds have their imitators among other butterflies that don't taste bad at all. A number of black butterflies with shimmering blue-and-white spots on the tips of their hind wings belong to a species other than the pipevine swallowtail, which they deceptively resemble and which is unpalatable to birds. Others—females of the eastern black swallowtails, dark-phase tiger swallowtails, spicebush swallowtails, Diana fritillaries, and red-spotted purples among them—would be perfectly tasty to a bird, but the pipevine resemblance may help protect them.

This lie has a catch to it, however. Since birds are not born knowing that they should avoid eating bugs of certain colors, shapes, or patterns, they have to learn to avoid them by sampling this one or that, and can sometimes be seen spitting out those that taste bad or hurt them, wiping their beaks afterward in disgust. If a bird that has just ventured out into the world by itself tries to eat a pipevine swallowtail for one of its first dinners, it *may* avoid all butterflies thereafter that resemble it; however, if instead its first meal is a tasty female Diana fritillary, it has no reason not to believe that black butterflies with shimmering blue edges to their hinder wings aren't nice dinners and will continue eating them until it finally runs into a pipevine swallowtail. Indeed, if the bird has eaten many palatable black and shimmering blue butterflies and been made happy by the experience, it may even go on eating them until it gets a run on pipevines. So this particular lie, the one we call Batesian mimicry, works well only when the mimics are met less often than the real thing.

This all sounds very neat and pat, but it is good to remember that "mimicry" is merely a word that we humans have invented. It stands for a complex of events and conditions that are supposed to answer questions about what we see in the world. However, mimicry is a spooky sort of thing, rather Escher-like, and the closer the events and conditions are examined, the more the answers we have formulated seem to become questions. Mimicry is deception, and answers to questions about it turn into deceptions themselves. It is one of biology's oddities, one that seems to wander off and turn into jokes on humans who think they understand it.

As a start, let's take one of the simpler jokes. For years biologists taught their students (who dutifully wrote it down) that the viceroy butterfly, a splendidly beautiful orange-and-black monarch look-alike, which harbors toxic glycosides from the milkweeds on which it feeds as a caterpillar, was a prime example of an edible Batesian mimic. The textbooks said so, too, as did the guidebooks. Then along came David Ritland, a graduate student working under Lincoln Brower, the University of Florida lepidopterist and authority on mimicry, who asked what all good scientists are supposed to ask: Is this so? He offered wild blackbirds butterfly abdomens (minus their wings, so that the birds would not be warned by any aposematic colors they had already learned) from a variety of species, both those presumed to be edible and those thought to be inedible. He made the startling discovery that the viceroy tasted just as bad to a blackbird as a monarch did. When presented with either one, the birds would taste it, shake their heads, become agitated, and afterward reject both butterflies in over one third of the cases. However, when offered other apparently succulent butterflies they gobbled down 98 percent of them without hesitation. "It still pays to mutually advertise," says Ritland. The viceroy's orange-and-black coloring reinforces the monarch's message, but it is a case of Müllerian mimicry, not Batesian, and all the lecture notes and guidebooks will have to be rewritten.

Another set of aposematic colors are yellow and black. Many wasps, hornets, and bees are thus colored, so often that the yellow-and-black combination almost seems like a signpost that says "stinging insect" and therefore protects insects that have no stingers. *Aganacris pseudosphex* is a katydid that is not a chubby, green-leaf mimic but is yellow and black and as wasplike in behavior and appearance as an orthopteran lacking a wasp's slim waist or stinger can be. As noted, yellow and black is also the color pattern flaunted by many syrphid flies, many of which have also come to resemble bees in other ways. They buzz, they are fuzzy, and the imitation is such a good one that it often fools humans.

I have written elsewhere about the time I was called to rid a dairyman's milk barn of what he assumed were my honeybees, which he insisted in believing even after I had told him they were flies. He was not convinced until I snatched one out of the air and held it in my fist, proving that it had no stinger. I remembered my experience with that dairyman the day I was staring out the window watching the syrphid fly on my flowers. How do they live their lives? How does it serve them to look like bees? What are they up to?

Before I went to California for the ladybug harvest, I spoke several times on the telephone to Ken Hagen and I knew even before I met him in person that I would like him because he really enjoyed talking about bugs. I have never had a short interview with an entomologist. Some of the happiest hours of my life have been spent in their company, for I have come to them with specific questions and they have gone beyond them. They have spun buggish tales from other entomological fields, describing their research and that of their colleagues with zest beyond the conventions and cautions of academic publishing. They speculate and wonder. They are incurable gossips. They are irreverent. They are funny. They like to talk bugs.

"Syrphid flies? You interested in syrphid flies?" asked Ken.

"Well, we work on them, too," he said. "Some species eat a lot of aphids, you know." I hadn't known; nor had I known many of the things he had to tell or show me about syrphid flies.

Like other members of the order Diptera, syrphid flies undergo a complete metamorphosis. The brightly colored, nectar-sipping adults emerge from pupae in which the larvae rearrange their maggot selves into mature, winged forms. Although all adult syrphids feed on nectar, the larvae, depending upon the species, eat different things and therefore live differently. The people at the Beneficial Insects Laboratory are interested in the species that are aphid eaters. As well they might be. Although an individual syrphid larva is not quite up to the ladybug mark of consuming 5,000 aphids in a lifetime, it has been estimated that it can eat up to 1,200. In one of those idle calculations made from time to time, the eighteenth-century French natural historian René-Antoine Ferchault de Réaumur once figured that any single fertile female aphid could, if unchecked, produce 5 million offspring in its reproductive lifetime of four to six weeks. Hence, for the comfort of all the rest of us animals who inhabit the planet, it is reassuring to have lacewings, ladybugs, and syrphid-fly larvae around to keep this from happening.

Harold Oldroyd, the dramatic British dipterist, turns the syrphid's feeding into theater:

> The feeding of these larvae has been studied and several times filmed. The maggot-like larvae hatch from eggs laid under a leaf, and are blind, of course: that is to say, though they may detect light and darkness by a general sensitivity of skin, they have no eyes, and no power of forming an image of their surroundings. They could not actively chase an elusive prey—no maggot can—but the aphids on a stem present what is literally a sitting target. In fact what impresses me most when I see films of aphids and ladybird larvae feeding among greenfly is the way in which the aphids show no reaction at all while the one next to them is being devoured. I suppose it is what one would expect, but the effect is macabre in the extreme.
>
> The Syrphid larva finds its victim by raising the front end of the body and swinging it from side to side until it touches and seizes an

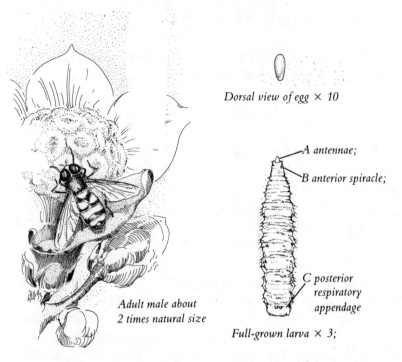

Dorsal view of egg × 10

A antennae;

B anterior spiracle;

C posterior respiratory appendage

Adult male about 2 times natural size

Full-grown larva × 3;

Metasyrphus americanus *(American hover fly)*

aphid. When a victim has been seized, it is held up, away from the surface, and sucked dry, while the fly-larva clings to the plant by the grip of its abdominal segments. Though at first this would seem a difficult way to attack prey, it has the advantage that the aphid cannot escape by running away.

The American hover fly, *Metasyrphus americanus,* is one of these aphid eaters, and is found throughout the northern part of the continent. Adult females lay their eggs on plants that have aphids on them, and the pale-gray larvae that hatch out eat the aphids. After they have had their fill, they drop to the ground under the plant, pupate, and emerge in the summertime. This may be the first time we become aware of them. It was an American hover fly I saw outside my window in Missouri sipping nectar, and it was another of the same kind who came to check me out on my porch in Washington. These adults are fat insects, just under half an inch in length, with three gleaming yellow bands across their black abdomens. They have yellow faces with black markings, and they often just stand in the air, looking things over, shining in the sun. Oldroyd writes:

> If it were not to risk being branded as anthropomorphic and sentimental, it would be pleasant to think that Syrphids enjoyed their hovering as much as we who watch them. After all, flies have to do something all their waking hours. Carnivores have to hunt, and if their prey is hard to find, hunting may take up most of their time. Flower feeders have an easier time. They can feed at any time, and unlike bees they do not have to collect food for a never-ending succession of larvae in a hive or, worse still, to make honey for an insatiable beekeeper. Many flower-feeding flies bask in the sunshine, while others strut about in an absurd way. Syrphidae spend much of their time, weather permitting, hovering in the air, with every appearance of enjoying it: or, if you prefer to express it differently, the state of hovering seems to be one of content, from which they are disinclined to depart.

Other species, including one of the most famous bee mimics, *Eristalis tenax,* commonly called the drone fly, and others of the prettier syrphids, spend their larval lives feeding on the usable organic bits they can filter out of what we humans consider loathsome: polluted water, decaying animals, drains, sewage seeps, and open latrines. Keeping them and studying them is not to everyone's taste, I suppose, for the standard advice for raising larvae of *Eristalis* and other genera that share their habits is to feed them on a decaying mouse submerged in water or moist rabbit droppings. The larvae of these species have an unusual structure that permits them to live in liquids and that gives them their name: rat-tailed maggots.

The "rat-tailed maggot" of the syrphid fly Eristalis, *a larva that creeps about underwater*

Eristalis tenax,
the drone fly
(½x)

They have a long, taillike appendage with a tube extension that can telescope in and out. Extended, this organ becomes a snorkel that pierces the surface of whatever ooze they find themselves in, allowing them to take air while feeding. When they are ready to pupate, they seek out a patch of soil and bury themselves just beneath its surface. When the adults emerge from the pupae and have allowed their wings to expand and dry, they fly in search of flowers that will give them the nectar needed to bring their sexual organs to maturity. They will continue to feed on nectar throughout their adult lives. They prefer daisies and other flowers with yellow in them. Because drone flies are fuzzy, like bees, they catch the pollen on flowers that they visit and spread it from blossom to blossom, aiding in the pollination of plants that are not self-fertilizing. They are easy to confuse with bees because they are patterned so similarly. They are large, a little bigger than an American hover fly. The males search for mates near flowers, courting the females by hovering close to them while they feed, emitting all the while a distinct buzzy sound. The females who accept them mate and then, fertile, winter in a protected spot. In Europe they sometimes migrate to the south and can be seen flying over the Alps or the Pyrenees, where the funnel effect in the passes concentrates them in such numbers that they appear to be in swarms. Taking a page from the ladybug book, their aphid-eating syrphid cousins also migrate if aphid populations are low.

It is this particular syrphid, the drone fly, in its adult form, which is such a good bee mimic that it is generally considered to be the deceiver that tricked literary gents, including Virgil, into repeating for 1,500 years the canard that honeybees can be generated from the rotting carcasses of cows. Virgil even suggested it as a way in which beekeepers could acquire new stocks of honeybees. It is true that Baron C. R. Osten Sacken, who in 1894 published his version of this fanciful idea, could find only one account of *E. tenax* larvae being discovered in the wild in a rotting carcass, but one may have been all that was needed in antiquity to start this foolishness. Scientists certainly have had no trouble raising other closely related species of syrphids inside dead animals, and after the larvae have fed they could pupate in the ground under the carcass, mature, and seem to fly out of it. Whatever is behind it, the story's origins are lost in the mist of history. Virgil claimed that he had it from the Egyptians, and it was repeated by Pliny, Ovid, and other classical writers. Virgil gave it poetic stature in his beautiful Fourth Georgic, and it was repeated on his authority by others afterward, including the medieval natural historian Aldrovandus, on whose work T. H. White based his *Bestiary*. The most recent reference that Osten Sacken lists of the "fact" that bees come from carcasses was written in 1663 by a man named Bechart.

In the Fourth Georgic, Virgil elevated Aristaeus, son of a nyad, to godhood for his (mistaken) notion about producing honeybees from dead cattle. Aristaeus, a beekeeper who had lost all his bees and supposedly acquired new ones this way, spent the remainder of his years on earth traveling and peddling this tale far and wide. He was not the first beekeeper, I'll wager, to hand out noddy clothed as divine wisdom, and I know he wasn't the last, but he may have been the only one made into a certified god as a result. His recipe for bees is not a pretty one, but the description of maggots is accurate, if overly poetic. The translation used below is by L. A. S. Jermyn. First Virgil lays out a bit of history:

> But if a keeper loses his whole breed
> Suddenly, and is doubtful whence he may
> Get him new stock, it will be time to expound
> The noted lore which the Arcadian taught,—
> How, oft ere now, when cattle have been slain,
> The blood in ferment has giv'n birth to bees.
> More deeply will I probe—trace the whole tale
> From its prime source. For where the fortunate race
> Of Pellaean Canopus hug the shores
> Beside the sluggish overflow of Nile,

209

And sail around their farms in painted skiffs,
Where the drawn Parthian bow threatens the marches,
And where the river splits his stream and flows
In seven months from the dark Ethiop land,
Making an Egypt from its black-laid loam
Rich, green and fertile,—men of all this plain
Build on this art sure hope of livlihood.
A spot is chosen first, constricted, small,
Apt for its special purpose, more confined
By four close walls narrowly overarched,
In which thin air-holes, facing the four winds,
Admit a slanting light. A two-year-old
Bull-calf is then procured, whose crescent horns
Already burgeon. Though it fiercely fight
Against its captors, both the nose and mouth
Are gagged: the beast is clubbed to death, the flesh
Pounded to pulp through the unbroken hide.
So closeted they leave it, underlaid
With brushwood, thyme and Cnidian bay fresh-picked.
This do they when the driven waves gleam white
Before the rising West, or e'er the meads
Are pied with colours new, or e'er the martin,
Chirruping, hangs her nest beneath the eaves.
Meanwhile, warm moisture in the softened bones
Begins to seethe: strange worms remarkable
Limbless at first, soon with loud whirr of wings,
Swarm in it, more and more essaying flight,
Until, like tempest from a summer cloud,
Or storm of arrows from the Parthian bows
When their light horse opens the fray,—they're off!

Virgil then concludes the poem with the advice given to Aristaeus by his mother, the nyad:

"My son, let gloomy care fall from thy heart. . . .
   Choose thou four bulls that now
Crop the green pastures on Lycaen hills,
In beauty excellent; four cows likewise,
With necks as yet unblemished by the yoke.
For these set up four altars near the shrines
Consecrate to the goddesses, and, thy knife

Severing the throats, let flow the holy blood.
Then leave the corpses in the shady grove.
And when nine times the dawn has risen and passed,
A black sheep shalt thou slay, and, visiting
The grove again . . .
Do worship with a calf for sacrifice . . ."
    Then Aristaeus, instant to obey
His mother's precepts, tarried not, but went.
Unto the shrines he came, and there upraised
The altars as ordained, leading four bulls,
In beauty excellent, four cows likewise
With necks as yet unblemished by the yoke.
And when nine times the dawn had risen and passed . . .
[He] to the grove returned. Lo! here was seen
A sudden miracle: bees with loud buzz
Seethed in the sodden flesh, hummed in the wombs,
And, bursting from the parted ribs, took wing
In huge and trailing clouds, and now their swarm
Hung on a tree-top, bending low the boughs.

Could Virgil have believed this? Elsewhere in the poem his knowledge of bees seems so exact that one suspects he may have kept them, but any rustic who had bees would have known the tale false after once bludgeoning his bull and cow to death and watching yellow-and -black-winged creatures emerge from them, creatures who, however beelike in appearance, would neither hive nor make honey. But such was the great Virgil's authority that the method was handed down unquestioned among the literate for centuries. One is sorry for the cows and bulls whose lives may have been ended so cruelly (though I doubt that they were many) to generate bees who turned out to be flies, but the whole deception stands as an unwitting triumph of animal mimicry, a joke upon us humans, or at least those of us who become literary gents unwilling or unable to put authority to a test. In reality, the whole process is special enough to inspire awe without resort to myth-making. We think of offal, carrion, the slurry of our sewage, dung, and waste as a problem in disposal, but the fly regards them as opportunity, a source of life and development, and tidies up what we have no use for, transforming it into pretty insects, black

211

and golden sexually mature adults who cheer a summer day and pollinate our flowers.

The joke is a good one. Nevertheless, nature is not purposeful, nor a source of pranks played upon literary gents. The question remains: How does the resemblance to a bee serve a fly? I discovered that this has been puzzling entomologists for a long time. Various theories have been handed around, and the answers, as with many answers in entomology, are only partial. First, it should be said that aposematic coloration doesn't make any difference at all to some important predators, for they happily eat wasps and bees, and therefore the flies' mimicry is wasted on them. Among those predators are the syrphids' own cousins, members of the order Diptera, flies of the family Asilidae, commonly called bee killers. They kill not only bees, but beelike flies as well. The aposematic coloration warns them of absolutely nothing. The same is true of many other insect and spider predators whose vision probably does not even give them the same information about color, shape, and pattern as ours does. In addition, a number of plants—sundews, pitcher plants, several of the dogbanes, and a variety of water lily—kill syrphid flies, entrapping them just as they do other insects that visit them.

It was noted a long time ago that certain species of beelike flies, including syrphids, resemble certain species of wasps and bees in whose nests they lay their eggs. Rather than deducing from this that the flies gained some protection from predators through this association, as is theorized in the case of the ant-mimicking spiders, it was suggested that these flies were fooling the wasps and bees, whom, it was said, they parasitized. But the nineteenth-century student of insect behavior Jean-Henri Fabre discovered that the wasp mimics were housecleaners, not parasites. Females of species of the genus *Volucella,* which closely resemble wasps, enter their nests to lay their eggs. They carefully keep to the outer combs, Fabre observed, to avoid the wasps, which readily recognize them as intruders and will sting them to death if they are discovered. But the female *Volucella* can lay her eggs even as she is dying. Once hatched, the larvae that emerge from those eggs drop

212

to the floor of the nest and feed on debris there—dead wasps and excrement. Later studies showed that bee mimics behaved similarly. The visual mimicry cannot fool bees; they have such keen chemical senses that they can tell their own nest mates from those in the hive next door, and will sometimes kill them if they try to enter. Distinguishing a fly from her sister bees, no matter how winsomely colored the fly might be, is no big deal for a bee.

Toads are another matter. They are fly predators and can be taught, at least under laboratory conditions, to avoid both bees and syrphid-fly bee mimics, so the mimicry could trick a toad. Jan van Zandt Brower and Lincoln Brower once conducted an experiment with toads and found that under controlled laboratory conditions the toads quickly learned to avoid the stinging insects, and after that also avoided the syrphids which imitated them. What is more, they could remember the painful lesson for at least several months thereafter.

The picture is not so clear among birds. Over the years studies have shown that various birds—among them starlings, crows, a few of the tits, and catbirds—do indeed avoid eating both bees and the flies that mimic them, and so in these cases Batesian mimicry works for the flies. But for such mimicry to succeed, as was mentioned earlier, there must be more of the harmful or hurtful population present than the edible one, or else those crows, catbirds, and all the rest would learn the *opposite* lesson: They would believe that big, fuzzy, buzzing, yellow-and-black insects were good food. G. P. Waldbauer, from the University of Illinois, presented a paper at a 1988 symposium on mimicry that suggests at least a theoretical explanation of how this might work for the kinds of birds which believe the lies told by syrphid flies. In northern Michigan and Illinois, where he conducted his census, Waldbauer found bumblebees, wild bees, and wasps present throughout the growing season, but in large numbers only toward the end of the summer. Hymenoptera of this sort start their colonies from a single overwintered fertile female and build in numbers throughout the summer.

The syrphids, on the other hand, live just a short time as sexual, beelike adults, and were present during only a part of the growing season, chiefly the early part, although there was another smaller population peak, especially in Illinois, later in the summer. At first this seems to violate the Batesian principle that more harmful models must be present than mimics. But Waldbauer theorizes that during the early spring the birds, whose memories for aposematic colors have been found to last well over a year, would avoid eating the bee and wasp mimics because they had learned their lesson the previous summer. The situation might be even better for the mimics if fewer models existed to which the sharp-eyed birds could compare them. The late-summer bloom of syrphids comes at a time when bees and wasps are plentiful: The fledgling birds have only recently learned that black-and-yellow flying food bits are hurtful, but now they need not risk eating them anyway, for other sources of food are around.

Waldbauer's census does not report whether or not the birds are actually eating or not eating bees or their mimics and it was not set up to do so, but it is interesting and suggests a theory that can be tested. However, one study has been done of what insects birds actually *do* eat, and this is particularly interesting because it does not use birds such as starlings, catbirds, and the like, which have a varied diet, but flycatchers—those birds which, along with martins and swallows, are specialists in eating flying insects and who are therefore the most important syrphid predators. This study shows that flycatchers eat both stinging insects and their mimics, and, what is more, can tell the difference between them.

N. B. Davies, of the Edward Grey Institute at Oxford, England, made this field study of the spotted flycatcher's prey selection. He recorded what these birds eat in the wild. He found that they took many fewer wasps and bees than other flying insects, but that when they had hungry nestlings they would capture the stinging bugs and render them harmless. This was particularly true in the early morning hours when it was cool, for bumblebees, which can raise their own body temperatures, are early flyers and are more abundant than other insects at that time of day. One reason why the flycatchers did not take a great many wasps or bees appears to be that they took more time and energy to prepare. The flycatchers understood that such insects stung, so in order to protect their nestlings they would scrub the captured wasp or bee against a tree limb to rub off its stinger. Sometimes the insect would break apart in the process and fall to the ground, and the parent bird would have nothing to show for its effort. Perhaps that is the way martins handle bees and wasps too, as well as the phoebes (which are a kind of flycatcher) and swallows outside my honey house. But—and this is the fascinating part of Davies's study—the flycatchers caught lots of bee-mimicking syrphids, big, fat, nutritious insects, for their youngsters, and when they did so they would *not* rub them against the branch but would feed them directly to the nestlings. They knew they did not sting. The mimics might fool the human observer but not the sharp-eyed birds, to whom a nice distinction among insects is a matter of survival.

In sum, about all that can be said from these studies is that even though you can't fool all of the predators all of the time, you can fool some of them some of the time. This may be enough to cause changes, according to one theory. It runs something like this: Once upon a time, back in Upper Triassic days, a little over 200 million years ago next Tuesday, all the flies, specialized and therefore relatively recent insects, were a dull grayish, blackish, brownish color. They lived and were eaten by other animals, older insects, and small reptiles day after day after day. But after the sun began to rise in Cretaceous times flowers and bees came into the world, and then one day a fly was born different from all the rest of his dull kind. By some freak he emerged from his pupa with light splotches on his abdomen and flew away. A lizard who usually quickly ate flies, no questions asked, paused to look before he snapped this one up because he wanted to check to see if it might be one of those black-and-stripy yellow food bits which had stung him on the lip two days ago. The pause allowed the fly to escape, breed, and pass on his light-splotch genes. In the meantime, the hungry lizard *did* eat up the next dull black fly he found, and so the dull one did not pass on his genes at all. In subsequent generations of splotchy-marked flies, those which had, by chance, more stripy splotches or which had a deformation that looked like a hair or two and which looked at a certain angle a little fuzzy—in short, those which were more beelike, even if only a little—were the ones which had a greater opportunity to pass on the genes that expressed those features than did those who lacked them.

This is the way the theory runs. It sounds a little like a *Just So Story,* and not everyone is satisfied with it because too often the mimicry doesn't work the way the theory suggests it should.

Is it possible this is not mimicry at all? Are there some subtle forces at work producing a convergence of coloration in both the Hymenoptera and the similarly colored flies? Could their appearance be the end effect of genetic changes brought about by the same environmental, chemical, or physical forces acting upon both fly and bee? "Clearly there are problems in regarding many hoverflies as mimics," concludes Francis S. Gilbert, the British expert on syrphids, after reviewing some of the studies I have outlined above, "and we have to look for some other, as yet unknown, explanation for their bright colors."

Oldroyd says it even more simply: "Adult hoverflies are aesthetically attractive . . . but a great many that look like Hymenoptera seem to have no obvious reason for doing so."

CHAPTER XIII

ORDER ORTHOPTERA: CAMEL CRICKETS

One of my artist friends was sitting at my desk peering intently into the terrarium full of camel crickets I have there. "They look like shrimp with big legs," she said. This is a visually apt description. They are big bugs, an inch or more, so you can easily see the overlapping plates that, shrimplike, armor their backs. I think they are prettier than shrimp, however. Shrimp always make me think of lingerie, but these camel crickets are a lovely pale, buffy fawn in color, dappled with darker brown and black. The big hind legs that make them good jumpers have beefy haunches stylishly herringboned in black. Seen from above on the bare ground, on bark, or on leaf litter, they are perfectly camouflaged. They are silent, wingless crickets, distant cousins of the chirping house crickets, as well as of katydids and grasshoppers. They are deaf to airborne sound. They don't act as though they use their black eyes, which look like tiny shoe buttons, although Dave Nickle, the federal orthopterist, assures me they are perfectly well formed. But they have splendid, sweeping, graceful, active antennae, as long as their bodies or longer, studded with sensory receptors. They use them to know their world. I have been keeping them because no one else has, and for twenty years I have been trying to figure out what they were up to.

$♀$

Ceuthophilus *(life-size)*

When I drive back and forth between the Ozarks and Washington I am accompanied by two dogs, one cat, and camel crickets of varying number, egg to adult. The people whose motel I use halfway between the two places welcome all of us mammals; I've never mentioned the camel crickets to them. There would be too much to explain. Camel crickets are immaculately clean, harmless animals whose dearest wish is to be left alone. They are found everywhere in the United States. My species is *Ceuthophilus seclusus,* in the *maculatus* group, which means, roughly, "Shy Spotty Bug Who Loves to Hide in Holes." Couple this with "A Shrimp with Long Legs" and you have a pretty fair description—better, I think, than some of its other common names: stone cricket or devil's coach horse; better, certainly, than that of a 1918 writer, who referred to it as "an ungainly insect with a cringing attitude." Another common name is cave cricket, but this more properly refers to the pale cave-dwelling cricket cousins on another branch of the cladistic tree, the Hadenoecini. Although camel crickets are extremely common, they are not familiar to many people, for they are nocturnal insects which hide away in bunches during the daytime in caves, basements, hollow logs, under piles of rocks or boards, in burrows, or inside beehives. They come out at night to socialize and scavenge dead bugs or other things we have no use for. Entomologists call them detritivores: they tidy up the world for us.

In my college years I was acquainted with the
world authority on camel crickets, but I didn't
know it. At eighteen I was self-absorbed,
and as Mary Webb once wrote in her
lush Victorian prose, (*The Golden Arrow*,
1916), "It is the tragedy of the self-
absorbed that when the great moments
of their lives go by in royal raiment with
a sound of silver flutes, they are so
muffled in self and the present that
they neither hear nor see." I missed
the flutes and didn't see the raiment.

Theodore Huntington Hubbell died
a few years ago, just about the time
I started keeping camel crickets in the
Ozarks. He was a professor at the
University of Michigan and curator
of insects at the museum when I was
an undergraduate there. I was part of an

Ceuthophilus maculatus
(life-size)

admiring band who surrounded Marston Bates, a flamboyant professor and celebrated star of the zoology department. Some of my
courses met in the museum, and I often saw the quieter, more
modest, white-haired Dr. Hubbell in the hall and exchanged greet-
ings with him. I had heard he was a famous entomologist, but I
never had wit enough to ask what his specialty was; I am ashamed
to say the only question I ever asked him was if he and the young
man with the surname of Hubbell whom I was soon to marry
might be related. It is a testament to the kindness and graciousness
of Dr. Hubbell that he seriously discussed the matter with me and
concluded that they were not. In those days I couldn't have asked
him about camel crickets even if I had known they were his specialty, for I didn't know what a camel cricket was.

I continued in my ignorance until 1972, when I began living in
a damp Ozark cabin, remarkably cavelike, with rotting wooden
floors, home to bugs of many sorts, but especially to camel crickets. At night I would be awakened by them insouciantly jumping

across the bed, finding hop-hold on my cheek or bare arm. I determined they were camel crickets quickly enough—their appearance is so distinctive that they can be mistaken for nothing else —even though species identification is harder. But I could find out little about their biology and behavior. Were they good or bad bugs? I asked an Ozark neighbor if I should do something about all the camel crickets in my cabin. "Do?" she asked in a voice full of wonder. "Do? They don't hurt nothin'. Learn to love 'em."

It was good advice. My Ozark cabin is now a tight, trim house with good foundations and a rock floor but I still have a resident population of camel crickets; they have become the Lares and Penates of my home. In January I start seeing small ones, just a few instars old, in the bathtub in the mornings, trapped there during the night when they fell into it while they were taking a stroll across the slippery tile wall. Later I see larger ones, even during the daytime, wandering across the living-room walls or hopping across the rock floors. This morning when I changed the bed I found two camel-cricket nymphs under the mattress pad. I captured them, one in each hand, and put them in the second terrarium I have started for wild camel crickets to compare with my others, born and bred in terrarium number one. The latter are the second resident generation, grandbabies of my first captives.

Nearly every entomologist I know has an affectionate story to tell about Dr. Hubbell, who not long after my time at Michigan became director of the museum there. He inspired, cossetted, and prodded class after class of graduate students and sent them on their way better people for their contact with him. On the day I was talking to Rob Brooks about water striders at the University of Kansas, he took me in to meet George Byers, and I noticed a single portrait hanging on the retired museum director's wall. I must have looked startled when I recognized the white-haired professor of my undergraduate days, for George Byers glanced up at the picture, too. "Now *that* is the man you ought to be writing about," he said, temporarily dismissing my questions about Torre-Bueno with a wave of his hand. "The-o-dore Hunt-ing-ton

Hubbell," he said, drawing out the syllables of the name of his mentor. "Great entomologist. *Great* man. Are you related?"

In 1936, Hubbell published his five hundred and fifty-page, two-inch-thick *Monographic Revision of the Genus Ceuthophilus.* Still the standard text, the book contains descriptions based on 17,430 specimens of the commonest genus of North American camel crickets and summarizes the author's observations on their biology and behavior. But it is detailed and highly technical. When I discovered it in the Library of Congress on the day I went there to read about camel crickets, I didn't have the competency to be able to use it to figure out what species it was I had begun keeping in 1991. There were few other papers besides Hubbell's. In one of them I read: "Only an expert can make a positive identification." Washington is a city full of experts, so I turned to those at the Smithsonian.

This was how I met Dave Nickle, whom I was later to interview about katydids. He is the man at the Smithsonian to whom all questions about orthopterans, even those outside his katydid specialty, are referred. He looked at the camel cricket I had pickled to bring him. "It's a female, not yet fully grown. Females are hard to identify," he told me. "I'm not sure what species this is. But I know someone who could tell you. His name is Ted Cohn, and he was a student of Hubbell's. . . . Say, you aren't related, are you?" He paused to tell me, with a warm smile of remembrance, how Dr. Hubbell had once helped him out of an awkward situation. "Ted Cohn teaches biology at San Diego State University, but he goes back to Michigan every summer to work on Hubbell's collection there. You could send Ted some specimens. Try to capture a fully mature male for him to work with. They are identified by the sexual parts of the male. I don't have Ted's phone number, but you could probably get it from the museum at the University of Michigan."

Dave thought it was interesting that I was keeping camel crickets for observation. "I don't think anyone has ever done that before," he said. "See if you can't get some Cricket Chow to feed them. Purina makes it for people who raise crickets as fish bait. If you can't get that, they also make an all-purpose Lab Chow, and you might try the camel crickets on that. Make sure they have water, but be careful how you give it to them so they don't drown in it. Keep the sand in the bottom of their cage damp, but not wet. And, oh, yes, every now and then they might like a slice of fresh apple. Let me know how you get along with them. I don't think much is known of their life histories."

I telephoned the University of Michigan Museum of Zoology, identified myself, and asked for Ted Cohn's phone number. "Are you related to Dr. Hubbell?" the woman asked after she gave me the number. An eighteen-year-old's question was coming back to haunt me at every turn.

I called Ted Cohn. His voice sounded more of New York than it did of California. I explained who I was *not,* and he agreed to take a look at my camel crickets and also kindly promised to spend some time with me if I wanted to visit him in Ann Arbor the following summer. "Always glad to help someone named Hubbell," he said. Across the continent, linked only by a telephone line, I felt a blush spread across my face.

I waited until I could capture what I hoped was a fully mature male to send Ted as a sample, and for good measure stuck in a female too. Like most members of their order, camel crickets are easy to sex, for the females wear their egg-laying equipment, their ovipositor, where it is easy to see, outside the tail end of their body, spikily extending from it, frightening the unknowing who suspect it may be a stinger of monstrous proportions. Female camel crickets have long, curving ovipositors, and even without my reading glasses I could sex them readily, although I couldn't tell if, in their bigger instars, they were mature or not. By the time I had a pair preserved in a 70 percent alcohol solution and ready to send to Ted, I had learned something about raising them and had pages and pages and pages of observations, even though I still did not know their species names.

Cricket Chow, it turned out, was available only in 2,000-pound lots, rather more than my two dozen pets would ever need, so instead I got a fifty-pound bag of Lab Chow, which came in pellets. Even after I had pounded the pellets to powder, it was of little interest to the camel crickets, who preferred crushed kitty kibbles. But the dogs loved the pellets, and so I used Lab Chow that spring as dog treats to reward particularly good behavior, especially for Louie, whom I was training to enter the civilized world of Washington, where I was soon to take her. Now and again I would also sneak one to Tazzie, the Good Dog, to lighten her jealousy of the intruder.

The camel crickets preferred their protein in a more direct form: dead flies, spiders, moths, or even the fresh corpses of one another. Because it was easily available I settled on giving them, as a staple, bloodworms, those chironomid larvae, available, neatly packaged, in the pet shop. Camel crickets do indeed like a bit of apple now and then. Occasionally but faddishly, they also eat fish flakes, shrimp bits, peanut butter, oatmeal flakes, molasses, wheat germ, crushed cat and dog food, bananas, and pears. They will wolf down these foods for a day or two and then scorn them. Do they have different nutritional needs at different development stages? I feed and water them by using milk-bottle caps for their dishes. They refuse marshmallows, brewers' yeast, bacon, leaves, and paper. In popular handbooks they are described as greenhouse pests. This, I believe, is a calumny, at least for my species, because I have repeatedly offered them fresh greens, and except for a very occasional nibble on a lettuce leaf when their water is low, they ignore them. I have even tried planting alfalfa and bean sprouts in their terrarium; the sprouts thrived and the camel crickets treated them as furniture, not food.

The only paper I could find on the eating habits of camel crickets was published in 1944 by F. E. Whitehead and Floyd D. Miner, economic entomologists, who investigated reports of seedling crop damage in Oklahoma by *Daihina brevipes,* another species. After two years of study the authors concluded, "Serious crop damage was not observed," but, economic entomologists that they were, they went on to add darkly, "the habits of the insect indicate that it *may* [italics added] become injurious under certain conditions." Perhaps the camel crickets found in greenhouses or in fields are scavengers of dead insects.

I fitted out my terrarium with a red light so that I could watch my crickets when they are most active: at night. In 1920 William S. Blatchley, who, along with Scudder, was one of the few entomologists who made much of camel crickets before Hubbell came along, described a group he found one evening in a cave:

> They were grouped in a circle, in a space about six inches square, with their antennae pointing toward the center of the circle and appeared to be holding a conference or a camel cricket convention.

Night after night, at least while my camel crickets were not yet sexually mature, I saw livelier versions of these same circles. My conventioneers kept in constant antennal contact with one another, dreamily stroking and sliding their antennae over their immediate neighbors' antennae, as well as those of more distant circle members, delicately reaching over one another to do so. Here are my notes from April 24, 1991, at 9:30 P.M.:

> Three in semicircle, touching one anothers' antennae, stroking slowly, deliciously. No. 1 reaches across No. 2 to contact antenna of No. 3. No. 4, nearby, but not quite in group, waves antennae in background as others do. What's going on? No. 3 leaves, joins another and feeds. No. 1 and 2 stay, fondly stroking one another. No. 1 eats. No. 2 begins eating, too. Then they begin attacking each other, apparently in order to push each other away from food dish, striking out with right and left, respectively, forefeet. *Bam! Bam!* No. 1 is the bigger and actually shoves away No. 2 with foot. No. 2 backs off. All this time they have maintained constant antennal contact.

Over the months of observation I began to appreciate the capabilities of those antennae, but began to wonder if they didn't also have some kinds of sensory receptors in their long palps, the two fingerlike structures descending from their mouthparts, as well as their hinder quarters. Are their cerci, which both sexes bear, sense receptors? What about the spines that bristle from their rear legs? As they walk along, palps to the ground, their long antennae sweep ahead of them, alternately tapping and touching whatever is in the way. Stroke, stroke. One, two, one, two. Their eyesight is good enough to allow them to tell day from night and to see a moving shadow overhead that might represent danger, but they do not act as though they see much more. I wonder if the pairing of their antennal tapping may give them something equivalent to binocular vision? In social contact their antennae do not keep up the one, two, tap, tap tattoo, but stroke gently. In fact the right antenna of a stroker may be on one fellow camel cricket while his left may be on another.

A year later, on April 8, 1992, I made a note about one of the offspring of the camel crickets described above. She was perched on the stick trellis I had built inside their terrarium to add to their contentment. They like to climb, and without the trellis would attempt, with frustratingly little success, to go up the sheer glass sides of their cage:

> 3 P.M. I experiment with touching the antennae of a mature female. In response she strokes my finger with one of them and experimenting, in turn, upon the experimenter, she moves it as far up my hand as she can reach without shifting from her resting position on the trellis. She remains calm. I suppose she has identified me as uninteresting and not dangerous.

These antennae are not only tactile organs but appear to allow the camel crickets to sample the tastes and aromas of their world. If not exactly "smelling" as we understand the word, they do something that is the equivalent. Here are my notes over two days, December 10 and 11, 1991:

> 8:30 A.M. I put out peanut butter. One small nymph comes out of cave immediately, antennae vibrating toward it. Comes to it directly, starts feeding ravenously. Aroma? 7 P.M. Put in apple slice, the first in weeks. A male antennas it from cave top, comes to it rapidly, making only a slight error when he reaches peanut butter

225

feeder. When he touches apple with antennae he clambers up on to it excitedly and touches it with palps all over. He doesn't bite into it, however, but walks away.

And again on March 4, 1992:

Female comes immediately to a piece of fresh apple as soon as I put it in, her antennae beating in its direction, sensing it from afar, rushes to it, touches it all over with antennae, then palps excitedly. Eats.

Those who have dissected camel crickets write that they lack auditory organs. They certainly do ignore the snap of a finger, the tinkle of a bell shaken directly inside their terrarium, or the bark of dogs outside it. One evening when my crickets and I were paying a visit to Asher, who began his academic work with the physiology of hearing, he experimented by blowing a dog whistle, too high-pitched for humans, into their terrarium. They reacted not at all. They certainly seem to lack the ability to hear airborne sound. However, that does not mean that they cannot pick up other vibrations. They are very good at this. A tap on their terrarium or a thump on the desk on which it stands causes them to turn accurately toward the disturbance and quiver their antennae rapidly toward its source. With eerie precision they flick their antennae in the exact rhythm of repeated taps or thumps. I often wonder what they make of the vibration they receive while I am driving the thousand miles between Washington and the Ozarks. It must bother them, for they neither eat nor drink during the trip, and it always takes them a couple of days to return to normal activity after they get home.

Camel crickets' matings are preceded by an excited, tremulous vibration of their antennae toward a potential mate, the males rotating their heads this way and that to keep the process going. Since they mate end to end, his penis to her genital opening under her ovipositor, this means that during lovemaking their antennae tremble and quiver rearward over their backs. The final positioning of copulation requires legwork, with the male locating and precisely determining his mate by reaching and touching her with his spiny, spurred rear legs as he backs into her, twisting his hind parts as he goes, so that he mates her for twenty minutes or less with his abdomen rotated nearly 180 degrees. During the height of the breeding weeks the males continually back up to anything that moves past them—young, mature, male, female—soliciting copulations. When their solicitation can be preceded by some antennal niceties, the males never make the mistake of soliciting another male, but when they use only their rear legs for guidance they do so as often as they approach females.

The antennae and legs are obviously very important to camel crickets, though as they begin to age they frequently lose parts of them (and manage fairly well, at least in benign captivity). They take good care of whatever legs and antennae they have, however, by cleaning them often and thoroughly. Later Ted Cohn told me that an insect's cuticle is surprisingly fragile, and that grit can scratch through it and damage the insect. Just as daddy longlegs do with their front legs, camel crickets bow their long antennae with their palps, pulling them through their mouths like a man chewing his mustache, working along the length of them until the tip end snaps free and they pop back into place. The males also frequently bend double under themselves and groom the tips of their abdomens, often after copulation, but at other times too. I don't know whether this is strictly a cleaning process or if something else may also be happening. Healthy camel crickets spend a lot of their waking hours grooming, so I have learned to recognize the ones that will soon die because they walk about encrusted with sand and bits of litter, having lost all interest in keeping clean.

By mid-May of my first year of caged-camel-cricket watching, I began to see copulating camel crickets linked end to end, sometimes with the female dragging the male along behind her until she could pull free. But this event was a rarity; more often the females were rejecting the males who sidled or backed up to them. They would run away from the males or even kick at them with their long hind legs. I believe that the males mature before the females, because many of my females still have one more molt to make when the males begin courting them. As the days progressed there were more and more linkages, and soon the crickets were copulating more than they were eating, drinking, grooming, or resting. They copulated on their trellis, they copulated on the ground, they copulated in the cave I'd made for their comfort and on it, they copulated hanging upside down from the screenwire ceiling of the terrarium. The males ceased hopping and began to pursue the females, striding heavily, ponderously, their abdomens dragging on the ground, important and weighty.

One day I received a telephone call from Ted Cohn, who sounded excited. He had identified the pair of camel crickets I had sent him as *Ceuthophilus seclusus,* a common enough species, but the male of the pair had an unusual anomaly that might be a clue to a puzzle that even Dr. Hubbell had not been able to solve during his lifetime. Later he gave me a copy of a paper Dr. Hubbell had presented in 1984 at a symposium on insect behavioral ecology, so I can present readers with the puzzle in his own words. He was eighty-seven at the time and the title of his paper was "Unfinished Business and Beckoning Problems." In it he outlined a number of questions for future research, and ended by saying:

> I shall conclude by describing [a] problem among the camel crickets (the group Theodore Cohn and I are currently studying)— [a] problem that can only be solved by behavioral studies. [It] involves the presence in a single species of two kinds of males—major and minor—that differ strikingly in body conformation but not at all in genitalic structure. . . . [Among] *Ceuthophilus seclusus* [which] I described in 1936 . . . in every collection from a sizable area centering on the Ozarks every male is a major with a pronotum [The pronotum is that scale of armor just below an insect's head that covers what we would like to call the neck but we musn't. Its name is prothorax, the first segment of the thorax] that is strongly elevated and deformed; such a modification occurs in no other species of the genus. Outside that area, forming a complete ring around it and extending into Arkansas, westernmost Indiana, Illinois, Iowa, eastern Nebraska, Kansas and Oklahoma, is a zone in which the male pronotum is entirely ordinary. Only in a few specimens from

the northern part of that zone does a hint of the modification occur. Furthermore, the constricted neck of the pronotal elevation has been traumatically destroyed in a high percentage of the major males seen—almost surely by the jaws of the female during or prior to mating. Can it be that there is an abrupt behavioral change at the edge of the area where only major males occur? How could there be a behavioral cline [a degree of change] when the structure involved is either present or absent? Is the major morphotype so successful that where it is present only majors can secure mates, and is it consequently spreading into peripheral territory at the expense of minors? And how do provincial females acquire their taste for the pronotal juices or pheromones or whatever it is that the sophisticated major males provide? Questions such as these can only be answered by observation, but I find behavioral observations frustrating. Last year I watched a female and major male *seclusus* in dim light for several hours, and then suddenly it was all over; they were in copula, apparently with no more preliminaries than a nudge or two by the male, and the female did not even give him a nibble.

The reason Ted was excited was that the pair of camel crickets I had sent him were from the precise region Hubbell had described in his paper. The male had an indented pronotum, but it was not bitten through. Ted had received others collected in this same area, but all had bitten and damaged pronota. Mine, collected on May 20, was the earliest he had ever received, and the female, though big, was not yet mature. "The theory is," he explained, "that perhaps the females, as part of courtship or mating, climb up on top of the males and bite through the pronotum, but we don't know for sure, and except for that one brief glimpse by Hub, no one has ever seen them mate. Have you?"

I felt like a gossip at a ladies' lunch. "Well, let me tell you!" I began, and launched into a colorful description of what I had been seeing over the past weeks.

"Fascinating! Just fascinating!" Ted exclaimed, but was disappointed that I had not seen females bite into the males' pronota. "Well, how in the world do they get damaged, then?" he wondered.

Among, for example, cockroaches and tree crickets, the males have a special gland, often on their backs, that secretes a substance attractive to females, who mount them and bite into it or drink of it before they are willing to mate. In more than a year of camel-cricket watching, however, I have yet to see a female bite a male pronotum, although several times I have seen them climb onto a male's back. Just before they are ready to mate, the males show the notch in the pronotum, at the head of which is an orange bulb, bulging and full. After they begin mating the bulb decreases in size and darkens. Some of my male camel crickets have damaged pronota after mating begins, but some do not. The males with damaged pronota continue to copulate, and by the end of the mating period the orange bulb can no longer be seen on any of their pronota. It is all very puzzling. I wonder whether the gland, if that is what it is, does not simply rupture from the wear and tear of life when it does so.

Here are my notes from March 5, 1992, at 7:30 P.M. The camel crickets I am watching are from the first ones to be raised entirely in captivity, offspring of the first batch I had captured the year before:

Big female trying repeatedly to mount the back of mature male with bulging pronotal gland. But, like a bronco, he bucks her off. However, he does try to back into her for a copulation. She'll have none of *that,* despite his wildly backward-beating antennae and the stylish, lusty twisting of his head. An hour of this and no copulation. Much cleaning of antennae in pauses.

The puzzle is compounded, Ted told me on the phone, by the fact that from a mere twenty-five miles to the south of my farm he receives specimens from a collector in the county seat there which are of the same species, *C. seclusus,* but the males have a smooth pronotum, and it is never broken. I asked Ted if he thought that females would mate with both males with smooth and indented pronota. "I don't know," he replied, and then added, "Maybe you could find out. You could cage a virgin female with both modified and unmodified males and watch to see what happens." He launched into a detailed proposal with me for the collection of camel crickets at a point halfway between my farm and the county seat, then halving the distance until I came to the place where the two kinds of males intergraded. And wouldn't I like to set up some metal barriers around a wild area and conduct a census study within it in order to estimate the population density? What about a nice capture, mark, and release study? I was due to leave the Ozarks for Washington soon and couldn't do most of the work he suggested, but I told Ted that I had friends with badly underemployed ten-year-olds in the area between my farm and the county seat, and that the following spring I would hire them to collect specimens.

Even though I may not have any serious research to report of the sort Ted would like, I have over the course of a year and three camel-cricket generations learned something about the ones in my terrarium. Each observation, however, has raised more questions than it answers, so the sum of my watching has caused me to grow in ignorance, not knowledge. None of what I have discovered has been published before, so it may be useful to record it here.

Camel crickets hatch out of pearly, oblong eggs, approximately ⅛ of an inch in length, laid by their mothers at least six weeks earlier. Here are my notes, taken over several days, from my original captive population:

30 August, 1991. Blessed event in P.M. Babies! Babies! At least six, several of whom have already made first molt. Look like miniatures. But a couple have just emerged, little bitties, scarcely bigger than one of their own eggs, white, tender, fragile, with long whisking antennae several times their own length. Scamper about. Come from an area where I once saw a female ovipositing, i.e., just west of the water dish.

31 August. 9 A.M. See a couple of first molters scampering around stick trellis, over rocks. The four adult males, the sole survivors of their generation, pay them no attention whatsoever. N.B. Since the last mature female died on 22 July and the last time I saw her oviposit was 18 July, it has to take about six weeks at a minimum for eggs to hatch.

3 September. 8:45 A.M. Snowy white tiniest of nymphs just emerged from sand back behind water dish and scampered for cover. 9:30 P.M. Watch all with hand lens. A nymph which has at least one molt is clearly visible on log. Sits there dreamily waving antennae one to one side, one to the other, in an uncoordinated way. Appears to have a tiny ovipositor.

A few hours after hatching or molting, the nymphs harden and darken—entomologists call the process tanning—and begin to show the characteristic splotchy markings and herringboned hind legs. In the benign terrarium environment they grow rapidly by molting. Dr. Hubbell's opinion was that there are probably seven or eight molts before adulthood. This seems right, although individuals would have to be marked in order to count the instars with exactitude. They like to find a high place in which to molt, a terrarium corner four inches off the ground or a trellis branch. When ready to molt, they hang upside down, gripping with their claws; their back splits open and the new, bigger camel cricket emerges and eats his shed former self.

It is only the middle-sized nymphs, several instars old, that are sociable, grouping together and stroking one another, though at all stages they sometimes bundle and huddle together during periods when they are inactive, or "sleeping." I keep them in each of my offices, the one in Washington and the one in the Ozarks, rooms without much natural light, and turn on the electric lights, for my convenience, not theirs, so I may have thrown off their natural diurnal rhythms; to some degree their behavior still mirrors the activity of the wild camel crickets in my Ozark house. Through their earlier instars they are seclusive and hide. Later they grow bolder and walk about in the light, but usually, during the very early morning, both young and old are somnolent and limp, antennae drooping on the ground in a state that is hard not to think of as sleep. (In 1988, W. Kaiser, in a study of bee "sleep," tested honeybees in a similar state and described its characteristics: increase of reaction time, relaxation of muscles, lessening of body activity, drop of body temperature to ambient, wilting of antennae. The similarity to my dozing camel crickets is striking.)

In my captive populations, mature males and females mate repeatedly over a six-week period, and during the latter part of it, as well as long afterward, the females lay eggs. How long, I wonder, does a given female take before she is ready to lay her eggs, and what is it that readies her? Some of the adults live well after some of the youngsters have begun to hatch out, which explains the mixture of nymphs and adults found in the wild. The females lay their eggs separately in the sand, although I saw one female who dribbled eggs on the surface of it on top of the cave, exposed everywhere, and these were promptly eaten by her fellows except for the few that I sneaked out, pickled, and sent to Ted Cohn. Although the eggs are laid singly, an ovipositing female—at least those in the terrarium—often picks as a promising spot one in which she has laid an egg before, so that clusters of eggs may be found together. Oviposition takes one to three minutes, with some ceremonial niceties beforehand to prepare the site, and afterward to cover it.

Here are my notes for July 18, 1991, beginning at 2 P.M.:

Writing check at desk and look up idly to watch big female nibbling on an oatmeal flake. She drops it after pausing contemplatively, and moves back to center front stage and begins probing sand with her ovipositor. Digs with her front two legs, scoots over hole made, and augers down her ovipositor, rotating it until it's fully down, twitching her abdomen as she does so. A great stillness then comes over her; her abdomen throbs. She rotates her ovipositor back out and uses it to tamp down sand over spot where it has been. Scrapes sand backward over it with front legs, using scraped spot to repeat oviposition. This brings her to feed dish. Nibble, nibble on Lab Chow. Other female comes up and they touch antennae. The ovipositing female acts disgusted, horrified. Ack! Withdraws hurriedly, moves on, starts to make another hole. Male starts butting her with his abdomen. She kicks him away . . . [She lays several more eggs as before] oviposits, but male interrupts her before she is able to tamp down sand. He is quite aggressive and in process

233

flips her over on her back. She climbs log to escape. Males all around frenziedly interested in her. Other female now crawls on top of male (but does not bite pronotum). Ovipositing female tries to drill hole in log but is unsuccessful. . . . She returns to sand and continues ovipositing, sometimes successfully, sometimes interrupted by males. Male copulates with other female. I try to time them, but after four minutes a telephone call interrupts. By 4 P.M., when I am able to look again, all is quiet. Female who laid eggs is "asleep" on screen ceiling. At 8 P.M. she copulates again, but briefly, and pulls away from male.

This egg-laying is hungry work. Once I watched a female who had been diligently fending off excited males and laying eggs for half an hour. Experimentally I dropped a dead fly just in front of her and she fell on it, devoured it greedily, and then resumed ovipositing.

Late in the summer of 1991 I drove to Ann Arbor for my appointment with Ted Cohn. He is a dark-haired man with an expressive face and a buoyant, enthusiastic manner. He is full of affectionate stories about Dr. Hubbell and is zestful about the systematics of camel crickets. His office contains a fraction of the museum's total collection, but nevertheless seems to overflow with small jars of camel crickets in preserving fluid. I hand him a dessicated but well-preserved camel cricket I had found in the bottom of a pressure canner in our basement in Washington. It looked very similar to my Ozark pets, but I assumed they were not the same. They were not. Ted grimaces and with a mock groan says, "Another *Tachycines asynamorus!!* It's an Oriental exotic, originally found in this country in the Southeast in greenhouses, where it came in on plant imports. It's widely distributed now." He rolls his eyes. "I get student-collected specimens from Arkansas and they contain too many of these."

Camel crickets, Ted tells me, are common throughout the temperate zones of North and South America, but are surprisingly rare in Europe, where they are represented by two genera found only in the southern part of the continent. In addition, there are tropical species that are bigger and heavier-bodied than our North

American ones. In this country camel crickets are to be found coast to coast, even in dry country.

Ted pauses to show me some pale white specimens adapted to living undetected in the shimmering desert sands of the Southwest. There are, he says, about 200 species in the United States, only half of which have been described. Those in the genus *Ceutophilus* are the commonest. He has spread out some specimens to show me under the microscope, *seclusus* males with pronota smooth, *seclusus* males with pronota deformed and ripped; he shows me their pseudosternites, structures next to their phalluses. Their use is unknown, but since they vary from species to species, they are diagnostic for identifying a specimen. Indeed, the genitalia vary completely from species to species, as he proves to me by putting one set after another under the microscope.

Over lunch at a nearby Korean restaurant I ask Ted how he got interested in entomology. "Oh, I always have been," he says with a smile. "My earliest memory of myself is as a toddler trying to dissect a camel cricket with a clothespin at my grandmother's house in the Poconos."

Back in his office Ted places in my hand a fine gift, a copy of Dr. Hubbell's *Monographic Revision of the Genus Ceuthophilus,* from the first and only printing of 1,000 copies.

Early in September, proud as any grandparent, I wrote Ted about the hatch of young camel crickets. He replied:

> Congratulations, congratulations. Now, do you think you can find it in your heart to pickle a few of the youngsters for me of both stages? These will be unquestionably *seclusus* and it will be very useful to have authentic specimens of a very early stage well enough preserved so that we can determine how early the distinctiveness of the color pattern is established—something we have never been able to do. Please also record the numbers and the day on which you think they molted into the next instar.

I went over to the terrarium and looked at my thirteen newly hatched camel crickets, young, but already the survivors of a number of perils. While they were still in the egg there had been an infestation in the terrarium of *Macrocheles rodriguezi,* a mite kindly identified for me by G.W. Krantz, the world authority on this genus. Although they prey upon small arthropods, he wrote me, he thought it unlikely that they could get a grip on camel-cricket eggs, so I stopped worrying about them. More serious, however, was a growing population of pretty little moths with orange-splotched wings. I had furnished the terrarium with what was attractive to me and I hoped would be to camel crickets: a bit of moss, the stick trellis, a cave made of small rocks, and a spongy fragment of decaying log with a tendency to grow toadstools. Perhaps the moth eggs of what Asher identified for me as *Pyralis farinalis,* the common meal moth, were in some of those pieces of furniture I had brought in from outdoors. During midsummer these moths fluttered about in the terrarium, but I did not know then who they were or what they were capable of doing. Obviously they mated, and their larvae burrowed into the sand. In food-storage bins, where they often become a pest, Asher told me, they spin tubular webs and feed from the open end. They spun these same webs in the terrarium, runnels in the sand, and ate from the camel-cricket feeding dishes. They preferred the bloodworms and fish flakes to meal-based food, so I feared they were also gobbling down the camel-cricket eggs buried in the sand. Was this happening? I tried picking the moths out with tweezers, but, closed off from natural predators in the protected world of the terrarium, they became too many. Eventually I discarded all the sand in the terrarium and built a new one with fresh sand and a new trellis. I washed the stones before remaking the cave and admitted to myself that the moss and rotting log had been there only for my aesthetic pleasure, not the camel crickets' need, so I left them out. Then I painstakingly set about catching the now quarter-inch camel cricket babies, hoping that I would not break a fragile leg or antenna in the process, and transferred them to their new quarters.

Hence when Ted Cohn's letter arrived, it took very little time to conclude that I would disappoint him. I couldn't sacrifice a single one of them. And a good thing, too. Despite the fact that these were a late-summer hatch and that outdoors the days were shortening and cooling, my terrrarium youngsters were living in an artificially warm and light environment, with plenty of food. Probably their wild kind were slowing down their growth and would overwinter as small nymphs, but my captives grew rapidly and one of them treated me to as good a Christmas present as I have ever had. Here are my notes for December 25, 1991, beginning at 9 A.M.:

Big female in spectacular molt, perhaps her final one. I find her hanging translucent white upside down from her previous cuticle, attached to the very end of the highest peak of the trellis. Only the tips of her abdomen and antennae hold her inside it. Antennae bowed severely in front of her. Arne takes photo of this and next several stages. She is quiet. Moves her mouth a little. Her legs are tightly bent against body. *9:40:* Kicking a little with rear legs and tugs on antennae which gives a wider loop of antennae and allows her back to curve more toward trellis. Front leg touching (grasping?) old front leg of cuticle for balance. Struggles, gets one antenna out. Struggles more. Releases abdomen tip. Holding on by legs to old cuticle. All free, even last antenna. Grapples for tarsi hold. Wiggles cerci. *9:45:* Now clinging partly to trellis, partly to shed exoskeleton. *9:50:* She rearranges herself to cling more to stick, encircling and appearing to hug shed cuticle to her in process. Other camel crickets are quite active, and the mature male with notched pronotum has particularly active antennae. *10 A.M.:* She is noticeably darker, more marked. Rear leg herringbone pattern quite apparent now; black splotches, too. This curving and grasping at stick of trellis brings her mouth into position to commence eating her shed cuticle. *10:15:* Palps on cuticle, eating. *10:25:* ovipositor now brown. *10:30:* raises and lowers ovipositor, wiggles cerci. *10:40:* mature male climbs up trellis, backs up to her in mating position, his antennae all achatter, touches her front leg with his cerci. She pulls back, clutching her shed cuticle to her, mouth and palps pressed into it. He flutters his antennae backward over his body at her, adjusts his posture to keep touching her front tarsus with his cerci. They become quiet. She wiggles her antennae toward him. *10:50:* she's pulled herself right side up to top end of trellis, rotated 180 degrees so that her ovipositor now points toward rear of male, but she still clutches her shed cuticle and is still eating it. He acts excited. Both flutter their antennae. He jabs his abdomen at her. She kicks him, fusses with her palps at old cuticle. Male now has his abdomen under her, shoving. She drops from trellis to ground, still holding old cuticle and drags it away, eating rapidly. He, palps moving frantically, antennae vibrating, descends, appears to search for her. He finds her outside at back of cave and backs up to her in mating position. Her antennae quiver also, even though she is eating voraciously. *11:10:* Antennae quivering, he clings to rock next to her with his abdomen as near as she will tolerate it. She is nearly finished eating old cuticle. Looks much darker now, but still light around edges, and her antennae are still white. Vibrating, they touch his. *11:15:* Old cuticle all gone. She cleans her palps, rotating her head to do so. *11:20:* She turns around, tries to move, but he has one rear leg over her that blocks her way. She struggles, pulls up and away on cave top. *11:30:* She walks, circles cave, comes back, and finds head bit and antennae of old cuticle. Eats these. *11:45:* He pursues her unrelentingly. She keeps escaping but stays in antennal contact. *12 noon:* She eats banana. Her suitor stomps,

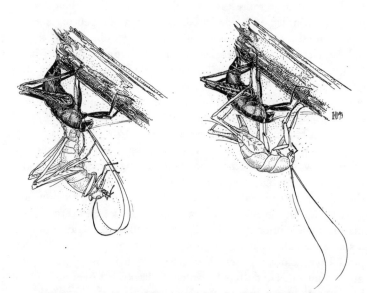

Christmas morning. A female camel cricket in molt. Note that her antennae are still caught by their tips in old cuticle in the left-hand drawing. In the drawing on the right, they are free, and she is nearly out of her cast cuticle, which can be seen, still clinging to the trellis, close to her hind legs.

overturns a crippled camel cricket. Searches for her. Stomps another nymph. We have to leave to pay a Christmas call. *1:10 P.M.:* His pronotum still intact. *10 P.M.:* Pronotum undamaged. He wanders around restlessly. All others, including this morning's star, are in cave, tucked up together.

It is springtime once again. Most of the ten-year-olds I have employed to capture and pickle camel crickets in the area between my farm and the county seat have proved to be too tender-hearted to kill them, except for one, who has already furnished me a jarful of specimens that I have sent to Ted Cohn. My second generation have produced a third, proving that at least under favorable conditions these insects can be double-brooded. A male and female of the second generation still hop about among the newcomers, who are too lively for me to count. I am suspicious of the mature male and female, however, and wonder if perhaps they are gobbling up the youngsters when the latter molt, for the only ones I see are of the smallest size, though the first began hatching out weeks ago. Are my suspicions justified, or is the third generation suffering from a decline in vitality because of captivity? I will raise and nurture as many of their descendents as I can.

Nearby, on my other desk, I have started a new terrarium, a bigger one that will give them more scope, and filled it with thirty-six wild camel crickets scooped up, mostly, from the bathtub. From these I have isolated a big female in a fish bowl and a big male in a cookie jar and will watch them until their final molts. That way I will know for sure that they are virgins. However, I have noticed that singly, they have succumbed to sloth and despondency. Both spend their time with their heads buried in a corner. Without the companionship of their fellows, will their behavior and biology be affected? Will it alter their attempts to mate when they are mature? I have telephoned my friend Nancy over at the county seat and asked her to collect a jarful of camel crickets from her pump house. These should be, according to Ted Cohn's theory, of the unmodified pronotal type. Once I have them, I will present one of the males to my isolated female. Will she prefer him to the home male, with his modified pronotum, now living in the cookie jar? And if she mates with one, the other, or both, what kind of offspring will she have?

In another week I must pack up my various terraria, jars, and bowls and drive back to Washington. I expect camel crickets will be my companions for years to come.

Bibliography

Introduction: General Reading

Barth, Friedrich G. 1985. *Insects and Flowers: The Biology of a Partnership.* Princeton University Press.

Borror, Donald J., and Richard E. White. 1970 *A Field Guide to the Insects.* Boston. Houghton-Mifflin.

Davies, R. G. 1988. *Outlines of Entomology.* London. Chapman & Hall.

Milne, Lorus, and Margery Milne. 1980. *The Audubon Society Field Guide to North American Insects and Spiders.* New York. Knopf.

Richard, O. W., and R. G. Davies. 1977. *Imms' General Textbook of Entomology.* Vol. I & II. London. Chapman & Hall.

The Torre-Bueno Glossary of Entomology. 1989. Compiled by Stephen W. Nichols and edited by Randall T. Schuh. New York Entomological Society.

Chapter I   ORDER LEPIDOPTERA: Butterflies

Douglas, Matthew M. 1986. *The Lives of Butterflies.* University of Michigan Press.

Klots, Alexander B. 1979. *Field Guide to the Butterflies in North America East of the Great Plains.* Boston. Houghton-Mifflin.

Opler, Paul A., and George O. Krizek. 1984. *Butterflies East of the Great Plains.* Baltimore. Johns Hopkins Press.

Pyle, Robert. 1981. *The Audubon Society Field Guide to North American Butterflies*. New York. Knopf.

―――. 1984. *The Audubon Society Handbook for Butterfly Watchers*. New York. Scribners.

Scott, James A. 1986. *The Butterflies of North America*. Stanford Univ. Press.

Stokes, Donald, Lillian Stokes, and Ernest Williams, 1991. *The Butterfly Book*. Boston. Little Brown.

Tilden, James W., and Arthur Clayton Smith. 1986. *A Field Guide to Western Butterflies*. Boston. Houghton-Mifflin.

The butterfly count is sponsored by the Xerces Society. Its address is 10 West Ash Street, Portland, Oregon 97204

Chapter II   ORDER DIPTERA: Midges and Gnats

Curran, Charles H. 1965. *Families and Genera of North American Diptera*. Woodhaven, N.Y. Henry Tripp.

Johannsen, O. A. 1909. *The Mycetophilidae of North America*. Maine Agricultural Experiment Station Bulletin No. 172.

Needham, James G., et al. 1905. *Mayflies and Midges of New York*. Albany. New York State Education Department, N.Y. *State Museum Bulletin No. 343*.

Oldroyd, Harold. 1964. *The Natural History of Flies*. New York. Norton.

Chapter III   ORDER COLEOPTERA: Ladybugs

Blatchley, W. S. 1910. *On the Coleoptera Known to Occur in Indiana*. Indianapolis. Buford.

Crowson, R. A. 1981. *The Biology of the Coleoptera*. New York. Academic.

Evans, Glyn. 1975. *Life of Beetles*. London. Allen & Unwin.

Hagen, Kenneth S. 1954. "The significance of predaceous Coccinellidae in biological and integrated control of insects." In *Entomophaga (Mem. H.S.)*, No. 7.

―――. 1962. "Biology and ecology of predaceous Coccinellidae." In *Annual Review of Entomology*, Vol. 7.

―――. 1970. "Following the ladybug home." In *National Geographic*, April 1970.

Hodek, Ivo. 1973. *Biology of Coccinellidae*. Prague. Academia.

Lawrence, John F., and Alfred F. Newton, Jr. 1982. "Evolution and classification of beetles." In *Annual Review of Ecology and Systematics,* Vol. 13.

Reither, Ewald. 1961. *Beetles*. London. Hamlyn.

Rùžička, Zdenek, and Kenneth S. Hagen. 1985. "Impact of parasitism on migratory flight performance in females of *Hippodamia convergens.*" In *Acta. Ent. Bohem.,* Vol. 82.

―――. 1986. "Influence of *Perilitus coccinelliae* on the flight performance of overwintered *Hippodamia convergens.*" In *Ecology of Aphidiophaga,* ed. by I. Hodek. Prague. Academia.

Sasaji, Hiroyuki. 1971. *Coccinellidae*. Tokyo. Academic Press of Japan.

White, Richard E. 1983. *Field Guide to the Beetles of North America*. Boston. Houghton-Mifflin.

Chapter IV ORDER OPILIONES: Daddy Longlegs

Bishop, Sherman C. 1949. "The Phalangida (Opiliones) of New York." In *Rochester Academy of Sciences Proceedings,* Vol. 9, No. 3.

―――. 1950. "Life of a harvestman." In *Nature,* Vol. 48, No. 5.

Blum, Murray S., and Arlan Edgar. 1971. "4-Methyl-3-Hepatone: identification and role in Opilonid exocrine secretions." In *Insect Biochemistry,* Vol. I, No. 2.

Bristowe, W. S. 1949. "The distribution of harvestmen in Great Britain and Ireland with notes on their names, enemies, and food." In *Journal of Animal Ecology,* Vol. 18.

Cloudsley-Thompson, J. L. 1958. "Harvest-spiders." In *Spiders, Scorpions, Centipedes and Mites*. N.Y. Pergamon.

Cokendolpher, James C., and Jean E. Cokendolpher. 1982. "Re-examination of the tertiary harvestmen from the Florissant formation, Colorado." In *Journal of Paleontology,* Vol. 56, No. 5.

―――, and Dolly Lanfranco. 1985. "Opiliones from the Cape Horn archipelago." In *Journal of Arachnology,* Vol. 13, No. 3.

Edgar, Arlan, L. 1963. "Proprioception in the legs of Phalangids." In *Biological Bulletin,* Vol. 124, No. 3.

―――. 1966. "Phalangida of the Great Lakes region." In *American Midland Naturalist,* Vol. 75, No. 2.

———. 1971. "Studies on the biology and ecology of Michigan *Phalangida (Opiliones)*." *University of Michigan Museum of Zoology Miscellaneous Publication No. 144.*

Eisner, Thomas, et al. 1971. "Defense of Phalangid: liquid repellent administered by leg dabbing." In *Science,* Vol. 173.

Ekpa, O., et al. 1984. "N, N-Dimethyl-β-Phenylethylamine and Bornyl esters from the harvestman *Sclerobunus robustus*." In *Tetrahedron Letters,* Vol. 25, No. 13.

Hooke, Robert. 1665. "Observation XLVII: of the shepherd spider or the long legg'd spider." In *Micrographia.* 1961 reprint. Codicote, Herts., England. Wheldon, Westfield & Hafner.

Jennings, Daniel T., et al. 1984. "Phalangids associated with strip clearcut and dense spruce-fir forests of Maine." In *Environmental Entomology,* Vol. 13.

Kaestner, Alfred. 1980. *Arachnids and Myriapods,* Vol. II of *Invertebrate Zoology.* Huntington, N.Y. Robert E. Krierger Pub. Co.

Klee, George E., and James W. Butcher. 1968. "Laboratory rearing of *Phalangium opilio*." In *Michigan Entomologist,* Vol. I, No. 8.

Meade, R.H. 1855. "Monograph on the British species of *Phalangiidae* or Harvest-men." In *The Annals and Magazine of Natural History,* Vol. 15, No. 90.

Sankey, John. 1956. "How to begin the study of harvest spiders." In *Countryside,* Vol. XVII, No. 9.

Savory, Theodore. 1962. "Daddy longlegs." In *Scientific American,* Vol. 107.

———. 1974. *Introduction to Arachnology.* London. Frederick Muller.

———. 1977. *Arachnida.* London. Academic.

Schroeter, Wolfgang C. 1977. "Behavioral aspects of southwest Michigan Opilonids." Kalamazoo, Michigan. Western Michigan University thesis, unpublished.

Tulk, Alfred. 1843. "Upon the anatomy of *Phalangium opilio*." In *The Annals and Magazine of Natural History,* Vol. 12, No. 76.

Chapter V ORDER DIPTERA: Black Flies

Crosskey, Roger W. 1990. *The Natural History of Blackflies.* Chichester. John Wiley.

Gibbs, K. Elizabeth. 1986. "Experimental applications of B.t.i. for larval black fly control: persistence and downstream carry, efficacy, impact on non-target invertebrates and fish feeding." *Maine Agricultural Experiment Station Technical Bulletin 123.*

―――. 1988. "Experimental stream applications of B.t.i. for human nuisance black fly management in a recreational area." *Maine Agricultural Experiment Station Technical Bulletin 133.*

Kim, Ke Chung, and Richard W. Merritt. 1987. *Black Flies, Ecology, Population Management and Annotated World List.* University Park, Penna. Pennsylvania State University.

Merritt, Richard W. 1989. "A broad evaluation of B.t.i. for black fly control in a Michigan river: efficacy, carry, and non-target effects on invertebrates and fish." In *Journal of the American Mosquito Control Association,* Vol. 5, No. 3.

―――. 1991. "Changes in feeding habits of selected nontarget aquatic insects in response to live and *Bacillus thuringensis* var. *israelensis* de barjac-killed black fly larvae." In *Canadian Entomologist,* Vol. 123.

Molloy, Daniel P. 1990. "Are black flies a critically important element in the food web of a trout stream?" *New York State Museum Circular 54.*

―――, editor. 1981. "The biological control of black flies," conference held at Morgantown, West Virginia, on April 16–17.

Reiling, Stephen D., et al. 1988. "The economic benefits of late-season black fly control." *Maine Agricultural Experiment Station Technical Bulletin 822.*

Chapter VI ORDER HYMENOPTERA: Bravo Bees

The change in attitudes toward bravo bees is best documented in the twenty-five years of reporting in *The American Bee Journal.*

Current research is summarized in *The "African" Honey Bee,* ed. by Marla Spivak, David J. C. Flecther and Michael D. Breed. 1991. Boulder, San Francisco, Oxford. Westview Press.

Chapter VII: ORDER HEMIPTERA: Water Striders

Andersen, Nils Møller, and John T. Polhemus. 1976. "Water striders." In *Marine Insects,* edited by Lanna Cheng. New York. Elsevier.

Cheng, Lanna. 1966. "Studies on the biology of the Gerridae," Part I & II. In *Entomologists' Monthly Magazine,* Vol. 102.

———. 1985. "Biology of *Halobates*." In *Annual Review of Entomology*, Vol. 30.

———. 1989. "Factors limiting the distribution of *Halobates* species." In *Reproduction, Genetics and Distribution of Marine Organisms*, edited by John S. Ryland and Paul A. Tyler. Fredensborg, Denmark. Olsen & Olsen.

———, and C. H. Fernando. 1980. "The water striders of Ontario." *Royal Ontario Museum of Life Sciences Miscellaneous Publication.*

———, and John Wormuth. 1992. "Are there separate populations of *Halobates* in the Gulf of Mexico?" In *Bulletin of Marine Science*, Vol. 50, No. 3.

———, Martien A. Baars and Swier S. Oosterhuis. 1990. *"Halobates* in the Banda Sea." In *Bulletin of Marine Science*, Vol. 47, No. 2.

Foster, W. A., and J. E. Treherne. 1980. "Feeding, predation and aggregation behavior in a marine insect." In Royal Society *Proceedings* B, Vol. 209.

———. 1981. "Evidence for the dilution effect in the selfish herd from fish predation on a marine insect." In *Nature*, Vol. 293.

———. 1982. "Reproductive behaviour of the ocean skater." In *Oecologia* (Berl.), Vol. 55.

Hungerford, H. B. 1919. "The biology and ecology of aquatic and semiaquatic Hemiptera." *Kansas University Science Bulletin*, Vol. XI.

———, and Ryuichi Matsuda. 1960. "Keys to subfamilies, tribes, genera and subgenera of the *Gerridae* of the world." *Kansas University Science Bulletin*, Vol. XLI.

Järvinen, Olli, and Kari Vepsäläinen. 1976. "Wing dimorphism as an adaptive strategy in water striders." In *Hereditas*, Vol. 84.

McCafferty, W. Patrick, and Arwin V. Provonsha. 1981. *Aquatic Entomology*. Boston. Jones & Partlett.

Spencè, J. R., et al. 1980. "The effects of temperature on growth and development of water strider species." In *Canadian Journal of Zoology*, Vol. 58, No. 10.

Torre-Bueno, J. R. de la. 1917. "Life-history and habits of the larger water strider, *Gerris remigis* Say (Hem.)" In *Entomological News*, Vol. xxviii.

Treherne, J. E., and W. A. Foster. 1981. "Group transmission of predator avoidance behavior in a marine insect: the Trafalgar Effect." In *Animal Behaviour*, Vol. 29.

————. 1982. "Group size and anti-predator strategies in a marine insect." In *Animal Behaviour*, Vol. 32.

Wilcox, R. Stimson. 1972. "Communication by surface waves." In *Journal of Comparative Physiology*, Vol. 80.

Chapter VIII   ORDER THYSANURA: Silverfish

Angier, Natalie. July 24, 1990. "Nature switches roles for the mating game." New York. *The New York Times*.

Avebury, John Lubbock, Baron. 1873. *Monograph of the Collembola and Thysanura*. London. The Ray Society.

Boudreaux, H. Bruce. 1979. *Arthropod Phylogeny*. New York. Wiley.

Carpenter, Frank M. 1976. "Geological history and evolution of the insects." In Proceedings of the XV International Congress of Entomology, Washington, D.C.

Cornwall, J. W. 1915. "*Lepisma saccharina*, its life history and anatomy and its gregarine parasites." In the *Indian Journal of Medical Research*, Vol. 3, No. 1.

Delany, M. J. 1957. "Life histories in the Thysanura." In *Acta Zoologica Cracoviensia*, Tom II, Nr. 3.

Labandeira, Conrad C., et al. "Early insect diversification: evidence from a Lower Devonian bristletail from Quebec." In *Science*, Vol. 242.

Lindsay, Eder. 1940. "The biology of silverfish." In Proceedings of the Royal Society of Victoria, Vol. LII (New Series), Part I.

Morita, Helene. 1926. "Some observations on the silverfish, *Lepisma saccharina*. In Proceedings of the Hawaiian Entomological Society, Vol. VI, No. 2.

Packard, A. S. 1873. *Synopsis of the Thysanura of Essex County, Mass.* Salem. Peabody Academy of Science.

Rolfe, W. D. I. 1985. "Early terrestrial arthropods: a fragmentary record." In the Philosophic Transactions of the Royal Society of London. B309.

Slifer, Eleanor, and Sant S. Sekhon. 1970. "Sense organs of a Thysanuran, *Ctenolepisma lineata pilferata*, with special reference to those on the antennal flagellum (Thysanura, Lepismatidae)." In *Journal of Morphology*, Vol. 132, No. 1.

Sturm, Von H. 1956. "Die Paarung beim Silberfischen, *Lepisma saccharina.*" In *Zeitschrift für Tierpsychologie,* Band 13, Heft 1.

U.S. Department of Agriculture. 1939. *Silverfish.* Washington, D.C.

Wygodzinsky, Pedro. 1961. "On a surviving representative of the Lepidotrichidae (Thysanura). In *Annals of the Entomological Society of America,* Vol. 54, No. 5.

Chapter IX   ORDER ORTHOPTERA: Katydids

Alexander, Richard D. 1967. *Singing Insects: four case histories in the study of animal species.* Chicago. Rand McNally.

Allard, H. A. 1928. "Remarkable musical technique of the larger angular-winged katydid." In *Science,* Vol. LXVII.

Bailey, Winston J. 1991. *Acoustic Behaviour of Insects: an evolutionary perspective.* London. Chapman and Hall.

Bell, Paul D. 1981. "Transmission of vibrations along plant stems: implications for insect communication." New York Entomological Society, LXXXVIII(3):1980.

Belwood, Jaqueline J., and Glen K. Morris. 1987. "Bat predation and its influence on calling behavior in neotropical katydids." In *Science,* Vol. 238.

Blatchley, W. S. 1920. *Orthoptera of Northeastern America.* Indianapolis. The Nature Publishing Company.

Fulton, B. B. 1933. "Stridulating organs of female Tettigoniidae." In *Entomological News,* Vol. xliv.

Grove, Davison Greenawalt. 1959. *The Natural History of the Angular-Winged Katydid.* Ithaca. Cornell University Ph.D. thesis, unpublished.

Gwynne, D. T. 1988. "Courtship feeding in katydids benefits the mating male's offspring." In *Behavioral Ecology and Sociobiology,* Vol. 23.

Iseley, F. B. 1941. "Researches concerning Texas Tettigoniidae." In *Ecological Monographs,* Vol. II, No. 4.

Morris, Glen K., and James H. Fullard. 1983. "Random noise and congeneric discrimination in *Conocephalus.*" In *Orthopteran Mating Systems,* edited by Darryl T. Gwynne and Glen K. Morris. Boulder, Colorado. Westview Press.

————, Dita E. Klimas, and David A. Nickle. 1989. "Acoustic signals and systematics of false-leaf katydids from Ecuador." In *American Entomological Society Transactions,* Vol. 114.

Nickle, David A. 1976. "Interspecific differences in frequency and other physical parameters of pair-forming sounds of bush katydids." In *Entomological Society of America Annals,* Vol. 69, No. 6.

―――. 1990. *Katydids of Panama.* Washington, D.C. Smithsonian Institution.

―――. n.d. "Singing insects in the rainforests: the katydids of the Peruvian Amazon." In *Orion Nature Quarterly.*

―――, and T. C. Carlysle. 1975. "Morphology and function of female sound-producing structures in ensiferan Orthoptera with special emphasis on the Phaneropterinae." In *Journal of Morphology and Embryology,* Vol. 4, No. 2.

Riley, Charles V. 1874. *Sixth Annual Report on the Noxious, Benefical, and Other Insects of the State of Missouri.* Jefferson City, Mo. Regan & Carter.

Shaw, Kenneth C. 1968. "An analysis of the phonoresponse of males of the true katydid." In *Behaviour,* Vol. 31.

Spooner, John D. 1964. "The Texas bush katydid—its sounds and their significance." In *Animal Behaviour,* Vol. 12.

―――. 1968. "Pair-forming acoustic systems of the Phaneropterine katydids." In *Animal Behaviour,* Vol. 16.

Suga, Nobuo. 1966. "Ultrasonic production and its reception in some neotropical Tettigoniidae." In *Journal of Insect Physiology,* Vol. 12.

Walker, Thomas J. 1964. "Cryptic species among sound-producing ensiferan Orthoptera." In *Quarterly Review of Biology,* Vol. 39, No. 4.

―――. "Experimental demonstration of a cat locating Orthopteran prey by the prey's calling song." In *The Florida Entomologist,* Vol. 47, No. 2.

Chapter X   ORDER ODONATA: Dragonflies

Corbet, Philip S. 1963. *A Biology of Dragonflies.* Chicago. Quadrangle Books.

―――. 1980. "Biology of Odonata." In *Annual Review of Entomology,* Vol. 25.

Mickel, Clarence E. 1934. "The significance of the dragonfly name 'Odonata.' " In *Annals of the Entomological Society of America,* Vol 27.

Johnson, Clifford. 1972. "Tandem linkage, sperm translocation and copulation in the dragonfly, *Hagenius brevistylus.*" In *American Midland Naturalist,* Vol. 88, No. 1.

Miller, P. L. 1987. *Dragonflies.* Cambridge University Press.

Needham, James G., and Minter J. Westfall, Jr. 1955. *A Manual of the Drag-onflies of North America*. University of California.

Packard, A. S. 1867. "The dragon-fly." In *American Naturalist,* Vol. I, No. 5.

Tillyard, R. J. 1917. *The Biology of dragonflies.* Cambridge University Press.

Chapter XI ORDER LEPIDOPTERA: Gypsy Moths

Fernald, Charles H. 1897, 1898, 1899, 1900. *Special Reports on the Work of the Extermination of the* Ocneria dispar, *or Gypsy Moth.* Massachusetts State Board of Agriculture.

Forbush, Edward H., and Charles H. Fernald. 1896. *The Gypsy Moth.* Boston. Wright & Potter. 1977 reprint edition: Arno Press.

Gerardi, Michael H., and James K. Grimm. 1979. *The History, Biology, Damage, and Control of the Gypsy Moth,* Porthetria dispar *(L.)* Rutherford, N.J. Fairleigh Dickinson University Press.

Howard, Leland O. 1897. *The Gipsy Moth in America.,* Bulletin No. 11–New Series, U.S. Department of Agriculture. Division of Entomology. Washington, D.C. Government Printing Office.

————, and William F. Fiske. 1911. *The Importation into the United States of the Parasites of the Gipsy Moth and the Brown-Tail Moth.* Bulletin No. 91 of the U.S. Bureau of Entomology. Washington, D.C. Government Printing Office. 1977 reprint edition: Arno Press.

Lewis, Franklin B., and Donald P. Connola. 1966. *Field and Laboratory investigations of Bacillus thuringiensis as a Control Agent for Gypsy Moths.* U.S. Forest Service Research Paper NE50. Upper Darby, Pennsylvania. Northeastern Forest Experiment Station.

Medford Mercury, Medford, Mass. 1906. *Illustrations of the Ravages of the Gypsy and Brown Tail Moths.*

Schultz, Jack C. 1991. "The Multimillion dollar gypsy moth question." In *Natural History Magazine,* June 1991.

Chapter XII: ORDER DIPTERA: Syrphid Flies

Brower, Jane van Zandt, and Lincoln P. Brower. 1962. "Experimental studies of mimicry 6: the reaction of toads to honeybees and their drone fly mimics." In *The American Naturalist,* Vol. XCVI, No. 890.

Davies, N. B. "Prey selection and the search strategy of the spotted flycatcher." In *Animal Behavior,* Vol. 25.

Gabritschevsky, E. 1926. "Convergence of coloration between American pilose flies and bumblebees." In *Biological Bulletin*, Vol. LI.

Gilbert, Francis S. 1986. *Hoverflies*. Cambridge University Press.

Metcalf, C. L. 1913. "The Syrphidae of Ohio." *Ohio State University Bulletin*, Vol 17, No. 31.

Shipley, A. E. 1915. "The Bugonia myth." In *Journal of Philology*, Vol. 34, No. 67.

Svensson, B. G., and Lars-Åke Janzon. 1984. "Why does the hoverfly *Metasyrphus corollae* migrate?" In *Ecological Entomology*, Vol. 9.

Virgilus. 1947. *The Singing Farmer*, translated by L. A. S. Jermyn. Oxford. Blackwell.

Waldbauer, G. P. 1988. "Asynchrony between Batesian mimics and their models." In *Mimicry and the Evolutionary Process*, edited by Lincoln Brower. University of Chicago Press.

Chapter XIII ORDER ORTHOPTERA: Camel Crickets

Bell, Paul D. 1980. "Multimodal communication by the black horned tree cricket." In *Canadian Journal of Zoology*, Vol. 58.

Blatchley, William S. 1920. *Orthoptera of Northeastern America*. Indianapolis. Nature Publishing Co., p. 622–638.

Hubbell, Theodore Huntington. 1936. *A Monographic Revision of the Genus Ceuthophilus*. Gainesville. Univ. of Florida Press.

———. 1984. "Unfinished business and beckoning problems." In Symposium on Insect Behavioral Ecology 1984. Florida Entomological Society.

———, and Russell M. Norton. 1978. *The Systematics and Biology of the Cave Crickets of the North American Tribe Hadenoecini*. Miscellaneous publication 156 of the Museum of Zoology, University of Michigan.

Kaiser, W. 1988. "Busy bees need rest, too." In *Journal of Comparative Physiology*, Vol. 163.

Roth, Louis M. 1969. "The evolution of male tergal glands in the Blattaria." In *Annals of the Entomological Society of America*, Vol. 62.

Whitehead, F. E., and Floyd D. Miner. 1944. "The biology and control of the camel cricket, *Daihinia brevipes*." In *Journal of Economic Entomology*, Vol. 37, No. 5.

Index

Page numbers in *italics* refer to illustrations.

258

dragonflies (*cont'd*)
  mating posture of, *154*
  molt of, 163
  mouthparts of, *162*
  names of, 155, 159–60, 170
  nymphs of, *163*
  paired flight of, 153–54
  as pests, 155
  reproduction of, *154,* 166–68,
    169
  species of, 170
  speed of, 164
  territoriality of, 166
  vision of, 164
  white tail, 166, *167*
drone fly (*Eristalis tenax*), 207–8,
  207, 208, 209

ear mites, xix
Earth Day, 57
eastern black swallowtail, 202
eastern katydid (*Pterophylla
  camellifolia*), 136–37, 138
Eastern toe biters, 110
ecdysis, 150, 163
Edgar, Arlan, 63, 66, 68, 69–73
Egypt, 58
Ehrlich, Paul, 13, 19
elytra, 40
Endangered Species Act (1973), 83–
  84
English ladybug, 46*n*
English sparrow, 9
Entomologica Americana, 121
entomology, 21
  in Great Britain, 160–61
  microscope and, 139
  vocabulary of, 120–21
entomophobia, 159–60
Erebia magdalena, 13, 29
E. theano, 13–14, 16, 17, 20

Eristalis tenax (drone fly), 207–8,
  207, 208, 209
Erwin, Terry, 38
Euphydryas anicia, 19
E. gilletti, 4, 200
  eggs of, 18
European cabbage butterfly, 9–10
European skipper, 9–10
evolution, 21, 126–27
  of beetles, 40–41
  of black flies, 77–78
  of butterflies, 9
  coevolution, 126–27
  convergent, 26
  of ladybugs, 39–41
  of silverfish, 126–27
  of syrphid flies, 215–16
exoskeletons, 23, 150, 151
eye gnats, 37
eyes, 164–66

Fabre, Jean-Henri, 212
Fabricius, Johann Christian, 161–
  62
"false vein," 198–99
families, 23
*Families and Genera of North American
  Diptera* (Curran), 29, 35–36
father longlegs, 69
  see also daddy longlegs
feeding behavior:
  of black flies, 77–78
  in beetle evolution, 40–41
  of camel crickets, 221–23
  in courtship, 142–43
  of daddy longlegs, 63–64
  of dragonflies, 155, 162
  of katydids, 142–43
  of midges, 32–33
  of syrphid flies, 205–6
  of water striders, 111, 113

262

German bee (*Apis mellifera mellifera*), 95, 97
Germany, 181–82
Gerridae, 109, 110, 113, 119
    see also water striders
Gerris remigis, 112
Gibbs, K. Elizabeth, 76, 81, 83–84, 88–89, 138
Gilbert, Francis S., 216
Gillette, Clarence P., 4
Glaucopsyche xerces, 5
gnats, xv-xvi, 21–37, 76, 91, 155
    biting, 29–30, 32–33
    British meaning of, 33
    buffalo, 29–30
    definition of, 29–30
    eye, 37
    families of, 29, 33–34
    fungus, 33, 36, *36*
    gall, 33, 34
    larvae of, 36–37
    metamorphosis and, 34–35
    names of, 33, 37
    nonbiting, 29–30
    number of species of, 30
    reproduction and, 34
    swarming by, 116
    wood, 33
Golden Arrow, The (Webb), 219
golden cinquefoil (*Potentilla aurea*), *165*
golden-eye lacewing, *43*
Goliath beetle, 147
grasshoppers, 134, 135, 136, 147, 217
    chocolate-dipped, 161
    southern lubber, *104*
Great Britain, 5, 58, 181
    daddy longlegs in, 69
    entomology in, 160–61
    gnats and midges in, 33

peppered moth of, 201–2
silk trade and, 176
Great Gypsy Moth Escape, 184
green darner (*Anax junius*), 170
green lacewings, 43, 55
Grey, Paul, 17–18
grooming, 64, *64,* 227
ground spider, *62*
"Group Transmission of Predator Avoidance Behavior in a Marine Insect: The Trafalgar Effect" (Treherne and Foster), 116–17
Grove, Davison Greenawalt, 137–38, 139, 141–43, 145, 149, 150
Gryllidae, *see* crickets
Guatemala, 79, 81, 89, 90, 96, 100, 102, 103–4
Gwynne, D. T., 143
Gymnosperms, 40
Gypcheck viral spray, 195
Gypsy Moth, The, 193
gypsy moth (*Lymantria dispar*), 9, 82, 171–97
    appetite of, 172
    caterpillars of, 172, *173*
    control of, 171–72, 174–75, 187–92, 194–95
    droppings of, 172
    egg masses of, 172, *173*
    European outbreaks of, 181–83, 193
    French names of, 173–74
    fungus spinner, 181
    German names of, 181–82
    initial U.S. outbreak of, 184–87
    in Japan, 193
    modern range of, 195
    natural checks on, 193–94
    parasites and, 193–94
    predators and, 174, 193–94

locusts, 149
loons, 77
Los Angeles Times, 161
Loskiel, G. H., 32–33
Love, Sally, 159
Lubbock, John, 125
luna moth, 8, 178
Lycaenidae, 14–15
Lymantria dispar, see gypsy moth
Lymantriidae, 180

Machilidae, 126
McLachlan, Robert, 115
Macrocheles rodriguezi, 236
Maeterlinck, Maurice, 91
maggot, "rat-tailed," 207–8, *207*
Maine, 84–85, 88–89, 193
Maine Agricultural Experiment
    Station, 36–37
Mallis, Arnold, 121
Mansilla, Jorge, 101
mantids, 144
March flies (*Bibio*), 23–24, *24,* 91
marsh felwort (*Swertia perennis*), *165*
marsh treaders, 112
Massachusetts, 187, 193
Massachusetts State Board of
    Agriculture, 192
mass extinctions, 127
mating and reproduction:
  of bees, 24–25, 92, 98–99
  butterflies and, 14
  of camel crickets, 226–28, 231,
    233–34
  courtship feeding and, 142–43
  of daddy longlegs, 59, 65–67, 70,
    72, 167
  of dragonflies, *154,* 166–68, *169*
  of gnats, 34, 91
  of gypsy moth, 172–73
  of katydids, 139–40, 142–43, 167

of midges, 30–31, 91
paedogenesis and, 34
of silverfish, 130–32
singing in, 141–42, 144, 145
swarms in, 30–31, 91
of water striders, 112, 116–17
mayflies, 33, 76, 138, *139*
meal moth (*Pyralis farinalis*), 236
mealworms, 161
mealybug destroyer (*Cryptolaemus
    montrouzieri*), 56
mealy bugs, 44, 56, 110
mechanoreceptors, 145
Medford, Mass., 171, 175–76, 187,
    192, 195–97
Mediterranean fruitfly, 96
Megaloptera, 87
  see also dobsonflies
Merritt, Richard, 85–88
mescaline, 92–94
metamorphosis:
  of black flies, 80
  of butterflies, 7–8, 150
  of daddy longlegs, 66
  gnats and, 34–35
  of grasshoppers, *104*
  of honey bees, *104*
  incomplete, *104,* 150
  of katydids, 140, 150
  of ladybugs, *42*
  limits to, 150–51
  midges and, 34–35
  of syrphid flies, 205
  of water striders, 150
Metasyrphus americanus (American
    hover fly), 206–7, *206,* 208
methoxychlor, 81
Meudon Observatory, 186
Mexico, 97, 102
Michener, C. D., 26
Michigan, 213

moths (*cont'd*)
    day-flying, 8, 15
    diamond-back, 83*n*
    ear mites in, xix
    hawkmoths, 180
    large, 147
    luna, 8, 178
    meal, 236
    mimicry and, 201–2
    peppered, 201–2
    prometheus, 178
    tufted bird-dropping, 201
    tussock, 180
    see also gypsy moth; silkworms
mountain blue butterfly, 15
mulberry tree (*Morus multicaulis*),
    178
Müller, Fritz, 201
Müllerian mimicry, 201, 204
Multicaulismania, 178
Mycetophilidae, 33

Nabokov, Vladimir, 15, 158
naiads, 163
Napoleon III, Emperor of France,
    175
Natural History of Flies (Oldroyd), 36
Nature Magazine, 193
Needham, James, 30, 162
Nelson, Horatio, Lord, 116–17
nematodes, 54, 74
    filarial, 75
Neuroptera, 110, 161
New Guinea, 119
New Hampshire, 193
New Jersey, 193*n*
New York, 57, 83
New Yorker, 84
New York Natural History
    Conference (1990), 85
New York State Museum, 85

New York Times, xvii, 53, 157, 185
New Zealand sawyer, 134, 147, 148
Nickle, David, 134, 136–37, 143,
    146–48, 151, 217, 221
Norris-Elye, L.T.S., 155
North Carolina, 135
no-see-ums, 32–33
Nosema bombycis, 178
numerical taxonomy, 26–27

ocelli, 164, 166
Ocneria dispar, see gypsy moth
Odonata, 22, 161–62
    see also dragonflies
odor, 29
    of daddy longlegs, 60, 67–68, 70
    of ladybugs, 51
Oklahoma, 223
Oldroyd, Harold, 36, 207, 216
    syrphid fly feeding described by,
    205–6
Onchocerca volvulus (filarial
    nematode), 75
Onchocerciasis Control Program
    (OCP), 75–76
onchocerciasis (river blindness), 75,
    78
    treatment for, 81–82
Ontario, 155
operational taxonomic unit (OTU),
    27
Opie, Iona, 58
Opie, Peter, 58
Opiliones, 61–62
    see also daddy longlegs
Opler, Paul, 160
orb-weave spider, *62*
orchid, Jersey (*Orchis laxiflora*), *165*
orders, 23
    naming of, 21–22
    see also specific orders

pupae (*cont'd*)
of syrphid flies, 205
see also metamorphosis
Pyle, Robert, 4–5, 6, 12–13, 15, 16, 17, 29
Pyralis farinalis (meal moth), 236

Queen Alexandra (*Colias alexandra*), 13
queen bee, 92, 98, 102
question mark (*Polygonia interrogationis*), 11

races, 25
rat-tailed maggot, 207–8, *207*
Raupenleim, 181
Réaumur, René-Antoine Ferchault de, 205
red admiral (*Vanessa atalanta*), 11, 51
red-spotted purple, 202
Reiling, Stephen D., 88
reproduction, *see* mating and reproduction
respiration, 148–50, 151
Rhode Island, 193
rhymes, *see* verses
Riley, Charles V., 189–92
Ripley, S. Dillon, 5
Ritland, David, 203
river blindness (onchocerciasis), 75, 78
treatment of, 81–82
Robbins, Robert, 9, 25
Rodalia cardinalis (Vedalia ladybug), 46
rodents, 143
rose chafers, 156, *156*
Ross, Harold, 84
Roters, M., 64
Rouff, Lowell, 45–52, 55

ruby-throated hummingbird, 155
rufous hummingbird, 16

St. Victor, Hugo, 30
salmon, 79
Samuels, Edward A., 183–84
Sandal Test, 98
Savory, Theodore, 60
sawyers, *see* katydids
scale insects, 44, 110
scales:
of butterflies, 11, 21
of silverfish, 127–28
Scanning Electron Microscope Atlas of the Honey Bee, A, 139
scarab beetle," 58
Schaefer, J. C., 182
Schroeter, Wolfgang, 59, 67
Sciara militaris, 36
Sciaridae, 33, 36, *36*
Scientific American, 83n
scorpions, 48, 61
water, 112
whip-, *62*
Scot, Reginald, 160, 161
Scott, James, 10
Scripps Institution of Oceanography, 115
Scudder, Samuel, 189–90, 224
sea skaters (*Halobates*), 113–14, 116
seed plants, 40–41
segmentation, *xix*
Selenographical Society of Great Britain, 175
Selfish Gene, The (Dawkins), 142
sericulture (silk culture), 176–81
sex, *see* mating and reproduction
sexual dimorphism, 173
Shaler, Nathaniel S., 182–83, 184, 188–91
shepherd spider, *see* daddy longlegs

ABOUT THE AUTHOR

SUE HUBBELL writes for newspapers and magazines; she has written three previous books. She splits her life between the Ozarks of Missouri, where she keeps bees, and Washington, D.C., where her husband works.

ABOUT THE TYPE

This book was set in Bembo, a typeface based on an old-style Roman face that was used for Cardinal Bembo's tract *De Actua* in 1495. Bembo was cut by Francisco Griffo in the early sixteenth century. The Lanston Monotype Machine Company of Philadelphia brought the well-proportioned letter forms of Bembo to the United States in the 1930s.